OXFORD WORLD'S CLASSICS

THE MISANTHROPE, TARTUFFE,
AND OTHER PLAYS

MOLIÈRE, whose real name was Jean-Baptiste Poquelin, was born in Paris in 1622, the son of a wealthy royal upholsterer. When he was 21 he gave up legal studies, resigned the court post obtained for him by his father, and founded, with Madeleine and Joseph Béjart and others, a dramatic company called the 'Illustre Théâtre'. In 1645, after two difficult years failing to establish a theatre in Paris, the company began to tour the provinces, performing the works of others and plays and sketches written by Molière, influenced by the Italian *commedia dell'arte*. In 1658 the troupe returned to Paris where the favour of Louis XIV's brother secured them the *Salle du Petit-Bourbon* (in the Louvre), until the company moved to the Palais Royal in 1660–1. Molière's first great comedy of manners, *Les Précieuses ridicules*, was performed in 1659 and immediately established its author's reputation for topical social satire. In 1662 Molière married Armande Béjart, Madeleine's sister, and in the same year *L'École des femmes*, a five-act verse comedy, was first performed, prompting a series of attacks and counter-attacks between Molière's company and its rivals at the Hôtel de Bourgogne. Over the next eleven years Molière wrote and performed in a number of verse and prose plays (often with interludes of ballet and music), including *Don Juan* (1665), *Le Misanthrope* and *Le Médecin malgré lui* (1666), *George Dandin* and *L'Avare* (1668), *Le Bourgeois gentilhomme* (1670), *Les Fourberies de Scapin* (1671), and *Les Femmes savantes* (1672). *Tartuffe*, which satirized religious hypocrisy, was performed privately, condemned by ecclesiastical bodies and banned several times from 1664, before it was finally granted a public licence in 1669.

On 17 February 1673, during the fourth performance of *Le Malade imaginaire*, Molière collapsed on stage and died later the same evening.

MAYA SLATER is a Senior Research Fellow of Queen Mary and Westfield College, London University. Her publications include *The Craft of La Fontaine* (Athlone Press, 2000), and many articles on French seventeenth-century literature. For Oxford World's Classics she has edited La Fontaine, *Selected Fables* (1995), and translated *Three Pre-Surrealist Plays* (1997). Her translation of Molière's *Don Juan* was performed in London in 1999.

OXFORD WORLD'S CLASSICS

*For over 100 years Oxford World's Classics have brought
readers closer to the world's great literature. Now with over 700
titles—from the 4,000-year-old myths of Mesopotamia to the
twentieth century's greatest novels—the series makes available
lesser-known as well as celebrated writing.*

*The pocket-sized hardbacks of the early years contained
introductions by Virginia Woolf, T. S. Eliot, Graham Greene,
and other literary figures which enriched the experience of reading.
Today the series is recognized for its fine scholarship and
reliability in texts that span world literature, drama and poetry,
religion, philosophy and politics. Each edition includes perceptive
commentary and essential background information to meet the
changing needs of readers.*

OXFORD WORLD'S CLASSICS

MOLIÈRE

The Misanthrope
Tartuffe
and Other Plays

Translated with an Introduction and Notes by
MAYA SLATER

OXFORD
UNIVERSITY PRESS

OXFORD

UNIVERSITY PRESS

Great Clarendon Street, Oxford OX2 6DP

Oxford University Press is a department of the University of Oxford.
It furthers the University's objective of excellence in research, scholarship,
and education by publishing worldwide in

Oxford New York

Athens Auckland Bangkok Bogotá Buenos Aires Cape Town
Chennai Dar es Salaam Delhi Florence Hong Kong Istanbul Karachi
Kolkata Kuala Lumpur Madrid Melbourne Mexico City Mumbai Nairobi
Paris São Paulo Shanghai Singapore Taipei Tokyo Toronto Warsaw

with associated companies in Berlin Ibadan

Oxford is a registered trade mark of Oxford University Press
in the UK and in certain other countries

Published in the United States
by Oxford University Press Inc., New York

First published as an Oxford World's Classics paperback 2001
Reissued 2008

British Library Cataloguing in Publication Data

Data available

Library of Congress Cataloging in Publication Data

Data available

ISBN 978–0–19–954018–1

12

Typeset in Ehrhardt
by RefineCatch Limited, Bungay, Suffolk
Printed in Great Britain by
Clays Ltd, St Ives plc

CONTENTS

ACKNOWLEDGEMENTS

I should like to thank the following for their help in preparing this volume: Terence Allott, for his careful reading of the players; Craig Raine, for his helpful comments on *The Misanthrope*; Julian Kenny, for advice on legal language; my husband, for hours spent problem-solving; my family, for endless play-readings; also my mother, Lil Hara, Hal Lieberman, and Isaac Sonsino. Finally, I should like to thank Queen Mary and Westfield College for sabbatical leave to work on this project.

M.S.

INTRODUCTION

The Early Years

All his life, Molière courted controversy. The plays translated here prove it. So do the known facts of his life. His real name was Jean-Baptiste Poquelin: he adopted the stage name Molière in about 1644. Born in 1622, into a respectable Parisian bourgeois family, he could have been a lawyer, or succeeded his father in the honorific post of upholsterer to the King. But he rejected the career his family chose for him, took the money his mother had left him, and, in 1643, at 21, went onto the stage.

He started off as an actor, then became an actor-manager. The first steps of his theatrical career were disastrous. He spent his inheritance, got heavily into debt, was briefly imprisoned for failing to pay the bill for some candles, and was forced to leave Paris. For the next thirteen years, he and his troupe—his mistress, Madeleine Béjart, her family, and a gradual accumulation of other actors—toured the provinces. There was no prospect of their working in the capital. It was not until 1658 that the company was secure enough to risk coming back to Paris, under the patronage of the King's brother.

It was during this period of exile in the provinces that Molière first started writing plays. Mostly, the troupe performed tragedies and comedies by well-known writers like Corneille. But these were often preceded by short comic interludes. It seems that Molière's first plays were written to fill this gap. It is tantalizing to have so few details of them. One broad farce, *Barbouillé's Jealousy*, about a jealous husband, is almost certainly by him. By the time he was back in Paris, he was already writing more elegant verse comedies, like *The Bungler*, about a silly, thoughtless young man who unwittingly foils every attempt to help him get his girl.

When Molière started writing comedies, he was tapping into an established genre, with its own conventions and traditions. Theoretical writers in the earlier years of the seventeenth century divided comedy into two types. First was farce, a traditional form of theatre that had its roots in the Roman theatre of Plautus, and had been immensely popular in France till the early years of the century. More recently, the Italian *commedia dell'arte* had ousted French farce. Audiences loved its stock harlequinade characters, and its outrageous and often improper plots; Molière himself is known to have had a particular affection for Italian comedy (though Spanish comedy also exerted an influence, contributing fantastic plots, rich in abductions, duels, and matters of honour).

The second type of comedy, according to contemporary theoreticians, was the so-called 'belle comédie', a realistic, elegant comedy of manners. Earlier in the century, five-act verse comedies had already become popular. Molière's immediate precursor, Pierre Corneille, wrote elegant comedies of this kind. They have a contemporary setting and a happy ending, but are agreeable and civilized rather than sidesplittingly funny in tone. In addition, the authors of the 'belles comédies' were expected to obey the rules of tragedy, as laid down by the Académie Française earlier in the century, following the traditions of theatre that went back to Aristotle and Greek tragedy: the three unities of time, place, and action must be preserved, as must the rules of 'vraisemblance' and 'bienséance'. The result was plays whose action lasted no more than twenty-four hours (unity of time), in a single setting (unity of place), and with a single theme (unity of action). The plots were not implausible or outlandish (*vraisemblance*), and the characters' behaviour did not offend the conventions (*bienséance*). On the whole, Molière's verse plays fulfil these requirements, except that the characters' behaviour can at times be both outlandish and unconventional. This fact was to cause him considerable trouble.

It is not, however, quite true to say that Molière's precursors obeyed the rules implicitly. Not only Corneille, but other seventeenth-century playwrights, such as Scarron, were also interested in depicting eccentric characters, who formed the centrepieces of their best comedies. Molière was to follow them, and outdo them all. His great originality was to place memorably eccentric characters in a realistic setting. The result was a series of plays that were lively and entertaining, but also cast a vivid light on the life of his contemporaries. In *The School for Wives Criticized* Molière explains his aims as a playwright through his mouthpiece Dorante.

Newly arrived in Paris, with a name to make and a company's wages to pay, Molière might have played safe, offering the public uncontroversial theatre. Instead, he courted scandal—and achieved his first big success. He wrote a short prose play, *The Ridiculous Précieuses* (1659)—an innovative mixture of satire and farce which mocked the *précieuses*, affected society women with pretensions to literary sophistication. Molière defended himself half-heartedly, claiming that he was not targeting the *précieuses*, but the provincial women who imitated them. Nobody was taken in. If Molière's aim in provoking his contemporaries was to draw the public, he succeeded admirably. He says of himself, 'I know what he's like. He doesn't mind if people attack his plays, as long as they attract the audiences' (*The School for Wives Criticized*). But he had started on a dangerous path.

The School for Wives

Molière's next play to create a scandal, *The School for Wives*, made him enemies far more powerful than the *précieuses*. It is the first play in this collection.

The play opened on Boxing Day, 1662. It was a great hit, and it is easy to see why. The play sparkles with life. True, it explores a well-worn theme. Molière himself had written an earlier version of the story of a cantankerous older man who plans to marry his young and beautiful ward: *The School for Husbands* (1661). His enemies now accused him of plagiarism. But the character of Arnolphe was definitely new. Molière himself played the role, with a wealth of grimaces and comic exaggeration, stressing Arnolphe's ludicrous obsession with cuckoldry, and the eccentric measures he takes to protect himself. His exuberant performance irritated some of his contemporaries. The real strength of the play, however, is not in the clowning but in the innovative combination of broad farce, satire, and psychological insight. At first, Arnolphe thinks he is in control—he holds all the trump cards. But he quickly discovers that the naive bride he has chosen, and her callow suitor, are outwitting him. Much of the pleasure of the play lies in observing his discomfiture. To make things worse, when he realizes he is about to lose Agnes, he admits for the first time that he loves her. Molière means this to be a convincing emotion. That much is clear from a passage in *The School for Wives Criticized*, Molière's first apology for his play: 'Don't ordinary respectable people, at moments like that, do certain things?... Think! If we look at the way we behave, when we're really in love...' The role of Arnolphe is one of the most demanding that Molière wrote for himself to perform. Onstage for almost the whole play, he conveys much of the action through anguished speeches and soliloquies. Arnolphe deliberately surrounds himself with idiots, and his downfall is the more humiliating, as he is 'punished repeatedly by the very precautions he had taken to protect himself', as Molière explains in *The School for Wives Criticized*.

The other characters too are full of interest. Arnolphe's stupid bride Agnes turns out to be more than a match for him. Agnes is a fascinating portrait of a completely untutored mind, with a natural logic that cuts through Arnolphe's sophisticated reasoning. When Arnolphe explodes: 'So it's all right to let young men into your life?', she answers simply: 'Well, yes, because he says he wants me for his wife. | I've done just what you taught me—and you rubbed it in: | You have to marry, to remove all hint of sin.' Agnes is, in fact, a unique character in Molière. His most famous characters— his Misers, Hypochondriacs, or Misanthropes—are set in their ways. They have evolved into full-blown eccentrics before the action begins. The other characters are also fully formed, and their efforts to outwit or circumvent the destructive behaviour of the central character form the plots of his comedies. Agnes is different. She learns and evolves throughout the play. Having started off as a figure of fun, who thinks that 'women make their babies through the ear', she realizes her own ignorance: 'Do you think I'm deceived? Do you think I can't see | A stupid idiot is what you've made of me? | It hurts. I'm so ashamed—but now I've got a plan: | I'll try to seem less idiotic if I can.' By the end, her predicament seems touching rather than ridiculous: she has won the audience over.

The School for Wives earned Molière and his troupe a royal pension. But it also started a polemical war, known as 'The quarrel of *The School for Wives*'. Molière's many critics included other, less successful writers; actors from the rival troupe of the Hôtel de Bourgogne (whom he ridicules, in retaliation, in *The Impromptu at Versailles*); the leading playwright of the time, Corneille, whom he teases in the play; women angry at his improper language and innuendo; and, most importantly, religious groups indignant at his spoof account of a wife's duties to her husband in Act III scene 2, which seems to mock the sacrament of marriage. As his career progressed, the religious faction was to become ever more hostile.

The School for Wives Criticized

Molière addressed many of these criticisms, and poked fun at his critics, in a short polemical play, *The School for Wives Criticized* (1663), which is reproduced in this volume. He himself tells us to take this piece seriously: 'Many of the things I would like to say [in my own defence] are already in a discussion I have written in dialogue form' (preface to *The School for Wives*). Much more than an exercise in self-defence, this play is a witty, informal work, highly entertaining in its own right. It takes the form of a discussion about *The School for Wives*, in which its defenders are sensible, its adversaries fools—an affected *précieuse*, a half-witted marquis, a pedantic playwright. In a piece of self-mockery that will later become his trademark, Molière rehearses a number of arguments against his own play. He himself almost certainly played one of his own opponents, the Marquis, so that the contemporary audience would have had the additional pleasure of watching him on stage sneering at his own creation: 'I didn't even bother to listen. But I do know that I've never seen anything so pathetic.' The defence of *The School for Wives* is left to a 'straight man', Dorante, played by the actor Brécourt. Molière addresses a number of serious criticisms of that play. His comments reveal a thoughtful approach, which underlies the frivolity of the rest of this witty piece. The critics had attacked *The School for Wives* for its lack of verisimilitude, its failure to obey the rules, the inconsistency of the main character, and other fundamental flaws. Molière's mouthpiece answers all their points systematically—and incidentally gives us considerable insight into his own technique as a playwright. In particular, he makes it clear that his chief priority is to make his characters seem convincing, commenting, for example, that the outrageous views on marriage expressed by Arnolphe are justified 'by the eccentricity of Arnolphe, and the innocence of the girl he's talking to'. And the fact that Arnolphe can seem friendly and even generous is explained because 'it's not impossible for a person to be ridiculous in some respects, and decent in others'.

The School for Wives Criticized was performed in June 1663, only five months after *The School for Wives* itself. Molière's enemies swiftly retaliated with their own polemical plays. In August, a journalist called Donneau de Visé published *Zelinde or The True School for Wives Criticized*; then in September a young playwright called Boursault put on *The Painter's Portrait*. These plays repeated the attacks on *The School for Wives*, with their authors' own more or less trivial additions: for instance, Donneau de Visé complains that the stone that Agnes throws at Horace in Act III scene 4 is too big (Molière calls it *un grès*, a paving stone). Visé was later to become one of Molière's most fervent admirers. Boursault is content to imitate *The School for Wives Criticized*, simply reversing the roles, so that Molière's comic characters become serious in Boursault's version, and vice versa. Molière, on hearing about *The Painter's Portrait*, launched an immediate counter-attack with *The Impromptu at Versailles* (performed in October 1663, and reproduced here). Molière is said to have written it in only eight days, and it was indeed, as the title suggests, first performed at Versailles, before the King.

The Impromptu at Versailles

The Impromptu at Versailles is a second defence of Molière, and a second attack on his critics. It is just as lively as its predecessor, *The School for Wives Criticized*. It has a surprisingly modern feel, with the actors appearing in their ordinary clothes, playing themselves: the troupe is rehearsing. The pretence is, of course, disingenuous. Molière takes good care to produce an entertainment, not just a slice of life. He casts himself as the fall guy, comically despairing as he is let down by all his actors, one after the other. He second aim, no less important, is to answer criticisms of *The School for Wives*, this time offering the play's success as an argument for its quality. Again, he simultaneously mocks his opponents, and teasingly attacks himself: 'I mean! The impertinent fellow [Molière] doesn't believe that women can be brilliant! He criticizes all our refinements of speech. He wants us to use nothing but ordinary language.' He counters the arguments of his rivals with mischievous gibes. Boursault, for instance, is dismissed as a complete nonentity, whom nobody has even heard of: 'someone called Br... Brou... Brossaut.'

This short play provides a unique insight into Molière's own opinions. In one important speech, which he delivered himself, he reveals his views on acting techniques. It takes the form of a mocking account of the rival troupe at the Hôtel de Bourgogne, who specialized in tragedy. This is how he puts it: 'I thought of writing a play about a poet (I'd have played the part myself). He'd have gone to see a troupe of actors, just back from the country, to offer them a play. He'd say: "Do you have any actors and actresses who can do justice to my work? . . . Which of you plays the King? . . . Let's hear him recite a dozen lines." At that, the actor would say a few of the King's lines . . . He'd speak the lines as naturally as possible. And the poet would say: "What? Is that what you call reciting? You must be joking. You have to recite the line with the proper emphasis. Listen to this" [*and he imitates that excellent actor from the Hôtel de Bourgogne company, Montfleury*] . . . "Do you see the way I'm standing? Mind you take note. You see, you have to stress the end of the speech. That's how you get the audience going, and drive them wild." "But, Monsieur," the actor would answer, "I think that a king, having a private conversation with his Captain of the Guard, would use a more ordinary tone of voice, not shriek like a man possessed." "You don't know what you're talking about. Just try speaking the lines the way you do, you'll see. Nobody will say 'Ah!'"' (Scene 1). Molière's views seem very modern: he approves of speaking the lines naturally, adapting their delivery to the situation. He wants actors to show emotion, to look right for the part. It is appropriate for comic actors to have their own ridiculous, recognizable mannerisms; but tragic actors should speak simply, and avoid idiosyncrasies. These comments show that he had a very different attitude from most tragic actors of the time, who are known to have favoured a formal, artificial style of delivery, striking attitudes, and standing motionless as they intoned their words in a singsong litany.

Later in *The Impromptu at Versailles* (Scene 4), Molière expresses his views on writing plays as well. By a dramatic trick, he makes it quite clear that the speech we are to hear is to be taken very seriously. Another actor is supposed to be delivering the lines, but Molière interrupts: 'Wait a minute. You want to say all that bit more emphatically. Listen, this is how I want it spoken', and he goes on to make the whole speech himself. In it, he talks about his choice of material. He looks for faults in human nature, and explores them through drama. In his own view, the topic of all his theatre is 'man's ridiculous side'. He is an observer of human nature, who sees his role as pointing up the flaws in man. (Later, in the preface to *Tartuffe*, he will put it even more forcefully: 'The function of comedy is to correct the vices of men.') He is telling us that he is not merely a light-hearted entertainer: if he makes the audience laugh, it is with an ulterior motive.

Observations on Molière's Theatre

Looking at Molière's theatre as a whole, we can see that these words of his are indeed illustrated by his plays. Even the most light-hearted of his farces explores human folly. In the major plays, there is always a central flaw to be examined in detail, sometimes over more than one play. And these themes can be seen as variations on fundamentally warped attitudes to human relations: jealousy, fear, and suspicion; the need to bully and control; the desire to seem what one is not. These motives, in various combinations, lie at the heart of almost all his plays. Take the four verse plays in this selection: in *The School for Wives*, Arnolphe dreads the power of women, and seeks to control his future wife. Later, he adds jealousy to his problems. In *Tartuffe*, Tartuffe manipulates Orgon, who in turn controls and browbeats his family. In *The Misanthrope*, Alceste is suspicious of his fellow men, and a jealous lover too. In *The Clever Women*, Philaminte bullies her husband, family, and household. Molière's protagonists suffer from a further major defect, the inability to see things in proportion, or, to put it another way, the tendency to exaggerate. As Cleante tells Orgon in *Tartuffe*: 'You don't let reason govern you, or so it seems, | And your idea of sense is going to extremes.' The pattern is repeated in play after play; it gives a unity of theme to each individual work, and lends coherence to Molière's whole *œuvre*.

In addition, each play examines a specific problem. To take an example, *Tartuffe* explores the subject of straight speaking, or the lack of it. Hypocrisy is embodied in the sinister figure of Tartuffe, who destroys Orgon and his family, claiming the holiest of motives. His henchman, M. Loyal the bailiff, is unctuously polite as he turns the family out of their home. Two of Tartuffe's victims, the ladies of the house, Elmire and Mariane, are reluctant to speak their minds, though for a different reason: it is not a woman's place to speak

frankly. But Tartuffe's chief dupes—Orgon, and Mme Pernelle his
mother—are the opposite of hypocritical: they are uncontrollably
frank and outspoken. And Orgon's son Damis is just as bad, showing
a close family resemblance to his father and grandmother. The servant Dorine shares their plain speaking: her language is so crude
that, when she talks of Tartuffe burping, Molière feels obliged to add
a note to the reader excusing her uncouthness. In between all these
extremes is the reasonable Cleante, who addresses the problem directly, trying to persuade Orgon to see through the hypocrisy of
Tartuffe, and to control his own tongue. In this way, virtually the
whole cast reflects Molière's preoccupation with his theme. This
kind of approach can be seen in play after play—in *The Clever
Women*, for example, we have the intellectual snobs (the women, the
professional literati, the scribbling servants), opposed not only by
the sensible ignoramuses Henriette and Clitandre, but also by the
philistine Chrysale, who longs to ban all books from the house,
except for 'a tome of Plutarch to press down my neckerchiefs'.

So Molière is a systematic observer of human folly. But he does
not suggest a cure. On the contrary, he shows us that character flaws
cannot be remedied. I have already suggested that Agnes is more or
less the only character who really develops in Molière's theatre. He
paints a bleak picture of a world of eccentrics rigidly set in their
ways, monomaniacs out of touch with reality, who tend to call the
tune. The normal-seeming characters around them, and dependent
on them, have to duck and weave to try to get on with their lives.
Indeed, Molière sometimes has difficulty bringing his plays to a
close. Logically, they should never end happily—so long as the
eccentric progatonist is alive, we can expect more disaster for young
people hoping to marry, more misery for downtrodden wives, and
more unbridled behaviour on his part. Molière has to resort to
absurd twists of plot to turn the plays into comedies: long-lost relatives appear and overturn the plot in *The School for Wives*, *The
Miser*, or *Scapin's Trickery*. Or an unexpected event changes everything, as at the end of *Tartuffe*, or, more strangely, in *Don Juan*,
where a statue comes to life and drags the hero down to hell. Most
interesting are the occasions where a trick is played on the main
character to oblige him or her to relinquish his stranglehold, and let
the others be happy—though he himself will continue mad as
before. This happens in *The Clever Women*, or, more crudely, in *The*

Bourgeois Gentleman or Molière's last play *The Hypochondriac*, in both of which the main character thinks that his crazy ambitions have been achieved—the bourgeois believes he has become a Turkish nobleman, the hypochondriac that he has qualified as a doctor—and in the happiness of their fool's paradise they allow a longed-for marriage to take place. Perhaps they may later realize that they have been duped, when it is too late—but the audience does not waste time on such speculation. By this stage, these plays have lost all their realism, their central characters have become no more than caricatures. The most honest of the endings are those of *Amphitryon*, where it becomes plain that Amphitryon's wife Alcmène has been seduced by Jupiter, and of *George Dandin*, where the protagonist has married above himself and been humiliated by his wife. Amphitryon is advised to pretend not to notice; George Dandin announces that he is going off to drown himself. In the second play, Molière softens the blow by introducing a drunken ballet to round off the action.

The idea of writing comedies round an eccentric, flawed character was not invented by Molière. Corneille had paved the way with witty comedies like *The Liar* (1659), whose title is self-explanatory. What was new, and shocking, in Molière was the contemporary nature of the satire. The fact that he performed in his own plays greatly increased their controversial quality. I have already said that when, in the *Impromptu at Versailles* speech, Molière describes the character flaws he wants to criticize in his plays, he takes over the lines himself. The moment he does so, he focuses his attack: 'Even without going outside the court, can't you see at least twenty types of character that [I haven't] used yet?' He proceeds to enumerate the courtiers' faults. And this at Versailles, standing on stage in front of the King and assembled court. His satire of his contemporaries was more than brave—it was foolhardy.

Perhaps one of the reasons why Molière was so wedded to exploring eccentricity through comedy relates to his technique as an actor. It is plain that he excelled at portraying the central figures. Most of these parts were written for himself to perform—monomaniacs defying the world, driven to excesses of fury when thwarted. His catch-phrase, his leitmotif, was 'j'enrage!' ('I'm bursting with fury!'). He played Arnolphe in *The School for Wives*, Orgon in *Tartuffe*, Alceste in *The Misanthrope*, Harpagon the Miser, Argan the Hypochondriac, and most of the others. He did not play Philaminte, the bullying wife of *The Clever Women*, probably for two reasons: first, it was a *travesti* role, and he does not seem to have taken those (though audiences enjoyed seeing male actors in female roles. Mme Pernelle in *Tartuffe* is another example). Secondly, he was tired and ill, and probably unable to storm about the stage as tempestuously as before. Instead, he wrote for himself the part of the weak, ineffectual, henpecked husband, Chrysale. In other plays, those in which the monomaniac theme is not so strong, he wrote for himself the part of a servant. He must have excelled at long speeches, for the servant character is always very garrulous, a prattling fool in *Amphitryon* or *The Doctor in Spite of Himself*, an empty-headed showoff in *The Ridiculous Précieuses*, a superstitious coward in *Don Juan*, a brilliant manipulator in *Scapin's Trickery*.

The only plays that do not fit such a pattern are the two polemic plays, *The School for Wives Criticized* and *The Impromptu at Versailles*. They were the product of a particular situation, written with a strong ulterior motive, weapons in an ongoing battle—the quarrel of *The School for Wives*. Molière was not allowed to have the last word with *The Impromptu at Versailles*. There were several more salvos from his enemies. The son of Montfleury, the principal actor of the rival troupe, the so-called 'grands comédiens' ('great actors') ridiculed by Molière, wrote an answer, which he called *The Impromptu at the Hôtel de Condé*, since it was performed at the residence of that great nobleman. The play is remembered for its malevolent, but revealing, portrait of Molière on stage: 'He enters, nose to the wind, on bow legs, one shoulder thrust forward. His wig trails behind, stuffed full of bayleaves like a ham. He dangles his hands rather carelessly by his sides. His head sits on his back like a pack on a mule. He rolls his eyes. When he speaks his lines, the words are punctuated by endless hiccoughs.'

Though Molière generally thrived on the cut and thrust of controversy, he was hurt when his critics started on his personal life. In particular, he was wounded by the insinuation that his new wife Armande, whom he had married in 1662, was not the much younger sister of his former mistress Madeleine Béjart, but her unacknowledged daughter: the marriage, it was implied, was incestuous. On the whole, though, Molière emerged triumphant from the battle of *The School for Wives*—with vastly increased audiences, fame (or at least, notoriety), a royal pension. With his next great play, *Tartuffe*, he overreached himself.

Tartuffe

In May 1664, Molière was appointed master of ceremonies at a splendid entertainment hosted by the King at Versailles. The occasion was to be so memorable that it was given a name, 'The Pleasures of the Enchanted Isle.' Molière and his troupe performed in pageants as water deities; put on an elegant, courtly play, *La Princesse d'Élide*; and performed a new three-act comedy called *Tartuffe*. We do not know exactly what this play was like: the final version of *Tartuffe*, the only one that has come down to us, is a full-length, five-act play. Some critics speculate that the first three acts only were performed, in which case the play will have ended, with appalling bleakness, at the point when Tartuffe has tricked Orgon into disinheriting his son, promising him his daughter in marriage, and giving him unlimited access to his wife. Others believe that it was a three-act version of the whole. After this one performance, the play was immediately banned. Molière was to spend the next five years fighting to put it on.

What was the problem with *Tartuffe*? I have already described the play's treatment of hypocrisy. But influential contemporaries were incensed by a second theme woven into the structure: the abuse of religion. Tartuffe insinuates himself into Orgon's household by pretending to be devout. Orgon and his mother, who are genuinely pious, are taken in, and come to regard Tartuffe as their religious mentor. The preachings of Tartuffe are ludicrous, yet recognizable, versions of genuine Christian teachings: this is why they are so unnerving. Orgon says, besottedly: 'If you sat at his feet, he'd bring you peace, for sure; | The world would seem to you a great heap of manure. | I've learnt from him, and things are clearer in my eyes. | He's taught me to reject the things I used to prize. | The people that I thought I loved, I now deny, | And I could watch my mother, children, wife all die, | And, shall I tell you what? I just couldn't care less.' Molière was accused of lampooning a real person in his Tartuffe; and critics have suggested that he was targeting a number of religious movements. Suffice it to say that the religious faction was very powerful at court, and succeeded in having the play suppressed, despite the King's admiration for it. A violent anonymous pamphlet was published, denouncing Molière as 'a demon clothed in flesh and dressed as a man, the most outstandingly impious libertine that has ever lived'. When he finally published the play, Molière wrote a preface giving his view of the situation: 'The hypocrites, in an appalling fury . . . have all taken up arms against my play . . . they have claimed that their self-interest is the cause of God; in their mouths, *Tartuffe* has become an offence against piety. From beginning to end, the play is full of abominations; it should be burnt at the stake. Every syllable in it is impious; every gesture is criminal.' He claims that his enemies have misunderstood the play: 'I have devoted all my art and effort to making a clear distinction between the character of the hypocrite and the genuinely devout man.'

Molière's protestations are somewhat disingenuous. True, his play mocks at Tartuffe, his religious hypocrite; but the main butt of his satire is the genuinely religious man, Orgon. Not for nothing did Molière himself take this part, a much bigger, more rounded role than that of Tartuffe. Orgon is indeed devout; but his piety is not enough to keep him from destroying both himself and those for whom he is responsible. Religious belief, as Molière demonstrates, can go hand in hand with arrogance, cruelty, inhumanity, and gullibility.

Clearly reluctant to let a work of this quality disappear without being performed, Molière fought on. He performed it at private gatherings as often as possible. In 1667, he managed to get the King's permission to perform a 'milder' version, with the hypocrite being given a new name, Panulphe. But, after one performance, the play was again banned, this time by order of Parliament, whose president wrote that 'it is not the place of theatre to preach the gospels'. Molière was so discouraged that he closed his theatre for six weeks. He continued the struggle, however, and was finally allowed to perform the play in 1669, in the version that we have today, and that is translated here. It was a triumphant success.

During those difficult years, Molière had other problems to contend with. The play that immediately followed the first *Tartuffe* was *Don Juan* (1665), a strange story of an impious libertine who gets his come-uppance. Again his enemies attacked, and again the play was withdrawn, this time after some fifteen performances. He never put it on again. It was later to inspire Da Ponte, the librettist for Mozart's *Don Giovanni*. The following year, he showed the first symptoms of the tuberculosis that was to kill him, and had to stop performing for two months.

The Misanthrope

The year 1666 saw the production of what is generally acknowledged to be Molière's masterpiece, *The Misanthrope*. His contemporaries greatly admired the play. To his friend the poet Boileau, the arbiter of literary merit, Molière was simply 'the author of *The Misanthrope*'. However, the play was not much appreciated by the public, and the box-office takings were unimpressive. This is partly because the play lacks the farcical element that the audience had come to expect from Molière, and which is present in all his other plays (except his tragicomedy *Don Garcie of Navarre*, of which more later). Even in *Tartuffe* there is some quite crude comedy, mostly involving Orgon hiding under the table, chasing his maidservant round the room, and so on. Furthermore, to play Alceste, Molière changed his acting technique. For the first time, he removed the heavy black moustache that seems to have been as much his comic signature as it was Groucho Marx's. Alceste is acknowledged as admirable by the other characters, which suggests a completely new approach to character portrayal on Molière's part. Compare the opinions given on Arnolphe by other characters in *The School for Wives* ('the man's completely off his head', 'he's gone right round the bend'), with Eliante's verdict on Alceste, when she affirms that his sincerity 'does have a noble and heroic side to it'. Alceste is ridiculed, but should we be admiring him as well? If he is in trouble, it is because he is too frank (giving his honest opinion on a mediocre sonnet), and too honest (refusing to soften up the judge so as to win his court case). Most significant of all is the way that Philinte responds to Alceste. Philinte takes the part of the 'reasoner', the sensible character who, in all Molière's great verse comedies, steps in to try to make the crazed protagonist see reason. In all the other plays, the reasoner is as adamant in his stance as the central figure; but in this play, we see Philinte agreeing with Alceste's disillusioned view of society (though not with his bitter rejection of it).

Then, too, the play is puzzling, and may make an audience feel uncomfortable. There is the universal attack on contemporary life, which seems to target the entire audience. The attack on the court, in particular, is uncompromisingly cynical. And it is difficult to know whom to like or admire in the play. The heroine, Celimene (played by his own wife Armande), is a shallow flirt, who plays off her suitors against each other. Then the play contains too many ambiguities. What precisely is Molière's solution to Alceste's predicament? Does he favour Philinte—is he arguing that the right thing to do is to play the part of a society gentleman, while acknowledging that society is fundamentally corrupt? Or does he favour the more honest and radical stance of Alceste? Presumably the former, since it becomes clear that Alceste is not viable in society, as he himself admits: 'It stands to reason that I can't live here, among | My fellows, since it's clear I can't control my tongue, | And I can't answer for the things that I might say. | I'd find myself in constant trouble, every day.' But we cannot be sure. It is not even clear whether Alceste's honesty is really what it seems—could he possibly be making a stand partly to impress his friend? Is he secretly as anxious for the good opinion of society as the other characters, but in his own, eccentric way?

The play is rich in additional mysteries, one of which is the incompatibility between Alceste and his beloved Celimene. His attitude and language have a serious, almost tragic quality at times, while she remains witty, malicious, and flippant. Part of the explanation is a practical one: always reluctant to waste material, Molière adapted speeches from his one, unsuccessful, attempt at tragicomedy, *Don Garcie of Navarre* (1661), and included them in *The Misanthrope*, Act IV scene 3. *Don Garcie* was the story of a young man destroyed by his violent, unfounded jealousy. Molière took his speeches from a crucial scene in which he upbraids his innocent mistress Elvire, and put them into Alceste's mouth. But then he changes all Elvire's earnest answers, and makes Celimene reply pertly to Alceste's heartfelt tirades. The two characters seem to be living in different worlds. The clash between their values and attitudes works brilliantly. Molière insists throughout that Alceste and Celimene are thoroughly ill suited to each other. This makes for further tensions in the play: Alceste rejects and despises society and everything it stands for, but, as Philinte says, 'Apparently, young Celimene has turned your head. | Yet she's a little flirt, and has a spiteful tongue.' Much of the play has Celimene and her admirers showing off their wit in a lively, amusing yet somehow despicable manner, while Alceste demonstrates his righteous indignation, yet somehow seems ridiculous.

The Misanthrope is a complex work, composed with loving care. Molière, who could dash off a play in a few days if need be, is said to have spent five years writing it. The result may have disappointed a public eager to split their sides, but it remains the play at which, as Donneau de Visé wrote, 'we laugh in our souls'.

By this period in his life, Molière was a sick man, slowly dying of tuberculosis. He continued to work frenetically. In the last seven years of his life, he produced sixteen new plays, not counting the revised *Tartuffe*. Not only did he write them, but he produced, directed, and acted in them. Several of these works were courtly plays, written for the King's theatre at Versailles. Others were light-hearted farces; but it was at this stage that he wrote his most famous prose plays, *George Dandin* (1668), *The Miser* (1668), *The Bourgeois Gentleman* (1670), and *The Hypochondriac* (1673). In addition, he wrote two fine verse plays, *Amphitryon* (1668, a comic retelling of a classical myth) and *The Clever Women*, the last play in this selection.

The Clever Women

The Clever Women (1672) is Molière's penultimate play. It is possible to detect signs of fatigue in the playwright (I have suggested that he wrote a slightly easier part for himself to play). But overall, the play is as witty, lively, and innovative as ever. The central scene, Act III scene 2, in which the Clever Women indulge in an orgy of mutual admiration with their absurd poet, Trissotin, is one of the funniest in all Molière. It is also one of the most biting of his contemporary satires: Trissotin is modelled on a real poet, the Abbé Cotin, and the poems that Molière ridicules so mercilessly are genuine works by Cotin. The main thrust of the satire, though, is aimed at the women themselves. Throughout his career, Molière consistently laughed at women who push themselves forward and try to better themselves intellectually (there are examples in *The School for Wives Criticized*, and *The Impromptu at Versailles*). As the hero of *The Clever Women*, Clitandre, puts it: 'Pedantic women never have been to my taste. | Some schooling in a woman may not be misplaced, | But being passionate about it's a mistake— | She mustn't cultivate learning for learning's sake.' Nevertheless, ten years before, with *The School for Wives*, Molière seemed to be arguing for the freedom of women to choose their own lifestyle and partner. Now he is saying that women should know their place: 'It's not quite the thing | To be a clever woman, and a bluestocking. | The subject of your study, your philosophy, | Should be to keep the house, practise economy, | Bring up the children to know how things should be done, | See that the staff behave, and that the home's well run.' The speaker here is Chrysalde, whose views are exaggeratedly one-sided; but other characters express similar opinions. Henriette, the sensible young woman who is being parted from her chosen lover by her pedantic bully of a mother, claims that the one thing she wants is to obey her parents, provided that they make rational decisions on her behalf. Molière seems further to imply that being a bluestocking does not make a woman happy in her heart of hearts. This is demonstrated by the curious character of Armande (oddly named after Molière's own wife). She has a rooted aversion to physical love, and, before the play begins, has rejected Clitandre, who wanted to marry her. She claims she is on a higher plane, but when she realizes she is losing him to her sister Henriette, she is furiously jealous. At the end, when Henriette and Clitandre are about to marry, she rounds on her bluestocking mother Philaminte: 'You plan to sacrifice me to their happiness?' Philaminte retaliates: 'No, not at all. Just look at it another way: | You've got philosophy, to be your prop and stay. | So chin up, and enjoy the wedding. You'll be fine.' In his attitude to women, Molière remains firmly rooted in his age, and a modern audience may find this aspect difficult to empathize with; but it is well worth making the effort. *The Clever Women* is one of the best constructed of all his works: as his contemporary Donneau de Visé puts it, a 'beautifully polished' piece.

TRANSLATOR'S NOTE

Molière insisted that plays are written to be acted. I have kept this in mind when translating him, aiming to produce not just a reading text, but one that would work in performance. There have been many successful updated versions of Molière—the plays contain so much that is relevant to modern life that they lend themselves to such treatment. However, these versions are free adaptations. A true translation of Molière must retain some of the period feel of the plays. Accordingly, I have kept the original names, used the occasional French title ('Monsieur', 'Chevalier', and so on), retained the allusions to seventeenth-century Parisian life—mentions of seventeenth-century clothes, court etiquette, travel on horseback, archaic medicine, etc. At the same time, I have avoided old-fashioned language. In the original, the speeches are clear and lively; an over-literary version would give too stilted an impression. I have aimed for a modern idiom, though not excessively so, avoiding current slang and anachronisms.

My version is a line-by-line translation, as close to the original as is compatible with the exigencies of the rhyme scheme. Readers wishing to refer to the original French will find that the lines of my translation correspond exactly.

Unlike most other translators of Molière, I have chosen to render his verse into alexandrines, the verse form he uses himself, the chosen metre of French classical theatre. That being said, the alexandrine in English verse is not at all the same as the classical French equivalent. To give a very rough idea of the rules governing the French form, the classical alexandrine in French is a twelve-syllable line, each syllable being separately pronounced, and given equal weight. There is a subordinate stress on the middle syllable of each line, and a stronger stress on the final syllable. There is a short break between the two halves of the line. For example:

       1   2 3 4   5 6   7   8   9   10 11 12
       ÉpOUsEr Un - E sOtte | Est pOUr n' Ê - trE pOInt sOt.

(Note that the final e of 'une', which would be silent in modern spoken French, is given the value of a syllable, while the final e of 'sotte' is elided, because it is followed by a vowel—a glimpse of the complex rules of French versification.)

Effortless though they seem, Molière's alexandrines adhere rigidly to the rules. Luckily for the translator, the alexandrine in English is more relaxed: the natural rhythms of English speech will govern the stresses of the line. It may, however, sometimes be useful to count the syllables when working out how to deliver a line—I have sometimes allowed myself to count adjacent vowels as separate syllables at the end of the line, for example:

> 1 2   3   4   5 6   7   8 9   10 11 12
> ThE wOm - An's mAd. TO hEll wIth hEr Ill - Us - I - Ons!

The lines are quite frequently broken up between several speakers. But the twelve-syllable rule still applies throughout.

I have also chosen to make my couplets rhyme, as Molière does. Some translators prefer to use blank verse, arguing that rhyming couplets sound unnatural in English, whereas in France they were the accepted dramatic form for centuries. My own view is that the translator has a double task: not only to produce a text that reads naturally, but also to give a flavour of the original. The rhyming alexandrines are much closer to the original than blank verse can ever be. I have perhaps emphasised the rhymes less strongly than the original by a rather more frequent use of *enjambement*, running the sense of one line on into the next, so that there is no natural pause at the end of the first line of a couplet, for example:

> It's hard to bear when all the gentlemen forget
> Your charms.

But on the whole, I have not tried to underplay the rhyme. It is natural in comedy for language to draw attention to itself.

My original French text is the two-volume *Œuvres complètes de Molière*, edited by Robert Jouanny (Paris, Garnier, 1962), based on the first complete edition of Molière's works of 1682.

SELECT BIBLIOGRAPHY

General works on Molière

Bamforth, Stephen (ed.), *Molière*. Proceedings of the Nottingham Molière Conference, 17–18 Dec. 1993 (University of Nottingham: Nottingham French Studies, 1994). (Contributions on a variety of topics.)

Bermel, Albert, *Molière's Theatrical Bounty: A New View of the Plays* (Carbondale: Southern Illinois University Press, 1990). (Plays analysed from a director's point of view, recent productions discussed.)

Calder, Andrew, *Molière: The Theory and Practice of Comedy* (London: Athlone Press, 1993). (Emphasis on ideas, influence of ancients. Detailed material on *Tartuffe*.)

Dock, Stephen Varick, *Costume and Fashion in the Plays of Jean-Baptiste Poquelin Molière: A Seventeenth-Century Perspective* (Geneva: Slatkine, 1992).

Gaines, James F., *Social Structures in Molière's Theatre* (Columbus: Ohio State University Press, 1984). (The social background to the plays, the status of servants, the monetary system, etc.)

Gossman, Lionel, *Men and Masks* (Baltimore: Johns Hopkins Press, 1963). (Molière in the context of his age. Particular emphasis on *Tartuffe* and *The Misanthrope*.)

Gross, Nathan, *From Gesture to Idea: Esthetics and Ethics in Molière's Comedy* (New York: Columbia University Press, 1982). (Concentrates on character portrayal, the importance of language, gesture and farce, particularly in *The School for Wives*, *Tartuffe*, and *The Misanthrope*.)

Gutwirth, Marcel, *Laughing Matter: An Essay on the Comic* (Ithaca, NY: Cornell University Press, 1993). (General thoughts on comedy by a Molière specialist.)

Howarth, W. D., *Molière: A Playwright and his Audience* (Cambridge: Cambridge University Press, 1982). (Molière the actor-playwright in the intellectual and moral climate of his age.)

Lalande, Roxanne Decker, *The Dynamics of Gender in Molière's Comedies* (Madison: Farleigh Dickinson University Press, 1996). (A modern feminist approach—how Molière depicts women; the dynamics of opposition between the sexes in his plays.)

McBride, Robert, *The Sceptical Vision of Molière* (London: Macmillan, 1977). (Molière's ideas: is his philosophy consistent? Does it contain contradictory elements?)

Moore, W. G., *Molière: A New Criticism* (Oxford: Oxford University Press, 1949). (Molière as a man of the theatre.)

Nurse, Peter Hampshire, *Molière and the Comic Spirit* (Geneva: Droz, 1991). (Molière's wisdom, debt to the humanist tradition. Analyses of the great plays.)

Individual Plays

The following short studies are clear, interesting and informative:

Broome, J. H., *Molière: 'L'École des femmes' and 'Le Misanthrope'* (London: Grant & Cutler (Critical Guides to French Texts, 18), 1982). (On *The School for Wives* and *The Misanthrope*.)

Hall, H. Gaston, *Molière: 'Tartuffe'* (London: Edward Arnold (Studies in French Literature 2), 1960).

Molière, *Le Misanthrope*, ed. with an introduction and commentary by Jonathan Mallinson (London: Bristol Classical Press, 1996). (French text, with substantial introduction and bibliography.)

Peacock, Noël, *Molière: 'Les Femmes savantes'* (London: Grant & Cutler (Critical Guides to French Texts 78), 1990). (On *The Clever Women*.)

Slater, Maya, 'Molière's Women: A Matter of Focus', in James Redmond (ed.), *Themes in Drama 11* (Cambridge: Cambridge University Press, 1989), 75–85. (How far was Molière favourable to his female characters?)

Whitton, David, *Molière: 'Le Misanthrope'* (Glasgow: University of Glasgow (Glasgow Introductory Guides to French Literature 17, 1991).

Further Reading in Oxford World's Classics

Lope de Vega, *Three Major Plays*, trans. and ed. Gwynne Edwards.

Molière, *Don Juan and Other Plays*, trans. and ed. Ian McLean and George Gravely.

Jean Racine, *Britannicus, Phaedra, Athaliah*, trans. and ed. C. H. Sisson.

A CHRONOLOGY OF MOLIÈRE

1622   Baptism, on 15 January, of Jean–Baptiste Poquelin, son of Jean Poquelin, royal upholsterer and tapestry-maker, at the church of St Eustache in Paris.

1631–9[?]   Jean-Baptiste Poquelin at the Collège de Clermont in Paris; he completes his education in the humanities.

1640[?]   Begins university law studies.

1643   Abandons the law and renounces his association with his father's trade; together with members of the Béjart family, he founds the 'Illustre Théâtre' troupe and hires a theatre in Paris.

1644   Adopts the name 'Molière' and becomes the head of the troupe.

1645–58   After difficult beginnings, the Illustre Théâtre abandons the attempt to found a theatre in Paris and tours in the provinces, playing mainly in the south of France.

1658   Return to Paris, under the protection of Louis XIV's brother, Monsieur (who promises an annual pension but never pays it). The troupe is now known as the 'Troupe de Monsieur', and performs both comedy and tragedy in the Salle du Petit-Bourbon, which it shares with Italian actors; it also performs in court festivities and private houses.

1659   First performance, on 18 November, of the *Précieuses ridicules*, a topical satire which draws attention to the troupe.

1660   The troupe prepare the move to the Salle du Palais Royal: first performance of *Sganarelle ou le cocu imaginaire*, a successful one-act comedy.

1661   First performances of a heroic comedy *Dom Garcie de Navarre* (a failure), *L'École des maris* (a success), and *Les Fâcheux*, a three-act comedy commissioned for the court by the Chancellor, Fouquet. Molière attracts the attention of the king.

1662   Marriage to Armande Béjart, sister of Madeleine Béjart, Molière's rejected mistress (contemporary gossip claims that Armande is the daughter, not the sister, of Madeleine). First performance of *L'École des femmes*, a highly successful five-act verse comedy.

1663   Long public debate about the merits of *L'École des femmes*, carried on for the most part in the form of short plays produced by Molière's troupe (the *Critique de l'École des femmes* and the *Impromptu de Versailles*) and their rivals at the Hôtel de Bourgogne, who specialize in performing tragedies.

1664   Molière's first child, Louis, is born (he is to die on 10 November in the same year) and is baptized at the church of St Germain l'Auxerrois with the King as one godparent. A number of plays produced for the court, including an incomplete version of *Tartuffe*, which is immediately banned as sacrilegious, but which is commissioned for private performance by influential members of the nobility.

1665   *Dom Juan* first performed; Molière's troupe is now called the 'Troupe du Roi' and receives a substantial royal pension. Molière's second child, Esprit Madeleine, is born on 3 August.

1666   First performance of *Le Misanthrope* (a five-act verse comedy), *Le Médecin malgré lui*, and *Mélicerte* (a three-act pastoral comedy).

1667   One public performance of *Tartuffe*, followed by its renewed condemnation and banning by legal and ecclesiastical authorities.

1668   First performances of *Amphytrion* (a three-act comedy), *George Dandin* (with an accompanying ballet at Versailles; without a ballet at the Salle du Palais-Royal), and *L'Avare*.

1669   *Tartuffe* finally is granted a licence for public performance; first performance of *Monsieur de Pourceaugnac* (a three-act comedy-ballet).

1670   First performances of *Les Amants magnifiques* (a three-act comedy-ballet) and *Le Bourgeois gentilhomme*.

1671   First performances of *Psyché* (a five-act tragedy-ballet), *Les Fourberies de Scapin*, and *La Comtesse d'Escarbagnas* (a one-act comedy).

1672   First performance of *Les Femmes savantes*, a five-act comedy.

1673   Performance of *Le Malade imaginaire*, a three-act comedy-ballet; at the fourth performance, on 17 February, Molière collapses on stage and dies later in the evening.

THE SCHOOL FOR WIVES

1662

CHARACTERS

ARNOLPHE,* otherwise known as Monsieur de la Souche.

AGNES,* an innocent young girl, Arnolphe's ward.

HORACE,* lover of Agnes.

ALAIN,* country lad, valet to Arnolphe.

GEORGETTE,* country girl, servant to Arnolphe.

CHRYSALDE,* friend to Arnolphe.

ENRIQUE, brother-in-law to Chrysalde.

ORONTE, father to Horace, and friend to Arnolphe.

A LAWYER.

*The scene is set in Paris, in a town square.**

ACT I

SCENE 1

ARNOLPHE, CHRYSALDE

CHRYSALDE. You've come to marry her tomorrow, do you say?

ARNOLPHE. That's right. I want to sort things out without delay.

CHRYSALDE. We seem to be alone. Let's have a quiet word:
I want to talk to you, and not be overheard.
As your close friend, will you allow me to be frank?
When I heard of your plan, I must say my heart sank.
Whichever way I look at it, your project's wrong.
If you get married, we must dread the dénouement.

ARNOLPHE. My friend, you're very nervous. What you say is true
In some cases—not mine. It may apply to you.   10
A man like you feels threatened, and that's why he warns
That everyone who marries ends up wearing horns.*

CHRYSALDE. Well, nobody's immune, a man may come unstuck.
It's useless to take steps to circumvent bad luck.
No. I'm afraid for you, with your sarcastic wit:
A hundred married men have borne the brunt of it.
You haven't spared a single husband, great or small—
Your critical attacks destroyed them, one and all.
There's nothing you like more. With you it's quite a craze,
Exposing private scandals to the public gaze.   20

ARNOLPHE. Quite so: and where on earth is there another town
Where if you're cuckolded, you hardly even frown?
You find those husbands here, in every shape and size;
They're led a merry dance, as you must recognize.
One husband earns the money for his wife to give
To men who cuckold him as their prerogative.
Another one, no less corrupt in his own way,
Does well—his wife gets lavish presents every day.
He doesn't mind, and thinks it's nothing untoward:

She tells him it's her virtue getting its reward.   30
One husband makes a fuss. Why bother? It's no good.
Another plays it cool, preferring to collude,
And welcomes the young man he knows his own wife loves,
And most politely asks to take his hat and gloves.
The woman sometimes plays an artful, cunning part,
Makes sure the husband knows about her new sweetheart.
The husband takes the bait, and falls under her spell.
He pities his own rival, thinking that all's well.
Another tricks her husband, so he disregards
Her lavish spending, saying that she's won at cards.   40
Her husband thanks the Lord. If he knew what the game
She played was sometimes called, he mightn't feel the same.
If everything I see gives me good cause to mock,
I can't be serious: all the world's a laughing stock.
So why not joke?

CHRYSALDE.   Because it's dangerous to chaff.
Your victims will be keen to take their turn to laugh.
I know how people talk; there's nothing they like more
Than hearing all the gossip. Scandal, they adore.
But in society, if people spill the beans,
A wise man shuts his mouth, and never intervenes.   50
I'd rather play things down, and seem agreeable,
Not let on I find gossip unacceptable.
Of course, like you, I don't intend to imitate
The way that certain husbands let their wives dictate.
But I don't make a point of saying what I think:
The thought that it might turn against me makes me shrink.
To prophesy the steps you will or you won't take
And swear you'll never go the same way's a mistake.
If I should be unlucky—I can't tell you how—
And find my own disgrace displayed here, on my brow,   60
I'm almost sure that, since I've always been discreet,
Society would not rejoice at my defeat.
I might even be privileged in my despair
To hear some kind souls murmur, seems a bit unfair.
But you, my friend, you're not the most discreet of men.
You're running quite a risk, I tell you once again.

When you attack poor husbands, reputations fall.
You let your tongue run on to ridicule them all.
You've been a very devil. Now you must beware—
If *you* don't want to fall, you'll have to tread with care.   70
If all your enemies can find an opening,
They'll make a point of laughing at your suffering,
And...

ARNOLPHE. Hey! No need to panic, I know, there's no doubt—
No one can outsmart me—they'll never catch me out!
I know what women do: they use us as their pawns,
And do their best to trick us into wearing horns.
Their cunning plans are organized to dupe us all—
So I've taken some steps to make sure I *don't* fall.
The girl I plan to marry's perfectly naive,
And she'll spare my brow here from horns, that I believe.   80

CHRYSALDE. So, in a word, you plan a marriage with a fool?*

ARNOLPHE. To wed a fool is not to be one, as a rule.
Your wife may turn out very wise, much more than mine,
But if a woman's clever, that's an awful sign.
I know some men who've paid a dreadful penalty
For marrying a woman with ability.
What, let myself be lumbered with a witty wife,
Who visits all the salons? No, not on your life!
The sort who writes of love in prose and even verse,
And is at home to all the gentry, which is worse—   90
But me, the husband, I'm the one they all forgot,
Thrown on one side, discarded, left alone to rot?
The last thing that I want's a female raconteur.
A wife who writes knows more than can be good for her.
My wife won't be like that—a genius, sublime.
She mustn't even know what's meant by the word 'rhyme',
And if she joins in with their game of 'box'—you play*
By using words which rhyme with 'box' when you must say
What your box has in it,—I want her to reply,
When her turn comes to speak, 'I know—a custard pie!'   100
I want her ignorant, since all she needs to know
Is how to love me, pray to God, and spin and sew.

CHRYSALDE. So you're determined on an idiotic bride?

ARNOLPHE. Yes. I'd prefer an ugly moron by my side.
   I won't take on a girl who's clever, witty too.*

CHRYSALDE. But I think wit and beauty...

ARNOLPHE.   Decency will do.

CHRYSALDE. But how can your dull bride, with her deficiency,
   Begin to understand what's meant by decency?
   Apart from which, I think it might be rather grim
   To spend one's days in company with someone dim.   110
   So are you being sensible? Do you believe
   You'll keep your brow horn-free? And aren't you quite naive?
   A clever woman may dishonour you, indeed,
   But she'll know what she's up to, when she does the deed.
   A stupid one may fail her duty constantly,
   But you may find she's doing it unknowingly.

ARNOLPHE. Your argument's quite brilliant, but it doesn't weigh
   With me. I answer in the words of Rabelais:*
   'Oh, preach and plead with me until it's Pentecost'
   To take a clever wife—I say your cause is lost.   120
   By all means lecture on, but when you reach the end,
   You'll find I won't agree with you, my learned friend.

CHRYSALDE. I won't say any more.

ARNOLPHE.   I'll do the thing my way.
   I've chosen my own wife, I'm going to have my say.
   I'm rich enough: I can afford the luxury
   Of taking someone who owes everything to me.
   She's got no dowry: she can't fling that in my face,
   So she'll rely on me. I'll keep her in her place.
   I fell in love with her when she was only four:
   I'd never seen a child so well behaved before.   130
   Her mother was hard up and couldn't make ends meet—
   So I hit on a plan which struck me as quite neat,
   And asked her for the girl. The peasant woman was
   Delighted to agree in such a worthy cause.
   I had her sent to school, according to my plan,

In a small convent, never visited by man.
The nuns were told that it was indispensable
To bring her up as ignorant as possible.
Thanks be to God, my efforts brought complete success,
And, growing up, she was so lacking in finesse   140
That I blessed heaven's grace for having been so kind
As help me get the very wife I had in mind.
I took her out of school, and as my residence
Is full of visitors, chose, in my vigilance,
To make sure she was safe, and well under my thumb:
I placed her in this house, where visitors don't come,
And, not wanting to spoil her sheer naivety,
Engaged a pair of servants innocent as she.
Do you want to know why I'm telling you all this?
To show I've thought of everything, not been remiss.   150
And now I'd like to ask you, as a faithful friend,
To dine with us tonight. Come, will you condescend?
Then you'll see the result of my experiment,
And judge if my precaution's worthy of contempt.

CHRYSALDE. Oh, I'll be there.

ARNOLPHE.   You may, at your convenience,
Assess the girl, evaluate her innocence.

CHRYSALDE. As far as that's concerned, your strange account has
    led
Me to...

ARNOLPHE. The truth is even stranger than I've said.
It's wonderful what simple fancies she confides,
And she comes out with views to make you split your sides.   160
The other day (I tell you, this you won't believe),
She was in quite a state, came to me, all naive,
And in her innocence, I swear it was sincere,
She asked if women made their babies through the ear.*

CHRYSALDE. I'm pleased for you, Monsieur Arnolphe...

ARNOLPHE.   No, no! For shame!
How many times must you be told? Don't use that name!...

CHRYSALDE. However hard I try, it comes out in a whoosh—
    I just can't seem to call you Monsieur de la Souche.*
    What devil inspired you, if I may be so bold,
    To un-baptize yourself at forty-two years old,*   170
    To take a rotten tree-stump lying on your land,
    And use it for a name that's trying to be grand?

ARNOLPHE. Look, that's the name they give my country house;
    beside,
    La Souche sounds better than Arnolphe: it's not just pride.

CHRYSALDE. It's madness to give up the name your fathers bore,
    And choose a new one that's invented. Furthermore,
    You're not the only fellow bitten by this bug:
    Here's a comparison. Don't say it's pure humbug:
    A peasant that I know used to be called Fat Pierre;
    He owned a plot of land, of which he was the heir.   180
    He dug a ditch around it, then he seemed to feel
    His isle entitled him to be 'Monsieur de l'Isle'.*

ARNOLPHE. I could have done without that story—very louche.
    But anyway my name is Monsieur de la Souche.
    I changed it for a reason, I prefer it now:*
    You'd best forget the other, or we'll have a row.

CHRYSALDE. But people find it very difficult to change—
    They call you Arnolphe, and they find your new name strange.

ARNOLPHE. I can't object if people call me that, when they
    Don't know...   190

CHRYSALDE.   Oh, I won't argue. Have it your own way.
    My tongue's so disobedient. Hard work to induce
    My mouth to try and call you Monsieur de la Souche.

ARNOLPHE. Goodbye. I'm knocking at my door to say hallo.
    I've only just got back, the servants still don't know.

CHRYSALDE [*exiting*]. By God, I think the man's completely off his
    head.

ARNOLPHE. In some ways, he's a bit eccentric, I'd have said.
    It's strange to see how far we each have passions,

And are besotted with our own fixations!
Hey there!...

SCENE 2

ALAIN, GEORGETTE, ARNOLPHE

ALAIN. Who is it?

ARNOLPHE.   Open up now! I dare say
They'll welcome me. It's days now since I went away.   200

ALAIN. Who is it?

ARNOLPHE.   Me!

ALAIN.   Georgette!

GEORGETTE.   Yes, what?

ALAIN.   Open the door.

GEORGETTE. No. Open it yourself!

ALAIN.   No, you go.

GEORGETTE.   No, what for?

ALAIN. Well, I won't go, so there!

ARNOLPHE.   Look here, what's going on?
I'm waiting at the door! I've had enough! Come on!

GEORGETTE. Who's there?

ARNOLPHE.   Your master.

GEORGETTE.   Hey, Alain!

ALAIN.   What?

GEORGETTE.   It's Monsieur.
You open up.

ALAIN.   No, you!

GEORGETTE.   The fire—it needs a stir.

ALAIN. The cat's about. I better shut the birdcage door.

ARNOLPHE. If you don't come at once and open up, before
I count to three, you won't get anything to eat.*
Aha!   210

GEORGETTE. Hey, you, why rush? I'm on my way. Don't cheat!

ALAIN. I'm coming, Sir! Get lost, you with your monkey tricks!

GEORGETTE. Get out of it!

ALAIN.   No, you get out! This ain't for kicks!

GEORGETTE. I want to let him in.

ALAIN.   That's what I want to do.

GEORGETTE. You ain't going near that door.

ALAIN.   No more you ain't.

GEORGETTE.   Nor you.

ARNOLPHE. I can't believe I'm standing here so patiently...

ALAIN. Look, I'm the one, Monsieur!

GEORGETTE.   It was me, honestly!

ALAIN. Monsieur's here what deserves all the respect I got,
Or else I'd show...
                    [*makes to hit* GEORGETTE, *but accidentally hits*
                    ARNOLPHE

ARNOLPHE.   Ouch!

ALAIN.   Sorry!

ARNOLPHE.   Bungling idiot!

ALAIN. She was the one, Monsieur!

ARNOLPHE.   Be quiet, you clumsy lout!
Now try to answer me, and stop messing about.   220
Alain, I want to know, how are you keeping? Well?

ALAIN. Monsieur, we are... Monsieur, we have... Thank God, I
tell...

[*Each time* ALAIN *starts to speak,* ARNOLPHE *takes his hat off for him*

ARNOLPHE. When you talk to your master, take your hat off, oaf,
And mind your manners. Time you learned to use your loaf!

ALAIN. You're quite right, I was wrong.

ARNOLPHE.   Ask Agnes to come down.
When I went off, was she in any way cast down?

GEORGETTE. Cast down? No.

ARNOLPHE.   No?

GEORGETTE.   That's right.

ARNOLPHE.   How's that?

GEORGETTE.   See, probably
She thought you was about to come back presently.
We never heard no beast come down the avenue,
No horse, no mule, no ass, but she thought it was you.   230

SCENE 3

ARNOLPHE, AGNES, ALAIN, GEORGETTE

ARNOLPHE. Oh, look, that's a good sign—her sewing in her hand.
Well, Agnes, as you see, my journey's over, and
I'm back. So, are you pleased?

AGNES.   Yes, Monsieur, thank the Lord.

ARNOLPHE. I'm pleased to see you, too. That should be your
reward.
It looks as though you've been quite well, and happy too?

AGNES. But for the fleas which bothered me the whole night
through.*

ARNOLPHE. You'll soon have someone in your bed to give them
chase.

AGNES. I'll be delighted.

ARNOLPHE.   I imagine that's the case.
What are you doing?

AGNES.   Hemming kerchiefs for my hair.
Your nightcaps and your shirts are made, ready to wear.*   240

ARNOLPHE. That's very good. Now, that's enough. Be off upstairs,
And I'll be back soon, when I've seen to my affairs.
I've got important business to discuss with you.

[Exeunt all except ARNOLPHE

You modern heroines, you clever women, who*
Make such a show of feeling and of sentiment,
I here defy your learning—every document,
Your letters, novels, verse, all your intelligence—
To match her in her honest, blushing ignorance.

SCENE 4

ARNOLPHE, HORACE

ARNOLPHE. A woman's riches shouldn't blind us to her worth,
And if her honour's... No! It can't be!... What on earth?...   250
No, I'm mistaken... No... Yes... No, it has to be
Hor...

HORACE. Monsieur Ar...

ARNOLPHE.   Horace!

HORACE.   Arnolphe!

ARNOLPHE.   I'm thrilled to see
You here. When did you come?

HORACE.   Nine days ago.

ARNOLPHE.   I say!

HORACE. I called on you at once, but heard you'd gone away.

ARNOLPHE. Off to the country.

HORACE.   Yes, you'd been away two days.

ARNOLPHE. You think they're children, then they grow so many
     ways!
     I'm flabbergasted! Look at him! What handsomeness—
     Last time I saw him, he was no bigger than this!

HORACE. Well, there you are.

ARNOLPHE.   And how's your father, dear Oronte,
     The best, most worthy friend a man could ever want?   260
     So, what's he up to? How's his health? What does he say?
     He knows I care for him—that's always been my way.
     We haven't seen each other now for many a year,
     Nor written to each other all that time, I fear.

HORACE. Indeed, Monsieur Arnolphe, he's in tremendous form:
     He'd given me a letter for you, to inform
     You why I've come; but then he wrote again to say—
     Without explaining why—he'll be here any day.
     A local man went to America to make
     His fortune. He's succeeded, if I don't mistake.   270
     He's been gone fourteen years. You know him, I perceive?

ARNOLPHE. Not me. But what's his name?

HORACE.   It's Enrique, I believe.

ARNOLPHE. No.

HORACE.   Well, my father mentions him and says he's back
     As if he thought I knew him pretty well (alack,
     I don't), but Father writes that they're both due to meet
     For some mysterious business they've got to complete.

ARNOLPHE. I'll be delighted to play host to my old friend.
     And I'll make him most welcome here—you may depend
     On that.

                              [*Reads the letter*

          Why must our friends insist on being polite,
     Eh? All these civil greetings! It just isn't right.   280
     He didn't need to write—as I'm his friend indeed,
     He knows I'll gladly give you anything you need.

HORACE. Believe me, I'm a man to take you at your word.
I need a hundred pistoles, is that quite absurd?*

ARNOLPHE. You're doing me a favour. By a stroke of luck
I've got the money here, so you won't come unstuck.
No, keep the purse as well.

HORACE.   I must...*

ARNOLPHE.   No, let it be.
But now, I want the lowdown. How d'you find Paree?

HORACE. The buildings are superb, the population teems,
It's packed with splendid entertainments, so it seems.   290

ARNOLPHE. We all make our own pleasures. Time and time again,
Those clever fellows, widely known as ladies' men
In this fine city, quickly earn the epithet:
My lady tends to be a natural coquette.
The blondes and the brunettes are always well disposed,
The husbands, for their part, are all led by the nose.
It's fun to watch: I find the goings-on risqué:
I often view these antics like some private play.
But have you made a conquest? How are things with you,
Eh? Since you've been in town, have you been lucky too?   300
Your looks are worth a fortune, now you're in your prime:
A man like you can make a cuckold, any time.

HORACE. No, I won't try to hide the truth from you, my friend.
I have had an experience here, and I intend
To tell you all about it: I'd like you to know.

ARNOLPHE. Aha! A saucy story! This'll make me crow.
I'll write it in my notebook, it'll cause a riot!

HORACE. But please don't talk about it, keep my secret quiet.

ARNOLPHE. Of course!

HORACE.   You know that in such situations
Letting it out destroys all our precautions.   310
But, anyway, I'll tell you what's been going on:
I've fallen for a lovely girl—my heart's been won.
The way I set about it worked, right from the start—

I quickly found the way to occupy her heart;
I won't go into details. Let's just say, she fell—
And my new love affair's progressing very well.

ARNOLPHE. Who is she?

HORACE.   A young girl who lives in that house there,
The one with reddish walls that stands across the square.
She's terribly naive, but that's her guardian's fault.
He's kept her shut away, and this is the result.   320
He tried to make her stupid, but, though she's a dunce,
She's very charming, and you'd take to her at once.
She's really sweet and lovable, and with an air
That no man could resist, though she's no savoir-faire.
But wait a minute—do you know the girl I mean?
A perfect beauty, quite the best you've ever seen?
They call her Agnes.

ARNOLPHE [*aside*].   Oh, the pain!

HORACE.   As for the man,
They call him de la Zousse or Sauce—a gentleman.
I didn't really get the name; in recompense,
I learnt he's plenty money, but too little sense.   330
They say that he's a laughing stock, and no mistake.
Do you know who he is?

ARNOLPHE [*aside*].   This is too much to take!

HORACE. What is it? Won't you answer me?

ARNOLPHE.   I know him, yes.

HORACE. He's crazy, isn't he?

ARNOLPHE.   Mmmm...

HORACE.   What d'you say? Confess—
You're saying 'yes'. Ridiculously jealous, eh?
And stupid? You confirm what all the neighbours say?
But anyway, my pretty Agnes's won my heart.
She's quite adorable. I tell you, for my part,
I think she's lovely, and I'll do the best I can
To save her from the power of this eccentric man.   340

Yes, she's my heart's desire: there's nothing I won't do
To get control of her, and give that brute his due.
I need your cash because of this decision—
Your money will finance the operation.
An enterprise may fail, however hard we try,
And money is the key, you know as well as I.
It takes hard currency to turn a person's head:
In love as well as war it helps you get ahead.
You're looking glum. What is it? Can it be that you
Are in two minds about what I intend to do?   350

ARNOLPHE. No, I was only thinking.

HORACE.   I've gone on too long...
Goodbye. I'll come round later—please, don't get me wrong.

[*Exit* HORACE

ARNOLPHE. Ah! Must I...

HORACE [*re-entering*].   By the way, make sure that you're discreet,
And don't go spreading it around, now, I repeat.

[*Exit*

ARNOLPHE. My heart's so heavy, and I...

HORACE [*re-entering*].   Specially, my friend,
Don't tell my father; he may go off the deep end.

[*Exit*

ARNOLPHE. Oh!...

[*Looks round, thinking* HORACE *is returning*

              What a conversation! That was misery!
I've never been in such a dreadful quandary!
He didn't think twice, rushed to tell me everything.
He's so naive, the whole thing's most embarrassing.   360
Admittedly my other name helped to deceive
Him—but he's wild, and I think that he's taken leave
Of all his senses. Though I squirmed, I had to hear
The whole of it to find out what I had to fear,
To push him to the limit, make him indiscreet.

I've got to know the truth. However did they meet?
I'd better catch him up—he can't be far away.
I really must discover what he's got to say.
What's going to happen? I can't get it off my mind,
And people often look for what they dread to find.   370

ACT II

SCENE 1

ARNOLPHE. It turned out for the best, there's no call for dismay
Because I didn't catch him up, and lost my way.
I was in such distress I had no self-control:
My feelings would have showed—I couldn't hide the whole.
I'm eaten up with misery, and he'd have guessed.
I don't want him to know, that's why I've not confessed.
I'm not at all the sort of man to let things go,
And step aside in favour of this Romeo.
I've got to stop his game. I'll start by finding out
What all their private get-togethers were about.   380
My honour is at stake, I'm taking it to heart.
I see her as my wife, and that's what makes me smart.
Ah, if she's let me down, then I'll be filled with shame:
For everything she does, she's doing in my name.
O tragic banishment! Unhappy wanderlust!

SCENE 2

ARNOLPHE, ALAIN, GEORGETTE

ALAIN. Ah, Monsieur, this time...

ARNOLPHE.   Silence, both of you. You must
Come here at once. Come on, get over here, I say.

GEORGETTE. Ugh! I feel scared. My blood's gone curdled with
dismay!

ARNOLPHE. So this is how you both obeyed me when I went
Away—you both conspired to throw me off the scent?   390

GEORGETTE. Oh, please don't eat me up, Monsieur, I beg of you.*

ALAIN [*aside*]. A mad dog's bitten him, he's gone a bit cuckoo.

ARNOLPHE. Ouf! I can scarcely speak, my brain pan's caving in!
 I'm stifling! I wish I could strip down to my skin!
 You wretched riffraff, you allowed a man to come
 Into my house? Don't try to run away, you scum!
 I want to know at once... Don't you dare move!... I need
 The two of you to tell me... Hey, there!... Yes, indeed...
 The first of you to move will get knocked down, or more.
 This man, now. How did he get his foot in the door?   400
 Eh? Hurry up and tell me, look sharp now, be quick.
 Don't hang about. Come on, now...

ALAIN and GEORGETTE [*falling to their knees*]. Ah, ah!

GEORGETTE.   I feel sick.

ALAIN. I'm dead!

ARNOLPHE.   I'm in a lather. Mustn't rush at it.
 I'd better fan myself, and walk about a bit.
 When he was just a little boy, how could I guess
 He'd end up doing this? God, I can't stand the stress!
 It might be better if I talk to her alone,
 And coax her to own up to everything she's done.
 I must keep calm, and try not to make such a row:
 Oh, my poor heart, be patient! Easy, easy now.   410
 Get up, you, and go in, tell Agnes to come here.
 No, wait! I'll go myself. That's vital. I must hear
 How she reacts if her response is unprepared.
 She'd better not be warned, or else she may get scared.
 You two, wait for me here.

SCENE 3

ALAIN, GEORGETTE

GEORGETTE.   My God, he's horrible!
 The way he looked—it scared me something terrible!
 I never saw a Christian soul so hideous.

ALAIN. I told you that young man would make him furious.

GEORGETTE. Well, why must he be such a brute? It isn't right
To keep our mistress locked up here, way out of sight.   420
And why won't he let anyone so much as take
A look at the poor girl? It's barmy, no mistake.

ALAIN. It's all because he's suffering from jealousy.

GEORGETTE. But what's his problem? Why? It's downright lunacy.

ALAIN. I'll tell you why—because... because he's jealous, see?

GEORGETTE. But why's he jealous, eh? And angry as can be?

ALAIN. Well, jealousy, you see... now, listen here, Georgette...
It's something... here... which makes a man feel under threat...
And makes him look at other men with such dislike.
Look here, let me explain what jealousy is like,   430
And then you'll understand why master seems so stup-
Efied. Imagine if you've got a bowl of soup,
And then some greedy-guts comes running up to try
To help himself. Well? You'd go mad, you won't deny.

GEORGETTE. What then?

ALAIN.   I'll make it even clearer if I can—
You see, a woman is a soup-bowl for her man;*
And when a fellow sees how other men begin
To gather round his soup and dip their fingers in,
He blows his top at once, it's driving him insane.   439

GEORGETTE. All right; but why don't all the others do the same?
Why are so many husbands free and easy, when
Their wives are hanging round with all those handsome men?

ALAIN. Well, they're not selfish, and I think they know their place.
He wants her for himself.

GEORGETTE.   Oh, no! We'd better brace
Ourselves—he's coming back.

ALAIN.   You've got good eyes, it's him.

GEORGETTE. He's got his troubles.

ALAIN.   Yes—that's why he looks so grim.

SCENE 4

ARNOLPHE, AGNES, ALAIN, GEORGETTE

ARNOLPHE. The Emperor Augustus met a certain Greek
    Who told him of a useful, practical technique
    To help you keep your cool, when you feel under threat.
    Apparently, you have to say your alphabet,   450
    To give yourself the time to overcome your rage:
    You won't lose your control, or go on the rampage.*
    I saw Agnes just now, and followed this advice.
    I asked her to come for a walk, as a device
    To get her out, so I can talk to her alone.
    I'll work round cunningly to my suspicions, grown
    So horribly important, now my trust is gone.
    I'll put out feelers, try to learn what's going on.
    Come here, Agnes.

                                        [*To* ALAIN *and* GEORGETTE

                Be off.

SCENE 5

ARNOLPHE, AGNES

ARNOLPHE.   A fine day for a walk.

AGNES. Yes, fine.   460

ARNOLPHE.   Fine weather, too.

AGNES.   Yes, fine.

ARNOLPHE.   What's new? Let's talk.

AGNES. My little kitten's dead.

ARNOLPHE.   That's sad, but tell yourself

All men are mortal, and it's each man for himself.
When I was in the country, did you have much rain?

AGNES. No.

ARNOLPHE. Was it very boring?

AGNES.   No, I can't complain.

ARNOLPHE. What did you do while I was gone? Come on, do tell.

AGNES. I did you six new shirts, and six nightcaps as well.

ARNOLPHE. You know, Agnes, my dear, the world's a funny place.
There's so much idle gossip, it's quite hard to face.
Some neighbours told me that a young man no one knew
Came to the house when I was gone, just to see you,   470
And you let him come in, and even socialize—
But I told them their tattle was a pack of lies,
And I was keen to bet they'd made a bad mistake...

AGNES. Oh, goodness, please don't bet, because you'll lose your
stake!

ARNOLPHE. What! So it really happened, and this man...

AGNES.   It's true!
He hardly left the house for days, I promise you!

ARNOLPHE [aside]. At least she's quite sincere, and since she has
confessed,
It's clear her innocence at least has stood the test.

                                                       [Aloud

But if I'm not mistaken, surely I recall
I said to turn away all strangers who might call.   480

AGNES. Yes, but you don't know how it happened, do you see.
I tell you, you'd have acted just the same as me.

ARNOLPHE. Perhaps; but meanwhile, tell me how it came about.

AGNES. It's quite amazing, very odd as you'll find out:
As I was sitting sewing on the balcony,
I raised my eyes and saw, beneath that very tree,
A handsome, fine young man, who, seeing me up there,

Bowed most respectfully, and with a courtly air.
I wanted to be civil, that was my concern,
So I made a respectful curtsey, in my turn.   490
He bowed again most promptly, not to be outdone,
And I produced a curtsey. Well, we'd just begun,
For he reacted with a third obliging bow,
And I immediately curtsied back. And now,
He's starting to walk back and forth, and every time
He passes me, he bows politely. Meanwhile, I'm
Observing him most carefully as he goes past,
And curtseying to him, determined to hold fast.
And if the evening hadn't come, I'm telling you,
I would have gone on standing there, till now. It's true—   500
I'd never once have given in, it couldn't be
That he should think me less polite and nice than he.

ARNOLPHE. That's good!

AGNES.   As I was standing by the door next day,
An old woman came up, and spoke to me this way:
'My child, may the good Lord protect you, and preserve
Those lovely looks for many a long year. I observe
That God made you a pretty girl; but he did not
Intend you to misuse the gifts that you have got:
For you must know that you have practically slain
A heart, and forced a man to cry aloud in pain.'   510

ARNOLPHE [aside]. You devilish old hag, I hate you, damn your
    eyes!

AGNES. 'Me, wound someone?' I cried, in very great surprise.
'That's right,' she answered. 'And he's now in agony—
The man you saw last evening on your balcony.'
'Oh, dear, how can I have done this to him?' I said.
'Perhaps I carelessly dropped something on his head?'
'No, no, it was your eyes that struck the fatal blow—
They only had to look at him to lay him low.'
'Oh, goodness me,' I said. 'This is astonishing!
Are my eyes really dangerous? The very thing!'   520
'Oh yes, my child, your eyes can kill men, have no doubt—
For they contain a poison you don't know about:

To cut the story short, the poor boy's in a state,'
The kind old woman told me. 'If you hesitate,
Or won't repair the harm you did him with your gaze,
He'll be as good as dead, in just about two days.'
'Oh, goodness!' I replied. 'That would be sad, it's true.
Of course I want to help! Tell me what I must do.'
She told me: 'What he needs to stop him getting worse,
Is just to sit with you a little, and converse.   530
Your eyes are now the only cure for his disease—
Although they're both to blame, they still can bring him ease.'
'I willingly agree,' said I. 'If that's the case,
He's welcome to come round and see me at our place.'

ARNOLPHE [*aside*]. You execrable witch, you got me in this fix!
    May hell repay you for your charitable tricks!

AGNES. Now you know why he came to see me in his plight.
    I cured him. Don't you think, yourself, that I did right?
    It would have been too bad to turn him down, instead
    Of helping him to live, to let him drop down dead.   540
    You know how sad I am when I see people cry—
    I even get upset to watch a chicken die.

ARNOLPHE [*aside*]. All this is the result of too much innocence.
    I should have stayed at home, and showed a bit more sense!
    I left this kind, good-natured maiden all alone,
    Exposed her to the libertines—I should have known.
    Can it be the young whelp, in all the brouhaha,
    Has not played by the rules, and let things go too far?

AGNES. What can be wrong with you? You don't seem very glad.
    Have I annoyed you? Mmm? Did I do something bad?   550

ARNOLPHE. No, no, but tell me all about what happened, when
    The young man came to visit. What was it like then?

AGNES. Oh, dear—he was as overjoyed as he could be,
    And all his symptoms went the moment he saw me.
    He brought a most delightful casket which he set
    Before me, and gave cash to Alain and Georgette.
    You'd have been just as pleased as us, if you had known...

ARNOLPHE. Yes, but what did he do, when you two were alone?

AGNES. He swore his love for me was endless; in a word,
He said the sweetest things that you have ever heard.   560
I've never listened to such words as that before.
And when I listen, I just seem to long for more.
It's very nice, it tickles deep inside somewhere,
A most exciting part I didn't know was there.

ARNOLPHE [aside]. Oh, what an inquisition! And for once it's true
For me to tell her, this will hurt me more than you!

[To AGNES

It's clear that all his presents were a great success.
Apart from that, did he attempt the odd caress?

AGNES. Oh, lots of times! He gently took my hands and arms,
And kissed them endlessly, and talked about their charms.   570

ARNOLPHE. And didn't he try taking something else, Agnes?

[She looks embarrassed

Ugh!

AGNES.   Er, he...

ARNOLPHE.   What did he?...

AGNES.   took...*

ARNOLPHE.   Eh?...

AGNES.   my...

ARNOLPHE.   What?

AGNES.   Well, yes,
He did, but I can't tell, because you'll be upset.

ARNOLPHE. Not me.

AGNES.   It's true!

ARNOLPHE.   No, no!

AGNES.   You promise you won't fret?

ARNOLPHE. I swear it.

AGNES.   Well, he took my... This'll make you cross!

ARNOLPHE. No!

AGNES.   Yes!

ARNOLPHE.   No, no! Good grief! Look, I won't give a toss!
    What did he take?

AGNES.   He took...

ARNOLPHE [aside].   I'm suffering like hell!

AGNES. He took my ribbon, that you gave me. Let me tell
    You that I tried to stop him, but it was no good.

ARNOLPHE [recovering his cool]. Well, never mind about the   580
    ribbon; if he could,
    Did he do more to you, than kiss your arms, and sigh?

AGNES. Why? Are there other things that people like to try?

ARNOLPHE. No... When he wanted you to cure his malady,
    Did he ask you to try another remedy?

AGNES. No. If he had, as you can see, I'd have agreed.
    I'd have done anything, to help him in his need.*
ARNOLPHE [aside]. Well, well, thanks be to God, this time it seems
    I've got
    Away with it. Next time, call me an idiot.

                                        [To AGNES

    Your innocence can take the blame, you need feel none.
    We'll say no more about all this, what's done is done.   590
    But trusting that young man, you didn't know the half:
    He wanted to betray you, then to have a laugh.

AGNES. Not true. He told me so himself, repeatedly.

ARNOLPHE. Ah! Don't believe he spoke to you quite truthfully.
    It's time for you to learn that sometimes young men come,
    And try to give you presents. But, if you succumb,
    And let yourself be coaxed, and give in to their art,

And let them kiss your hands and arms, and touch your heart,
You're guilty of a mortal sin, and you must die.

AGNES. What, that's a sin, you say? How's that? Do tell me why. 600

ARNOLPHE. I'll show you where it says so, printed on the page.
Behaviour like that puts heaven in a rage.

AGNES. But what does it all mean, and why should heaven be cross?
It's much the most delicious thing I've come across.
I can't get over how delightful and how new
It is—I've learnt a secret that I never knew.

ARNOLPHE. I know: what could be sweeter than those murmurings,
Those tender gestures, and those other charming things?
But they must be experienced in their own good time,
And people must get married. Then, it's not a crime.   610

AGNES. So, if you're married, they don't count it as a sin?

ARNOLPHE. That's right.

AGNES.   Can I get married? When can I begin?

ARNOLPHE. It's what you want, and I want it as much as you,
Indeed, I've come back here today to marry you.

AGNES. Can this be true?

ARNOLPHE.   Yes.

AGNES.   How delightful! Let's make haste.

ARNOLPHE. Yes, I'm quite sure that marriage will be to your taste.

AGNES. You want the two of us...

ARNOLPHE.   The thing's as good as done!

AGNES. Well, if this happens, I'll make sure we have some fun!

ARNOLPHE. Hmm, hmm! You know, you may find I reciprocate.

AGNES. I'm not much good at telling when a thing is fake.   620
Do you mean it for real?

ARNOLPHE.   I do, you've got it right.

AGNES. We're to be married?

ARNOLPHE.   Yes.

AGNES.   But when?

ARNOLPHE.   This very night.

AGNES [*laughing*]. Tonight?

ARNOLPHE.   Yes, yes, tonight. I see that makes you
    laugh.

AGNES. Oh, yes!

ARNOLPHE.   I'm here to sort things out on your behalf.

AGNES. Oh, dear! I'm terribly obliged to you for this!
    And, oh! my life with him—that will be utter bliss!

ARNOLPHE. With whom?

AGNES.   With... there...

ARNOLPHE.   *There?... There?...*
        That's not quite what I plan.
    You've been a bit too quick to nominate your man.
    I've got another suitor lined up for you now,
    And as for that young fellow, *there*, I'll tell you how   630
    To treat him, even if it drives him to his grave:
    You're going to send him packing, and you must behave
    As follows when he comes round here: with charming grace,
    You'll most politely shut the door right in his face,
    And if he knocks, open the window, throw a stone,*
    And make quite sure he gets the message from your tone.
    Now Agnes, do you understand? I'll hide away
    And watch, so mind you do exactly as I say.

AGNES. Oh, no! He's so good-looking, it's not...

ARNOLPHE.   That's enough!

AGNES. I couldn't bear to see how he...   640

ARNOLPHE.   All this is stuff
    And nonsense. Go upstairs.

AGNES.   But why?...

ARNOLPHE.   You've had your say.
    I'm master here. I've spoken. Come on now, obey!*

ACT III

SCENE 1

ARNOLPHE, AGNES, ALAIN, GEORGETTE

ARNOLPHE. Yes, everything went well, I say that joyfully.
You really did obey my orders perfectly.
I think you showed that blond seducer what was what:
A wise adviser has his uses, does he not?
You were too innocent, he took you by surprise:
You didn't think, but got involved, you realize.
Without me you'd have gone too far, I know it well,
Along the primrose path that leads you down to hell.   650
A young seducer of his sort is a disgrace,
Decked out with ribbons, feathers, breeches edged with lace,*
With flowing locks, and gleaming teeth, says he adores
His girl, while all the time he's sharpening his claws—
For he's a very hell-hound, eager for his prey:
He's thirsting for a woman victim to betray.
Thank goodness, I was there to tell you what to do,
And you've emerged unscathed, I kept my eye on you.
The way you glared at him when you flung down that stone
And made him realize that all his hopes had flown,   660
Confirms me in the view we'd better not delay
The wedding, which I mentioned earlier today.
But first you have to hear, since there's so much at stake,
A salutary speech, which I propose to make.
A chair here, in the shade!

[*To* GEORGETTE

You, hurry up! obey...

GEORGETTE. We promise to remember everything you say.
That other gentleman, he really made us think
He meant it...

ALAIN.   If we let him in, I'll never drink

Another drop, I swear. Besides, the man's a knave—
There was a problem with those two gold coins he gave!*   670

ARNOLPHE. Make sure you get the dinner ready, as I said.
And organize the contract, you've the go-ahead.
As soon as you've a moment, make yourselves look neat,
And fetch the lawyer on the corner of our street.

SCENE 2

ARNOLPHE, AGNES

ARNOLPHE [seated]. Now, pay attention, put your sewing in its place.
Good. Lift your head a bit, and let me see your face.
As long as I keep talking, look at me right here.*
Take note of every word I tell you, do you hear?
I'm going to marry you, Agnes, and from now on
You should thank God that your good fortune has begun,   680
And bear in mind the lowness of your former state,
And realize how good I am to contemplate
Removing you from base and brutish village life,
And making you a decent, bourgeois, lady wife.
Oh, what a privilege! You'll share the marriage bed
Of someone who, till now, has never thought to wed.
I've had some opportunities, and good ones too,
But I've refused to honour them, like I do you.
You never must forget I saw fit to prefer
You to the others. Think how low and poor you were,   690
And every day, make certain that you have deserved
The high position as my wife that is reserved
For you. You must make sure I never once regret
My act. Remember, you're forever in my debt.
A marriage, Agnes, is a great experience.
A wife commits herself to strict obedience.
Once you embark on it, you'll find that you've begun
A life without amusement: don't hope to have fun.
Your sex exists to be meek and subordinate,
Us men, who wear the beards, are here to dominate.   700

Although there are two halves to our society,
That doesn't mean those halves share strict equality.
One is the better half, the other's—opposite.
One half must rule supreme, the other must submit.
A trusty soldier knows his place, however hard,
And shows obedience to the captain of the guard;
A valet serves his master, and a child obeys
His father, and a priest does what the bishop says:
All these are nothing to the meek docility,
The strict obedience, the low humility,   710
And the profound respect she must show, in a word,
To him, for he's her husband, ruler, chief and lord.*
If he looks at her soberly, it's best she tries
To do her duty humbly, casting down her eyes.
She never should presume to look him in the face—
Except if he looks kind, and smiles at her with grace.
All this is quite beyond the women of today;
But you should never care what other people say.
Don't try to imitate coquettes who make me frown:
Their shocking doings are the talk of all the town—   720
And never let the devil tempt you, in the shape
Of handsome blond young men, who get you in a scrape.
Just bear in mind that you're becoming half of me,
So you're the keeper of my honour, Agnes, see?
It's very fragile, is my honour, you can hurt
It too, and that's no joke, but something to avert,
For there are boiling cauldrons waiting down in hell
For torturing the women who have lived too well.
All this is far from frivolous, and, for a start,
You'd better try to learn these lessons off by heart.   730
If you make sure that you don't flirt, but do what's right,
Your soul will always be pure, clean, and lily-white;
But if you fail your honour, lose your self-control,
Then, from that moment, it'll be as black as coal.
You'll be on show, just like a monster at a fair;
You'll be the devil's own, and everyone will stare.
He'll take you down to boil eternally, in hell.
May God make sure you never fall under his spell.
Now curtsey, and imagine you're a novice, as

She enters her new convent, tries to learn the Mass: 740
You must be a good wife; try hard, and be intent.
Now in my pocket here, I've got a document,*
Which ought to help you with your marriage articles.
The author's quite unknown, but has high principles;
You must read nothing else—this tells you all you need
To know. Now come along, let's hear how well you read.

AGNES [*reads*].

THE MAXIMS OF MARRIAGE

OR

THE DUTIES OF A MARRIED WOMAN
With her Daily Devotions

MAXIM NUMBER ONE

She who, by legal right,
A husband's bed has known,
Must learn, despite the blight
That current trends have shown,   750
The man who takes her on, intends her for his own.

ARNOLPHE. Just wait a bit; one day you'll learn what those things
   mean.
But just for now, read on, and I'll not intervene.

AGNES [*continues reading*].

MAXIM NUMBER TWO

She must not dress to tease,
Except, of course, to please
The man with whom she's lain.
He is the only one for whom she must seem fair.
She truly should not care
If others find her plain.

MAXIM NUMBER THREE

Enough of those regimes   760
Of ointments, unguents, creams,
All the ingredients which make complexions glow!
On honour, every day, they make the wrong impact—

When wife seeks to attract,
Her husband's not her beau.

MAXIM NUMBER FOUR

As decency requires, she must go out with head
Well covered, and her eyes cast down demurely; for
To please the man she wed,
She must please no one more.

MAXIM NUMBER FIVE

Apart from people who are visiting her sire,   770
Good manners must require,
However hard she's pressed,
That she should have no guest:
The men who visit her
Do not content Monsieur.

MAXIM NUMBER SIX

She must learn to refuse
The presents men produce—
For in this century
You get nothing for free.

MAXIM NUMBER SEVEN

Although she may object, amongst her property   780
She must not have a desk, nor paper, ink, nor pen:
It's more above board when
The husband writes, not she.

MAXIM NUMBER EIGHT

Those rowdy happenings,
Called social gatherings,
Corrupt the minds of women who do not beware.
To their suppression I wholeheartedly aspire:
For lovers will conspire
Against poor husbands there.

MAXIM NUMBER NINE

A virtuous woman, who her precious honour guards,   790

Must never play at cards,
For they are things unblessed.
By playing at that game,
She'll lose her sense of shame,
And gamble all the rest.

MAXIM NUMBER TEN

In summer, if the talk's
Of picnics, parties, walks,
Refuse, that's my advice.
A prudent person says
A husband on such days   800
Will always pay the price.

MAXIM NUMBER ELEVEN...

ARNOLPHE. Just finish on your own, and then I'll sit with you
And tell you what it means, when you have read it through.
I've just remembered something urgent, it can't wait.
It won't take very long, then I'll be with you straight.
Go in now, take the book with you, and hold it dear;
And if the lawyer comes, just keep him waiting here.

SCENE 3

ARNOLPHE

ARNOLPHE. The best thing I can do is make the girl my wife.
Whichever way I choose, I'll shape her very life—
I'll mould her in my hands, just like a lump of wax,   810
And then I'll sculpt her, in whatever form she lacks.
She's innocent. I must take care what she's about.
For when I was away, it almost caught her out.
But if the truth be told, I think it's fair to say
It's better for a wife to fail a man this way.
For such mistakes are remedied quite easily:
A simple soul will learn, with great docility,
And if she's lured away, the husband, undeterred,
Can bring her back in line with one well-chosen word.

A clever wife is quite another kettle of fish—   820
Our destiny depends upon her lightest wish.
When she's an idea in her head, she won't be crossed,
And all our serious warnings will, I fear, be lost.
She makes use of her wit to mock at our advice,
And twists into a virtue what is really vice.
She's plenty up her sleeve, she takes the truth, and bends
It, tricking her poor Argus, for her selfish ends.*
There's just no point in warding off the bitter blow—
A clever woman's learnt her mischief, long ago.
And when she makes her mind up, you can be quite sure   830
Your honour will be gone, all you can do's endure:
A lot of decent chaps will vouch for what I say.
But that wild, silly youth won't have it all his way.
He should have kept his mouth shut—he's himself to blame.
The problem's nationwide—all Frenchmen are the same—
The moment something happens, furthering their ends,
They're itching to let out the secret to their friends.
Their stupid vanity fills them with such conceit,
That they'd much rather hang themselves than be discreet.
Ha! How the devil tempts a woman when he makes   840
Her fall head over heels for such a jackanapes,
And how... But here he comes. I won't let on I know.
I want to probe his thoughts now, while he's feeling low.

SCENE 4

ARNOLPHE, HORACE

HORACE. I've just been to your house, but all to no effect:
For you were out, I couldn't pay you my respects.
I plan to go on trying, and eventually...

ARNOLPHE. Good gracious! What a fuss! Why stand on ceremony?
These social niceties just irritate me, and
In my opinion, formal visits should be banned.
The way that people mind their manners makes me squirm—   850
Don't let's waste time on that, we'd much better be firm.

Let's put our hats back on. How has your business gone?
And what's the gossip, eh, Horace? What's going on?
I wasn't concentrating, when we met before,
But thought about it afterwards, and then, what's more,
I found your rate of progress most remarkable,
I'm interested—I find it so incredible.

HORACE. Well, since I opened up to you, and told you where
  I'd got, there's been a setback in my love affair.

ARNOLPHE. Oh! Oh! What can have happened?   860

HORACE.   Cruel fate, alack
  Has intervened, and brought my beauty's guardian back.

ARNOLPHE. Oh no, what a disaster!

HORACE.   Yes—and then, what's worse,
  He seems to have found out our secret intercourse.

ARNOLPHE. But how did he discover? Have you any clue?

HORACE. I've no idea—I simply realized he knew.
  As usual I'd come at my appointed hour,
  To make my little visit to my beauty's bower,
  When, with a different tone and face from yesterday,
  The valet and the maidservant both blocked my way.
  They yelled: 'Get lost! We don't want you, you're a disgrace!' 870
  And straightaway they shut the door right in my face.

ARNOLPHE. Right in your face?

HORACE.   Right in my face.

ARNOLPHE.   I say, that's rich!

HORACE. I tried to reason with them through the closed door, which
  Was useless—all they did was answer through the slit,
  'We will not let you in, Monsieur's forbidden it.'

ARNOLPHE. They didn't open up?

HORACE.   No. At the window, I
  Saw Agnes, who confirmed the tyrant was close by
  By ordering me away in an aggressive tone,

And for good measure chasing me, throwing a stone.

ARNOLPHE. What do you mean, a stone?   880

HORACE.   And heavy as could be.
She threw it at me, hard. That's how she welcomed me.

ARNOLPHE. Oh, what a shame! How odd—and how unfortunate.
I'm truly sorry your affairs are in this state.

HORACE. That man's return has messed the whole thing up, you're
   right.

ARNOLPHE. I really feel for you—I'm not just being polite.

HORACE. Now everything is spoilt.

ARNOLPHE.   But not for good, I'm sure.
It should be possible to find some sort of cure.

HORACE. If we can get together, we can try. We ought
To trick the jealous guardian. He's the man to thwart.

ARNOLPHE. It shouldn't be too hard, since, when all's said and   890
   done,
She loves you.

HORACE.   Yes, she does.

ARNOLPHE.   You'll very soon have won.

HORACE. I hope so.

ARNOLPHE.   That big stone came as a shock to you.
But never mind, it didn't mean a thing—

HORACE.   That's true.
I realized at once the fellow was around,
And masterminding everything in the background.
You'll not believe it when you hear another thing
That you must know, a most amazing happening.
That sweet young girl has made a move you won't believe—
Most unexpected in a girl who's so naive.
Love is the greatest teacher in the world—what's more*   900
It teaches us the things we never knew before.
The habits of a lifetime can be overturned

In just a moment, once the laws of love are learned—
In seconds it will overcome all obstacles
Thrown up by Nature, with effects like miracles:
Love makes the miser generous and bountiful.
The coward is a hero, and a sage the fool.
The dullest minds become as agile as can be,
And love will civilize the worst naivety.
Miraculously, Agnes has become aware,   910
For in rejecting me, she chose her words with care:
'Be off!' said she. 'I won't see you again, don't try
To talk. I know your views, and this is my reply.'
That stone, which you saw as my love's worst antidote,
Fell at my feet; and wrapped around it was a note.
I'm quite amazed to see how cleverly she planned
Her words to fit both stone and secret letter, and
I'm sure you'll be surprised at her behaviour.
Now didn't love step in, become her saviour?
And don't you wonder at the power that love brings   920
To make one capable of most amazing things?
And what about her cunning, and her secret note?
Eh? Isn't it fantastic? Makes you want to gloat?
But best of all, what of the figure that he cut—
I mean the jealous guardian—isn't he a mutt?
Well?

ARNOLPHE. Yes, it's very funny.

HORACE.   Come on, laugh at it!
This man was up in arms, determined to outwit
Our love, setting up barricades, and throwing stones,
As though I was ransacking property he owns.
He went to crazy lengths, he was so petrified,   930
And even got the servants working on his side.
Yet though he put this daunting mechanism in place,
A girl he kept in ignorance could still outface
Him! I confess, despite his premature return,
Which has to be a cause of ongoing concern,
I still find the whole episode an utter scream,
And every time I think of it, it makes me beam,
And cheers me up. But you don't seem to see the joke.

ARNOLPHE. Oh, yes I do, just look, I'm laughing fit to choke.

HORACE. But look here, you're my friend. Let me read you her 940
note.
You'll sense her deepest feelings in the words she wrote.
It's touchingly expressed, full of sincerity,
You'll feel her innocence, and sweet simplicity.
You'd think that Nature's learnt to talk—that's how it reads,
It shows you how a girl's heart feels when first it bleeds.

ARNOLPHE [aside]. You minx, you learnt to write, and see what use
you make
Of it. I knew that teaching you was a mistake.

HORACE [reads]. *I want to write to you, but I'm not sure how to begin. I*
have been thinking things that I'd like you to know, but I don't know
how to put them, and I don't trust my own words. I'm beginning to
realize that I've always been kept in ignorance, so I'm afraid of put-
ting down something that isn't right, and saying more than I ought. To
tell you the truth, I don't know what you've done to me, but I do know
that I'm desperately upset at what they're making me do to you, and I
can see that being without you will be horribly painful, and I'd be very
glad to be yours. It may be wrong to say this, but I can't help myself—
and I would like it to be something that's all right to say. They keep
rubbing in the idea that all young men are deceivers, so we mustn't
listen to them, and they tell me everything you say to me is aimed at
duping me. But I promise you I can't believe that of you, and what
you say moves me so deeply, I can't believe it's all lies. Please be honest
with me about this: I'm acting in good faith, so it would be very wrong
of you to deceive me. I think I'd die of misery.

ARNOLPHE [aside]. Hum! Bitch!

HORACE.   What's wrong?

ARNOLPHE.   It's nothing. Just a cough—I'm fine.

HORACE. Well, don't you love her letter? Isn't it divine?
That hateful tyrant muzzled her, but still you see 950
The beauty of her nature shine out splendidly.
To spoil a mind that innocent just makes no sense:
I think it ought to be a criminal offence.

What sort of man could try to keep a girl in stark
Stupidity and ignorance, quite in the dark?
But now, and through the power of love, the door's ajar,
And I can tell you, I shall thank my lucky star
If I can show that brute, that beastly animal,
That rotten thug, that filthy swine, that criminal...

ARNOLPHE. Goodbye.   960

HORACE.   What? Off so soon?

ARNOLPHE.   That's right. A while ago,
I thought of some most urgent business. I must go.

HORACE. But since she's kept locked up in here, have you a clue
Who might have access to the house? I hoped you knew.
I'm shamelessly exploiting you—it's no surprise
I need to ask a friend to help my enterprise.
I've lost the backup that I used to have, inside.
The servant and the serving girl, when last I tried
To get them to help out, no matter what I did,
Refused to listen, and, instead, tried to get rid
Of me. There was a wonderful old woman, who   970
Was very skilled at all this sort of thing, it's true.
She was extremely useful, spoke up in my stead.
But then, four days ago, the poor old thing dropped dead.
Can you think of a way to make my love secure?

ARNOLPHE. No, I'm afraid not, but you'll find something, I'm sure.

HORACE. Goodbye, then. You can see how much I've trusted you.

SCENE 5

ARNOLPHE

ARNOLPHE. How mortifying! I made sure he never knew,
But what an effort, hiding my discomfiture!
She's ignorant, but oh! the cleverness of her!
The minx was just pretending, knew it all along—   980
The devil must have shown her how to lead me on.

That dreaded letter has most surely sealed my doom.
The traitor's won her heart, he's in, and there's no room
For me. He's wormed his way inside—what treachery!
I'm left with nothing but despair and misery.
I'm suffering both ways—my honour is at stake,
He's made off with her heart, and oh, how mine does ache!
I'm furious: he's occupied my property
And thwarted all my plans by sheer duplicity.
The end will come, I know, it's very clear to me: 990
His destiny will be his own worst enemy,
And she'll avenge me by herself, for she can't choose
But do it. Yet it hurts, to love the thing you lose.
Oh, God! I worked the whole thing out so carefully—
How could I fall in love with her so shamefully?
She's got no family, no money, no support,
But she's betrayed me, let me down without a thought.
And yet I love her, even if she's led me on.
I love her so, I'll be destroyed if she is gone.
You fool, aren't you ashamed? I'm furious, I'm base,   1000
I've earned myself a thousand slaps around the face.*
I'd better go inside, I'm desperate to see
The way that she'll behave after betraying me.
Dear God, don't give me horns, I beg of you to spare
Me that; or else, if it's my destiny to share
The common fate, then help me, God, I beg of you,
To keep my feelings to myself, like others do.

ACT IV

SCENE 1

ARNOLPHE

ARNOLPHE. I must admit, I'm having trouble keeping still.
   I'm thinking of a thousand stratagems—they fill
   My brain. How can I keep control outside and in,   1010
   And make sure that young idiot can never win?
   The little bitch! She met my eyes so shamelessly.
   She seems quite unaffected by her perfidy.
   I'm at the point of death because of what she's done,
   But seeing her, you'd think she couldn't have begun
   To cheat on me. The more I looked, the more she seemed
   At peace. It made me furious—I almost screamed.
   But all the burning passions boiling in my heart,
   Just made me love her more, and tore my soul apart.
   I felt embittered, helpless too, and sorrowful,   1020
   And yet I'd never seen her look so beautiful.
   Her eyes had never pierced my soul like that before.
   I'd never realized the truth—that I adore
   That girl. I feel it here—I'm going to be destroyed.
   The worst may happen, if I find I can't avoid
   My fate. I brought her up so conscientiously,
   With every care, so cautiously and tenderly!
   What! Did I take her in when she was just a child,
   And live in hope for her, believing fortune smiled
   On me? I built my love upon her budding charms,   1030
   Waiting for thirteen years to take her in my arms,
   And now I find she loves some fool, and they propose
   To run away together right under my nose,
   When she's already more than half married to me?
   No, damn it! You won't get away with it, you'll see,
   You stupid oaf! You'll fail, and I'll do everything
   To stop you. You deserve your share of suffering,
   You won't have the last laugh. Not now, at my expense.

SCENE 2*

LAWYER, ARNOLPHE

LAWYER. Ah! There he is! Good day, Monsieur. Shall we commence
Our business, and draw up the contract as you ask?   1040

ARNOLPHE [*not seeing him*]. What's to be done?

LAWYER.   Let's be
     straightforward—that's our task.

ARNOLPHE [*not seeing him*]. Let's take precautions, think it over,
     that seems best.

LAWYER. I'll make sure everything is in your interest.

ARNOLPHE [*not seeing him*]. I must protect myself—one hardly
     understands...

LAWYER. The main thing is to put your business in my hands,
     And I'll advise you what agreements must be made—
     We won't endorse the contract, till the money's paid.

ARNOLPHE [*not seeing him*]. I'm very much afraid, if I make too
     much fuss,
     That in the town there'll be some gossip about us.

LAWYER. It's easy to prevent a scandal. What you do   1050
     Is get the contract drawn up secretly for you.

ARNOLPHE [*not seeing him*]. But how on earth do she and I sort out
     these things?

LAWYER. You fund her in proportion to the wealth she brings.*

ARNOLPHE [*not seeing him*]. I love her, and it's this that causes my
     disgrace.

LAWYER. A wife can be provided for in such a case.

ARNOLPHE [*not seeing him*]. How should I treat her? Mmm?
     There's bound to be some strife.

LAWYER. Well, normally the husband must endow the wife
     With just a third of all her dowry. I've known some

Who, thinking this inadequate, increased the sum.

ARNOLPHE [*not seeing him*]. If...   1060

[ARNOLPHE *notices* LAWYER

LAWYER.   As regards the death of one spouse, you decide
What's best between you, and a husband can provide
For his wife's needs.

ARNOLPHE.   What?

LAWYER.   Yes, he can increase the sum
If he wants her to have a sizeable income.
This is achieved by dowry, settlement, or claim,
Which shall be forfeit on the passing of the same.
It goes irrevocably to the legatees,
Or else, at the discretion of the said trustees,
By free disposal may be formally bestowed—
And that way you'll keep on the right side of the code.
Hey, why d'you shrug like that? Am I a silly pup?   1070
And aren't I competent to draw a contract up?
Do you presume to teach me? No, I'm confident.
Don't I know that the conjoints both, by precedent,
Their chattels real and personal as one unite,
Unless of course they have, by law, renounced their right?
Don't I know that the spouse presumptive holds a third
Of her estate in common...

ARNOLPHE.   Yes, of course—I've heard
You out: you know; but then, who asked you to explain?

LAWYER. You, and you're trying hard to show me up, that's plain!
I saw you shrug your shoulders—I caught that grimace!   1080

ARNOLPHE. To hell with him, with his repulsive doggy face!
Goodbye. That's much the quickest way to make you go.

LAWYER. You sent for me to write a contract, yes or no?

ARNOLPHE. I sent for you, but now the matter's been delayed.
I'll send for you again when next I need your aid.
The devil take him. Won't his chatter ever end?

LAWYER. I think, in fact I know, he's gone right round the bend.

SCENE 3

LAWYER, ALAIN, GEORGETTE, ARNOLPHE

LAWYER. Hey, did your master order you to fetch me here?

ALAIN. Yes.

LAWYER.   It's not up to me to say why he's so queer,
But could you find him, please, and let him know from me,   1090
That he's gone barking mad?

GEORGETTE.   We'll let him know, you'll see.

SCENE 4

ALAIN, ARNOLPHE, GEORGETTE

ALAIN. Monsieur...

ARNOLPHE.   Come closer, both of you, my faithful pair.
You've been good friends—I know the whole of the affair.

ALAIN. The lawyer...

ARNOLPHE.   Never mind, that's for another time,
For right now you must know that there's a dreadful crime
Been planned against my honour. Think about the shame,
The sleaze of your poor master losing his good name!
You wouldn't dare to show your faces in the street,
And you'd be pointed at by everyone you meet.
So this is your affair as much as it is mine.   1100
I want you both to make quite sure that you confine
That girl so the young man can't get inside the door.

GEORGETTE. We know all that—you told us what to do before.

ARNOLPHE. But when he pleads with you, you must be in no doubt.

ALAIN. What, us? I mean...

GEORGETTE.   We both know how to keep him out.

ARNOLPHE [to ALAIN]. If he comes up all kind: 'Alain, dear fellow,
say,

I need your help: I love her, and I'll pine away.'

ALAIN. 'You moron.'

ARNOLPHE [*to* GEORGETTE]. Good! 'Georgette, I need some
    comforting.
You look so kind, you're such a caring little thing.'

GEORGETTE. 'You flipping idiot!'   1110

ARNOLPHE [*to* ALAIN].   Good! 'Tell me, what's gone wrong
With what I want? I'm honest, please help me along.'

ALAIN. 'You nasty piece of work!'

ARNOLPHE [*to* GEORGETTE].   That's great! 'I'm sure to die
Unless you show some pity. Couldn't you just try?'

GEORGETTE. 'You ugly customer!'

ARNOLPHE.   You've understood, I see.
'I'm not the man to try to have my way for free.
You could do me a favour that I won't forget:
Meanwhile, as a beginning, here you are, Georgette.
Go buy yourself a petticoat. For Alain here,
Go drink my health. I'll give you plenty, have no fear.

                              [*They both take the money*

And all I ask is that you do one thing for me—   1120
Just take me to your mistress: her I want to see.'

GEORGETTE [*pushing him*]. 'Get out of it!'

ARNOLPHE.   That's good!

ALAIN [*pushing him*].   'Get lost!'

ARNOLPHE.   Good!

GEORGETTE [*pushing him*].   'Want a fight?'

ARNOLPHE. Good! Ouch! Ooh! That's enough!

GEORGETTE.   Why? Ain't I done it right?

ALAIN. We done just what you said, and he'd have been all bruised!

ARNOLPHE. But when I gave you cash, you ought to have refused.

GEORGETTE. Well, we just got a bit forgetful for a mo.

ALAIN. Hey, shall we do the whole of it again now?

ARNOLPHE.   No!
No, that'll do. Get in.

ALAIN.   You only have to say...

ARNOLPHE. No, no, I tell you! Go back in now. That's the way
I want it. Keep the money. Wait for me inside.   1130
And keep your eyes wide open. Let me be your guide.

SCENE 5

ARNOLPHE

ARNOLPHE. I've found a spy, to make quite sure she doesn't cheat:
The cobbler, who lives at the corner of our street.*
I plan to keep her permanently locked in here,
Under a constant guard, and I won't let her near
Those ribbon sellers, wig makers, and chic coiffeurs,
Those glove and kerchief makers, smart entrepreneurs,
Who toil away in secret, all the livelong day,
To make sure their intrigues will go the lovers' way.
I'm quite experienced, I know the sort of thing.   1140
That puppy's cleverness will be astonishing,
If he succeeds in making contact with the girl.

SCENE 6

HORACE, ARNOLPHE

HORACE. Oh, good! I'm glad to find you. I'm in such a whirl!
You won't believe! I've had the narrowest escape
Just now—I didn't mean to get into a scrape,
But Agnes chanced to come out on her balcony
To breathe the cool air in the shade, beneath that tree.

She made a little sign to me not to withdraw,
Then tiptoed down, and opened up the garden door.
We'd just got to her room, to talk of our affairs,   1150
When suddenly we heard her guardian on the stairs.
She had to hide me—you can guess the urgency.
She locked me in a cupboard—an emergency.
The man came in. I couldn't see him, but could hear
Him striding up and down, with me quaking with fear.
And every now and then, he'd heave a heavy sigh,
And aim a kick at furniture that stood nearby;
Or hit the little dog that got under his feet,
Or toss about her clothes, or otherwise ill-treat
Her things. At one point, in his search for some release,   1160
He broke a pair of vases on the mantelpiece.
I don't think the poor sap was acting on a whim:
He's got some inkling of the trick she's played on him.
He paced about a lot, and vented his disgust
On her possessions. What a temper! How unjust!
He didn't say a word, but still his fury grew—
Until he left. Then I came out of hiding too.
He terrified us both: you know, we didn't dare
Run any risks by staying on together there.
The danger was too great. But when it's dark, I plan   1170
To creep up to her window, quiet as I can.
I'll cough three times, so she will know that I'm outside,
And at my signal she's to fling her window wide.
I'll have a ladder, and she'll help me from above—
I'll get into that room, with guidance from my love.
I'm telling you all this because you're my best friend:
I like to have things out—it helps me to unbend.
Whatever happens, I have always found it's true,
You can't be happy till you've talked about it too.
I'm sure that you appreciate my sheer delight.   1180
Goodbye. I'm off to get things ready for tonight.

SCENE 7

ARNOLPHE

ARNOLPHE. Oh, fate has got it in for me. I'm in despair.
Why won't they give me time to draw a breath of air?
It happens every time. They get together, and
Succeed in overturning everything I've planned!
In my maturity, am I to be the dupe
Of this young innocent, and that young nincompoop?
Throughout these twenty years, I've tried to contemplate
How husbands are led on. I've seen their wretched fate:
I've made a detailed study of the things which can   1190
Result in the destruction of the wisest man;
I learnt from their misfortunes how to live my life.
When it was time for me to find myself a wife,
I thought that I could hold my cuckold's horns at bay:
I'd be the one to keep those wretched boys away.
I fought against the ghastly possibility,
With every means that human ingenuity
Could offer. Cruel fate rejected my attempt.
I realize now—nobody can be exempt.
With all the knowledge and experience that I   1200
Have managed to acquire, and to identify,
I've meditated carefully, for twenty years,
On how to take precautions, how to calm my fears.
Where other men were failures, I planned on success—
And now I find myself in just the same old mess!
Ah! Monstrous destiny, you've got it wrong this time,
For you forget the object of desire is mine.
Although her heart's been won by that blond saboteur,
At least I can prevent him taking all of her.
He thinks tonight's the night for winning her. It may   1210
Not work for them, they may not have it all their way.
In all this misery, it cheers me up to know
That I've been told about the trap they've set, and though
We're both at daggers drawn, this scatterbrained gallant
Has made his deadly enemy his confidant.

SCENE 8

CHRYSALDE, ARNOLPHE

CHRYSALDE. Good evening. Do we eat, before we take our walk?

ARNOLPHE. Forget it—I'm not hungry.

CHRYSALDE.   What a way to talk!

ARNOLPHE. I'm sorry, I'm not free. I'll see you when I can.

CHRYSALDE. Has something happened to upset your wedding plan?

ARNOLPHE. You shouldn't poke your nose in other folk's   1220
    affairs.

CHRYSALDE. Oh, oh! What's this? You're very touchy, full of cares.
    What is it, neighbour? Does your passion stand no chance?
    Eh? What's the matter? What's upsetting your romance?
    I'll swear there's something up—I see it in your face.

ARNOLPHE. Whatever happens, I won't suffer the disgrace
    Of realizing I'm just like some men I know,
    Who most politely welcome in their ladies' beaux.

CHRYSALDE. Oh, I'm amazed that you, with all your expertise,
    Should get so steamed up over matters such as these.
    You see them as the greatest threat to happiness—   1230
    Your honour is at stake. For all your cleverness,
    To be a brute, a fool, a liar, so you claim,
    Is perfectly all right, if you avoid that shame.
    It doesn't matter what you've done since you were born,
    The only thing that counts is not to sprout a horn.
    You take precautions. Can you possibly prevent
    Your good name being ruined by a chance event?
    And should a gentleman be driven to despair
    By something that he can't control? It's most unfair.
    Look here: must it be quite so hard to take a wife?   1240
    From that day on, must you be hounded, all your life?
    If she should fail to do her bit, must that disgrace
    Be seen as something monstrous, hideous, and base?
    Just get into your stubborn head that cuckoldry,
    If you're a decent chap, is not such misery.

It's just one of those trying things you can't avoid,
And you should face the whole thing out, not be destroyed.
Although the way that people talk is maddening,
Your problem's bound to lie in how you take the thing.
The secret of correct behaviour, so it seems,   1250
Is always to make sure you don't go to extremes.*
There's no need to be like those easygoing folk
Who treat their wives' affairs as if they were a joke,
And always have the lovers' sayings on their lips,
Admire their talents, praise them, imitate their quips,
Tell everyone the two of them are such good friends,
Are always there, stay on till every party ends,
Behave in such a way that people find them base,
And wonder that they're not ashamed to show their face.
A man who does all that is nothing but a cad.   1260
But I believe the opposite is just as bad:
Though I can't stand the man who takes the lover's part,
It doesn't mean I like his angry counterpart,
Whose clumsy outbursts are so turbulent and grim,
The whole world has to turn and fix its eyes on him.
It seems as if he's making such a fuss because
He's keen for all to know how he's been through the wars.
Between these two extremes, there lies an honest mean,
And that is where the prudent husband should be seen.
If he can take it well, he'll find that he pulls through,   1270
And he won't need to blush at what a wife can do.
I tell you, cuckoldry—whatever people say—
Is perfectly all right, it happens every day.
The thing that's difficult is trying to stay polite,
And knowing how to play the situation right.

ARNOLPHE. Well, thanks for that fine speech! The Hornèd
     Fellowship
Should give a vote of thanks for your group leadership.
If any of them get to hear how you uphold
Their rights, they'll all be queuing up to be enrolled!

CHRYSALDE. Yes, that's the sort of talk that makes me look   1280
     askance.
Look, since the kind of wife we get depends on chance,

I think we should treat marriage like a game of dice.
You play. You don't get what you want. You don't think twice,
But use your skill in lowering your sights a bit,
And make up for bad luck by what you do with it.

ARNOLPHE. You mean: eat well, sleep soundly, don't give way to
     stress,
     And let yourself believe it couldn't matter less.

CHRYSALDE. You're making fun of me; but in our universe,
     Quite frankly, we've known plenty things that are much worse,
     If those had happened, I agree, I'd have despaired—   1290
     But not a chance event like this. You're much too scared.
     If I were made to choose between two kinds of life,
     I promise you I'd rather have a cheating wife
     Than get myself a pillar of society,
     Who goes to law for every triviality,*
     A devil-woman, full of virtue, who sets store
     By prudish and and offputting manners, and, what's more,
     Rejoices in the fact that men can never tempt
     Her, giving her the right to treat us with contempt.
     Those women don't betray their husbands, but compel   1300
     The wretched fellows to endure a living hell.
     No, cuckoldry is only what you make of it.
     It's best to live with it, though it's unfortunate.
     There are some circumstances where it's good for you.
     It has its pleasures like the other things you do.*

ARNOLPHE. Enjoy it if you like—I know you and your sort.
     Not me. I've no intention, none, of being caught,
     I won't put up with it. On no account. I swear...

CHRYSALDE. I wouldn't swear, if I were you. You'd best take care!
     If fate has got it in for you, there's no defence,   1310
     And your opinion won't make any difference.

ARNOLPHE. What! Me, a cuckold?

CHRYSALDE.   Well, and so what if you are?
     I don't mean to be rude, but many men are far
     More decent, handsome, rich, and nobly born than you.
     There's no comparison. Those men are cuckolds too.

ARNOLPHE. Oh, stop comparing me to those pathetic folk.
  You laugh, but I'm afraid I just don't see the joke.
  Let's drop the subject.

CHRYSALDE.   Ah, you're angry. Tell me why?
  I'll find out soon enough, I rather think. Goodbye.
  You're taking a high moral tone in this affair—   1320
  Of you-know-what, I mean—but still, you're halfway there,
  If you insist on swearing it can never be.

ARNOLPHE. Well, I do swear it, and I'm going off to see
  How best to guard against it now. My plans are laid.

SCENE 9

ARNOLPHE, ALAIN, GEORGETTE

ARNOLPHE. My friends, the time has come for me to seek your aid.
  I'm very touched to find you're such a loyal pair,
  But now you're going to have to prove how much you care;
  And if you help me out, so honour is restored,
  You can be sure that I will give you your reward.
  Shh! This is secret. Look—the man you know about   1330
  Is planning an attack tonight, so I've found out.
  He'll climb a ladder up to Agnes's very room.
  But we must ambush him together. Get a broom—
  We'll have one each—and then we'll all three lie in wait.
  When he gets up his ladder, we won't hesitate,
  But charge! You must attack, and give him a good fright
  (I'll fling the window open, when the time is right).
  I want to teach him such a lesson, that he won't
  Forget. We'll let him have it, strike me if we don't!
  He won't be back. But never mention me by name,   1340
  And don't let on that I am joining in the game.
  Come on, now! Help me out! I'm going mad with rage!

ALAIN. If it's a fight you want, we'll go on the rampage.
  And how! I'll whack him good and proper, Sir. You'll see.

GEORGETTE. My hands are smaller, but they're big enough for me

To give him a good hiding. It'll be a riot!

ARNOLPHE. Well, go inside. Now, look! Be careful to keep quiet.
All this will be a useful lesson for mankind.
If all the husbands in this wretched town could find
A welcome like we plan for this young lover, then   1350
There wouldn't be so many cuckolds among men.

ACT V

SCENE 1

ARNOLPHE, ALAIN, GEORGETTE

ARNOLPHE. You fools! What have you done? You've knocked the
   boy out cold!

ALAIN. But, Monsieur, we was only doing what we was told.

ARNOLPHE. Don't make excuses. When I said: 'Give him a clout',
   I wanted you to punish him, not knock him out—
   I ordered you to thump his back, not break his head.
   You beat him to a pulp, and now the boy lies dead!
   Oh, heavens! How can I begin to contemplate
   My problems, now that he's been killed? Unhappy fate!
   Get back inside at once—and don't say anything   1360
   To anyone. Pretend this isn't happening.
   It's almost dawn. Have I the ingenuity
   To handle this? Oh, God, what a calamity!
   This business will be public knowledge, any day.
   What'll become of me? What'll his father say?

SCENE 2

ARNOLPHE, HORACE

HORACE. There's someone there. I'd better go and find out who.

ARNOLPHE. Oh, how could I have known?... Oh!... Who's there?
   Who are you?

HORACE. That you, Monsieur Arnolphe?

ARNOLPHE.   Yes. Who's that?

HORACE.   It's Horace.
   Look here, do me a favour! I'm in such a pass!
   But you're up early...   1370

ARNOLPHE [*under his breath*].   Oh, God! What confusion!
　　Can it be magic? Is he an illusion?

HORACE. To tell the truth, I've no idea what to do next,
　　So thank the Lord you're here. I really was perplexed,
　　But now I've met you, it's all right, for I can tell
　　You all about it. Everything's gone very well.
　　It's worked out better than I ever dared to hope:
　　By rights, we never should have managed to elope.
　　Somehow or other, Agnes's guardian got to know
　　About the secret meeting that we'd planned, and so
　　I'd almost reached her window on my ladder, when,   1380
　　To my dismay, three people came from nowhere, then
　　Made threatening gestures. Then they waved their sticks around.
　　I lost my footing, slithered back down to the ground.
　　I do have a few bruises, but my lucky fall
　　Meant that I wasn't hit with sticks and brooms at all.
　　The gang—including, I believe, my jealous clown—
　　Decided that it was their blows that knocked me down.
　　The pain was quite enough to silence me a space.
　　I lay there, motionless, for some time, on my face—
　　And they believed that they had really done me in,   1390
　　And one and all they went into a fearful spin.
　　They each accused the other two of trying to kill
　　Me. I could hear it all, although I lay quite still.
　　They had no lantern, couldn't see, so, full of dread,
　　Came timidly to feel, and see if I was dead.
　　Well, luck was on my side, because it was pitch dark.
　　I lay there like a lifeless corpse—no vital spark.
　　Appalled at what they'd done, they crept away to grieve,
　　And as I too was thinking it was time to leave,
　　My Agnes, deeply troubled at this so-called death, thought   1400
　　　　she
　　Must come down, to find out what had become of me,
　　For she'd heard all the frantic things that they had said
　　When they were moaning that they thought I must be dead.
　　They left her all alone, they were in such a state:
　　For once, it was quite easy for her to escape.
　　When she found I was safe, she let her feelings show—

I can't begin to tell—she just let herself go.
What more is there to say? This lovely girl, in short,
Is letting love dictate the things she feels she ought
To do. She won't go back, this much she understands.   1410
She wants to place herself entirely in my hands.
She's at my mercy, through her total innocence:
The madman who's responsible has no defence.
Just think what risks she might have run, if I had been
Unscrupulous or less in love—that man's obscene!
But no—I'm so in love, it sets my soul alight—
I'd rather die than take advantage of her plight.
Her beauty's made a deep impression on my heart—
I'll want to be with her, until death us do part.
I realize my father will be furious,   1420
But, given time, he can be reconciled to us.
I know I've let my feelings carry me away:
But we've only one life, I must live it my way.
What you can do for me, to help in this affair,
Is, let me put my lovely girl into your care.
It would help both of us, if she could stay with you,
And keep away from trouble, for a day or two.
We'll have to lie low, for a bit. That jealous brute
Will hunt for her, and never give up his pursuit;
Besides, you know how bad it looks, if couples spend   1430
A lot of time alone together. I intend
To put my trust in you. Your attitude is fair;
I've told you everything about my love affair;
I know you're on my side, and you're my friend indeed:
Will you take on my treasure, in my hour of need?

ARNOLPHE. Of course I will. You know you can rely on me.

HORACE. You're willing to take in my charming refugee?

ARNOLPHE. With pleasure, as I say, young man. Only too glad
  To help you out—this is the first chance that I've had.
  This opportunity is really heaven-sent,   1440
  And doing a favour never made me more content.

HORACE. I'm greatly in your debt—you've been so kind to me.
  I feared you might raise some objections, but I see

That you're unshockable: you understand the truth,
And make allowances for our unbridled youth.
She's with my servant, round that corner, out of sight.

ARNOLPHE. But what are we to do? It's starting to grow light.
There might be someone looking—best not bring her here.
But if I go inside the house, and you appear
With her, the staff will talk. I know—the safest thing   1450
Is pick a quiet spot. I'll wait there, you can bring
Her here. That alleyway will do. Go, fetch her now.

HORACE. You're right to take precautions. I could not see how
To hand her over. I agree, that's the best plan:
I'll bring her here, then leave as quickly as I can.

ARNOLPHE [alone]. Ah! Fortune! This one piece of luck I've had for
   free
Makes up for all the suffering you've heaped on me.

                                    [He wraps his face in his cloak

SCENE 3

HORACE, AGNES, ARNOLPHE

HORACE. Although I've got to go, you needn't be alarmed:
I've found a perfect way to keep you quite unharmed.
It would have ruined everything for you to stay   1460
With me. I've a much better answer. Come this way.

            [ARNOLPHE takes her hand without her recognizing him

AGNES. Why must you leave me here?

HORACE.   My darling, I just do.

AGNES. But try to come back soon, or I'll be missing you.

HORACE. I love you far too much to stay away for long.

AGNES. When I'm not with you, I'm afraid things may go wrong.

HORACE. When we're apart, I feel depressed and down, as well.

AGNES. Don't tell me lies. You never loved me, I can tell.

HORACE. I've said how much I love you. Don't you know it's true?

AGNES. No, you don't love me half as much as I love you.

[ARNOLPHE *pulls her away*

AGNES. He's pulling me too hard!   1470

HORACE.   Because it's dangerous,
Dear love, for anyone to catch a glimpse of us.
The man who's pulling you away is a good friend.
He's on our side—you'll see, he's faithful to the end.

AGNES. But he's a total stranger.

HORACE.   Trust him, life and limb.
Yes, take my word, you'll never come to harm with him.

AGNES. I'd be much happier, if I could stay with you.

HORACE. And I'd...

AGNES [*to* ARNOLPHE, *who pulls her again*]. Wait!

HORACE.   Dawn is breaking, I'll be going too.

AGNES. And when will you be back?

HORACE.   As quickly as can be.

AGNES. I won't be happy, till you're safely back with me.

HORACE. Thank goodness, everything has turned out for the   1480
best!
I'll go and have a nap, now that my mind's at rest.

SCENE 4

ARNOLPHE, AGNES

ARNOLPHE [*his face hidden in his cloak*]. It isn't wise to keep you
here, so come away.
I've got a better refuge for you; come, obey.
I plan to keep you in a place of safety, which
I know. You recognize me?

AGNES [*recognizing him*].   Hah!

ARNOLPHE.   You little witch,
You find my face a bit unnerving, now you've seen
It, eh? Are you reluctant? You don't seem too keen
To have me interfere in your new love affair.

[AGNES *looks after* HORACE *to see if she can still see him*

Don't gaze after the boy—it's no use. He's not there.
He won't be helping you, he's much too far away.   1490
Not much more than a child, and what a trick to play!
Pretending you're so innocent, and so sincere,
You ask if women bear their babies through the ear,
And then make assignations with young men, at night,
And run off with a boy, and stage a midnight flight.
His presence turns your tongue into a skilful tool;
You've had your education at some brilliant school.
Now who the devil taught you all those wicked things?
I thought you were afraid of what the darkness brings,
But now your lover helps you stay out late at night!   1500
You hussy! How could you betray me? By what right?
And after all I've done for you, commit such sin!
I see I've warmed a little frozen viper in
My bosom; once it's thawed, what base ingratitude!
It bites its benefactor. Monstrous turpitude!*

AGNES. Why are you shouting at me?

ARNOLPHE.   So, I'm in the wrong?

AGNES. There's no harm in what I've been doing, all along.

ARNOLPHE. So it's all right to let young men into your life?

AGNES. Well, yes, because he says he wants me for his wife.
I've done just what you taught me—and you rubbed it in: 1510
You have to marry, to remove all hint of sin.

ARNOLPHE. Yes, but you weren't intended for some profiteer;
I planned to marry you myself, I made that clear.

AGNES. You see, to be quite frank, and give you both your due,
Horace will be a better bet for me than you:

You paint a dreadful picture of the married state.
You turn it into something awful, that I'd hate;
With him, I've been entranced by what he has to say.
He makes me want to marry him, and straightaway.

ARNOLPHE. You shameless girl! You love him.   1520

AGNES.   Yes, indeed I do.

ARNOLPHE. What's more, you've got the face to tell me of it too!

AGNES. But that's because it's true. I mustn't lie, you know.

ARNOLPHE. You wicked girl! You know it's wrong to love him.

AGNES.   Oh,
How could I help it? He's to blame, you realize,
And when we fell in love, it took me by surprise.

ARNOLPHE. You ought to have controlled your feelings, for a start.

AGNES. But how can you control the instincts of your heart?

ARNOLPHE. You must have realized that I'd be angry too.

AGNES. What, me? No, not at all. How is it harming you?

ARNOLPHE. Quite right, I've every reason to be pleased, I   1530
guess.
So you don't love me, then?

AGNES.   What, do I love you?

ARNOLPHE.   Yes.

AGNES. No.

ARNOLPHE. What do you mean, no?

AGNES.   Do you want me to lie?

ARNOLPHE. Why don't you love me, then, you minx? Why don't
you try?

AGNES. Good gracious! Why on earth put all the blame on me?
And why not make yourself as lovable as he?
I never stopped you trying, and I never would.

ARNOLPHE. I tried my very best, by every means I could,

But all my efforts were a waste of time, it seems.

AGNES. He's better at those things than you, for all your schemes:
He made me fall in love, and with the greatest ease.   1540

ARNOLPHE. Just look at how she reasons with me, if you please!
God damn it! Could a woman of the world say more?
Ah, either I misjudged her, or in lovers' lore,
A silly girl knows better than a clever man!
My pretty reasoner, now tell me if you can,
Since you're so logical, do you think it makes sense
For him to profit from your life at my expense?

AGNES. No, but he plans to pay you back—yes, every bit.

ARNOLPHE. The things she says! She makes me feel inadequate...
So he's attractive. But do you think that your beau   1550
Can ever pay me back for everything you owe?

AGNES. I really don't see why I owe you anything.

ARNOLPHE. Oh, no? I brought you up—so that's not worth a thing?

AGNES. Oh, yes, my education's been a great success,
You had me taught—and now I'm in a fine old mess.
Do you think I'm deceived? Do you think I can't see
A stupid idiot is what you've made of me?
It hurts. I'm so ashamed—but now I've got a plan:
I'll try to seem less idiotic if I can.

ARNOLPHE. You don't want to be ignorant? Your boyfriend   1560
might
Give you a course of private lessons...

AGNES.   Yes, that's right.
I've learnt enough from him to know how ignorant
I am. I owe him more than you, that's evident.

ARNOLPHE. I don't know why I haven't punched you in the face.
My fist, here, longs to pay you back for this disgrace.
Oh, she's so cool, I've got to punish her for it,
And it'd calm me down to smack her face a bit.

AGNES. Oh, dear, I can't stop you. Go on. Do what you like.

ARNOLPHE. That look, those words. I'm quite disarmed, and I can't
    strike
    The girl. Instead, my heart is filled with tenderness.   1570
    I find myself forgetting all her wickedness.
    How very strange love is, and how is it that we
    Should melt with weakness for a monster? Look at me!
    The whole world is aware how foolish women are:
    Extravagance and madness are their repertoire.
    Their minds are mischievous, they're too inclined to sin,
    Pathetically feeble, lacking discipline.
    They're constantly unfaithful to their menfolk; still
    The little creatures bend us strong men to their will.
    All right, you little villainess, don't let's make war.   1580
    Yes, I'll forgive you, and I'll love you as before.
    You see, that proves I love you like a maniac,
    So, since I've been so good to you, just love me back.

AGNES. I'd really like to help you out, with all my heart.
    It should be easy, but I just can't play the part.

ARNOLPHE. My little sweetheart, you can do it if you try.

[Heaves a sigh

Oh, listen: did you hear that tender, loving sigh?
Look deep into my eyes, and you'll find out the truth.
Yes, I'm the one for you. Forget that callow youth!
He must have cast a spell on you. Oh, can't you see   1590
That you'd be so much happier, at home with me?
I see you always like to have a good time, so
I'll make sure that you get it, everywhere you go.
I'll stroke you, cuddle you, adore you, day and night.
I'll nuzzle you, and gobble you up, in a bite.
You'll do exactly what you feel like, have no fear.
There's no need to explain, I've made myself quite clear.

[Aside

Oh, how much can this passion make a lover do?

[Aloud

There's nothing that can equal how I feel for you.

You little monster, must I prove it? Watch me try!   1600
D'you want to see me hit myself, or watch me cry?
D'you want to see me tear my hair out on one side?
Or shall I kill myself? Will you be satisfied?
Oh, I'll do anything to show you how I care.

AGNES. Look, all this talk just isn't getting anywhere.
Horace has much more impact with a single word.

ARNOLPHE. You've gone too far this time. How dare you? That's
absurd!
You little beast, it's time you had a dressing-down:
I've had enough! I'm telling you, you're leaving town.
You turned me down, you thought you'd brought me to   1610
defeat.
I'll throw you in a convent. Ah, revenge is sweet!

SCENE 5

ALAIN, ARNOLPHE, AGNES

ALAIN. Monsieur, I've seen a funny thing. I'm not sure how,
Agnes and the dead man went walking off, just now.

ARNOLPHE. Yes. Here she is. Go in, and lock her in my room.
He won't come looking for her there, as I presume.
And anyway it's only for a brief half-hour.
I'm on my way to find a safer prison tower.
I'll get a carriage. Meanwhile, keep her shut up tight,
And, most of all, make sure she's never out of sight.
Who knows? Maybe a change of scene will do the trick: 1620
She'll realize her young man is a lunatic.

SCENE 6

HORACE, ARNOLPHE

HORACE. Monsieur Arnolphe, I've come to you in such a state:
I thought we'd won, but now my hopes are dashed by fate.

It's so unfair, that blow—it's struck me to the heart.
My darling love and me—looks like we've got to part.
My father's on his way—he thought he'd like a walk.
I met him, getting off his horse. We had a talk,
And, in a word, he let me know what brought him here—
His letters never said a thing, I'd no idea—
My marriage is arranged: I never gave consent.   1630
That's why he's here—to celebrate the glad event.
Oh, think of it! You'll guess how desperate I feel.
Oh, what a cruel blow! Oh, God! What an ordeal!
Remember that Enrique (I asked you yesterday
About him)? He's the cause of all my disarray:
He's come here with my father, hell-bent on my doom.
The bride's his only daughter: I'm to be the groom.
When they began to tell me this, I thought I'd faint.
I didn't stop to hear, or make any complaint.
I rushed straight over here, to ask you what to do.   1640
My father tells me that he's coming this way too.
I beg you not to breathe a single word about
My love. He'd be angry, if the truth came out.
But as you know, he sets great store by what you say:
Try to dissuade him from his choice of fiancée.

ARNOLPHE. Uh-uh.

HORACE.   Tell him he'd best not rush things, in your view.
    Oh, help me save my love: I know that you'll be true.

ARNOLPHE. I'll do what must be done.

HORACE.   You're worthy of my trust.

ARNOLPHE. Indeed!

HORACE.   You're like a father to me, and you must
    Explain that at my age... Oh, goodness me, he's here!   1650
    I need to talk to you, I've points I must make clear.

                  [*They move to a corner of the stage*

SCENE 7

ENRIQUE, CHRYSALDE, ARNOLPHE, HORACE, ORONTE

ENRIQUE [*to* CHRYSALDE]. The moment that I saw you here, with
    my own eyes,
  They didn't need to name you: I could recognize
  Your features—they're your dearest sister's, to the life,
  Your sister, who was once my own beloved wife.
  If cruel fate had let my faithful partner see
  Our homeland once again, how happy we would be!
  Yes, she'd have shared my rapture, and my joy, I know,
  At meeting all our loved ones, after years of woe.
  But it was not to be, and cruel destiny   1660
  Deprives us all, forever, of her company.
  I must try to have patience, try to be content
  With what she left behind her: that is my intent.
  My child concerns you closely, and I wouldn't dream
  Of marrying her to a man you don't esteem.
  Monsieur Oronte's son is a most distinguished choice;
  But still I won't proceed, unless I have your voice.

CHRYSALDE. The match is excellent! My judgement would be poor
  Indeed, if I professed myself to feel unsure.

ARNOLPHE [*to* HORACE]. Yes, yes, I'll help you, good and   1670
  proper, as you'll see.

HORACE. Wait, wait, just one more thing...

ARNOLPHE.   You can rely on me.

ORONTE [*to* ARNOLPHE]. Oh, how delightful! Been so long! My
  dear old friend!

ARNOLPHE. It's good to see you. Knew we'd meet up, in the end.

ORONTE. You know, I'm here because...

ARNOLPHE.   Don't tell it all again—
  I know why you've come here.

ORONTE.   You've heard the story, then?

ARNOLPHE. Yes, yes.

ORONTE.   Oh, good!

ARNOLPHE.   I know your son. He fears the worst.
  He doesn't want this marriage, says his heart will burst.
  He wanted me to try to make you change your mind.
  And, you know what? The only thing that I can find
  To say is, let him stew! The marriage must take place.   1680
  Yes, show him you're the father. Try not to lose face.
  Young men need firm control, or else they undermine
  Their elders. I say we should make them toe the line.

HORACE. You traitor!

CHRYSALDE.   If he doesn't want it, then, of course,
  It mustn't go ahead. It's not right to use force.
  That's what I think, Enrique. Well, do we speak as one?

ARNOLPHE. Don't listen. You must not be governed by your son.
  So, do you all believe that fathers should submit,
  And let their sons decide their futures—is that it?
  A fine state of affairs, if boys choose to ignore   1690
  Their fathers, don't do as they're told, lay down the law.
  No, no. You're my best friend. I care for your good name.
  Don't go back on your word—you'll fill us both with shame.
  You must stand firm—you mustn't go against your vow,
  But force your son to honour this agreement, now.

ORONTE. The wedding goes ahead—you're right to interfere.
  I'll answer for my son. Do I make myself clear?

CHRYSALDE [to ARNOLPHE]. For my part, I'm surprised at you.
    You seem so set
  On pushing through this business quickly. And I'll bet
  You've got a secret reason, which I still can't guess.   1700

ARNOLPHE. Maybe. It's what I've got to do, nevertheless.

ORONTE. Yes, yes, Monsieur Arnolphe.

CHRYSALDE.   Don't use that name. You know
  They call him Monsieur de la Souche—I told you so.

ARNOLPHE. It doesn't matter.

HORACE.   What's that?

ARNOLPHE [*turning to* HORACE].   Yes, it's news to you.
　Now do you understand? Oh, try to think it through!

HORACE. Oh, no!

SCENE 8

GEORGETTE, ARNOLPHE, HORACE, ENRIQUE, ORONTE,
CHRYSALDE

GEORGETTE.   Monsieur, you better come and help us, we
　Can't keep control of Agnes. She keeps breaking free.
　She wants to make a run for it, I'm that dismayed.
　She'll throw herself out of the window, I'm afraid.

ARNOLPHE. Go off, and fetch her here at once. My mind is set 1710
　On taking her away, right now.

                              [*To* HORACE

                    Don't be upset.
　If you had everything your way, you'd never learn—
　And, as the proverb says, each man must have his turn.

HORACE. Oh, heavens, I'm so wretched! I can guarantee
　That no one's ever been as miserable as me.

ARNOLPHE [*to* ORONTE]. Make sure you hurry up the wedding. For
　my part,
　May I invite myself? I take this thing to heart.

ORONTE. We mean to do so.

SCENE 9

ARNOLPHE, AGNES, HORACE, ORONTE, CHRYSALDE, ENRIQUE,
ALAIN, GEORGETTE

ARNOLPHE.   Come along, my pretty one.
I hear you won't stay still, you're spoiling for some fun.
Yes, there's your suitor. You can say your goodbyes, now,   1720
And bow to him, as gracefully as you know how.
It didn't turn out as you hoped, but, as you see,
In some affairs, a happy ending's not to be.

AGNES. Will you just let him walk me off like this, Horace?

HORACE. I don't know what to do—I'm in a sorry pass.

ARNOLPHE. Come on, now, chatterbox.

AGNES.   I'd much rather stay here.

ORONTE. Look here, what's going on? This whole thing's very
     queer.
We're staring at each other in astonishment.

ARNOLPHE. I'll tell you all about it, when convenient.
Goodbye, for now.   1730

ORONTE.   Where do you think you're going, though?
You're not saying the things you ought to say, you know.

ARNOLPHE. I did advise you not to listen to your son,
But get him married off.

ORONTE.   But if that's to be done,
We need the girl. Has nobody informed you that
The girl in question lives with you, and that, in fact,
She is the daughter of the charming Angelique,
Who had a secret marriage to Seigneur Enrique?
What made you say the things you said to us, I pray?

CHRYSALDE. Yes, I was most surprised at what he had to say.

ARNOLPHE. What?...   1740

CHRYSALDE.   Yes, my sister did get married secretly.
    She had a child, but never told the family.

ORONTE. Her husband kept the secret, and he chose to hide
    His baby with a nurse, out in the countryside.

CHRYSALDE. That was the time when fate heaped problems on him,
        and
    He had to run away, and leave his native land.

ORONTE. He was in fearful danger, so he had to flee,
    Away from all his loved ones, far across the sea.

CHRYSALDE. His bitter enemies maligned him. Though it cost
    Him dear, he finally regained what he had lost.

ORONTE. And, back in France, the first thing that he did was   1750
        find
    The nurse with whom the baby had been left behind.

CHRYSALDE. The woman told us that she hopes he understands—
    At four years old, she placed the baby in your hands.

ORONTE. She had no option: she was forced by poverty,
    And you were famous for your generosity.

CHRYSALDE. He was so thrilled to hear the story, that he thought
    He'd send for the old woman, so he's had her brought.

ORONTE. So she will soon be here. You'll see her, once again.
    The mystery will be solved—she's ready to explain.

CHRYSALDE. I think that I can guess the way you're suffering.   1760
    But in this matter, fate has done the decent thing.
    If cuckoldry seems such a fearful state to you,
    Avoiding marriage is the wisest thing to do.

ARNOLPHE [*departing, so overcome he is unable to speak*]. Oh!*

ORONTE.   Why did he run off without a word?

HORACE.   You'll see
    When I have told you what's behind this mystery.
    By chance, the very thing that you had wisely planned
    Just happened of its own accord, in this place, and

I fell in love with my sweet Agnes, she with me.
We promised that we'd stay together. Yes, you see,
To put it plainly, she's the one you've come to find,   1770
And she's the very girl on whom I've set my mind.

ENRIQUE. The moment I set eyes on her, I felt quite sure
She was the one. Oh, this is happiness most pure!
Ah! Daughter, I'm so thrilled. Come here, give me a kiss.

CHRYSALDE. Like you, dear brother, I want nothing more than
    this.*
But these are serious matters: this is not the place.
Let's go inside, and solve the problems of the case;
Since he's looked after her, let's recompense our friend,
And thank the Lord, that things came out right, in the end.

THE END

THE SCHOOL FOR WIVES
CRITICIZED

1663

CHARACTERS

URANIE*
ELISE*
CLIMENE*
GALOPIN*
THE MARQUIS*
DORANTE*
LYSIDAS*

The setting is in Paris, in Uranie's house.

SCENE 1

URANIE, ELISE

URANIE. What, no visitors, cousin?

ELISE. None at all.

URANIE. Well, really, I'm amazed. The two of us have been on our own all day.

ELISE. I'm just as amazed as you. It's not normally like this. All the court layabouts generally hang around your house, I'm happy to say.

URANIE. Yes, and the afternoon has dragged a bit, in my opinion.

ELISE. I thought it rushed past.

URANIE. Yes, you see, cousin, brilliant people like solitude.

ELISE. Oh, thanks very much. You know I don't claim to be brilliant.

URANIE. Well, me, I admit I like company.

ELISE. Me too, but I'm choosy; and so many idiotic visitors come along with the others, that I often feel I'd rather be on my own.

URANIE. If you can't stand anything but the pick of the visitors, you're being too difficult.

ELISE. If you put up with all and sundry, you're being too accommodating.

URANIE. I enjoy the sensible ones, and laugh at the outrageous ones.

ELISE. Actually, the outrageous ones soon bore you, and, after the first visit, they stop being amusing. But, talking of outrageous people, couldn't you get rid of that pushy Marquis* for me? Do you have to leave him on my hands? Must I always sit there listening to his endless witty jokes?

URANIE. But the way he talks is the latest thing—witty jokes are very popular at court just now.

ELISE. Too bad for the witty courtiers, who kill themselves trying to talk such rubbish. A fine thing, I must say, to fill the conversations at the Louvre* with stale old jokes picked up in the mud of the market place* and the student quarters of Paris!* A very courtly way of behaving, I'm sure! What a scream, when someone says to you: 'Madame, here you are in La Place Royale,* but you should be miles away outside Paris, because of your "bonney" looks'— the point being that Bonneuil is a remote little village.* How witty and elegant! Don't you think people who invent such brilliant repartee ought to be pleased with themselves?

URANIE. They're not really trying to be witty. Most people who talk like that know perfectly well how ridiculous it is.

ELISE. Once again, too bad. If they go to the trouble of saying such stupid things, and deliberately making feeble puns, they've got even less excuse. If I were a judge, I know what sentence I'd pass on all these gentlemen jokers.

URANIE. Let's stop talking about it: I can see you're getting rather heated. Dorante seems to be very late—we're supposed to be having supper together.

ELISE. He may have forgotten, and...

SCENE 2

URANIE, ELISE, GALOPIN

GALOPIN. Madame, Climene's here—she's come to see you.

URANIE. Oh, Lord! What a visitor!

ELISE. You were just complaining we didn't have any: now you're paying for it.

URANIE. Quick, go and tell her I'm not at home.

GALOPIN. She's already been told you're in.

ELISE. What idiot told her that?

GALOPIN. Me, Madame.

URANIE. You little horror! I'll teach you to put words into people's mouths.

GALOPIN. Madame, I'll go and tell her you'd rather be 'not at home'.

URANIE. No, stop, you little monster, let her come up: the harm's been done.

GALOPIN. She's out in the street, talking to a man.

URANIE. Oh, cousin, what an infuriating visit!

ELISE. I agree, the lady is naturally a bit infuriating. I can't stand her myself. I know she's well born, but she's a complete ass—and she will insist on debating every point.

URANIE. That's a bit strong.

ELISE. Oh, come on, she deserves it; let's face it, she deserves even worse. Have you ever known a more obvious *précieuse*,* in the worst sense of the word?

URANIE. But she objects to being called that.

ELISE. True, she objects to the name, but not to the thing. In actual fact, she's a *précieuse* from head to toe. She's the most affected person I've ever met. She looks like a doll with jointed limbs, and when she moves her hips, shoulders, and head, she jerks, as if she'd been wound up. She puts on a silly, drawling little voice, purses her lips to give herself a rosebud mouth, and rolls her eyes to make them look bigger.

URANIE. Hush, she might hear you.

ELISE. No, she's still downstairs. I'll never forget the evening she decided she wanted to have Damon* round, because he has something of a reputation and is in the public eye. You know what he's like, and how lazy he always is about keeping the conversation going. She'd invited him to supper to show off his brilliance, but he's never seemed stupider—and all this in front of half a dozen people she'd boasted to about him, who goggled at him as though he were a new species. They all thought he was there to entertain the company with witty remarks. They were expecting every word he spoke to be extraordinary; they were looking forward to impromptu masterpieces on every topic, and waiting for him dazzle them when he asked for a drink. But he disappointed them tremendously: he never said a word; the lady was as fed up with him as I was with her.

URANIE. Be quiet. I'm going to the door to welcome her.

ELISE. One more thing. I'd like to see her married to the Marquis we were talking about just how. What a marvellous combination, a *précieuse* and a punster!

URANIE. Oh, do be quiet! Here she is.

SCENE 3

CLIMENE, URANIE, ELISE, GALOPIN

URANIE. Well, really, it's getting a bit late, and...

CLIMENE. Darling! I'm simply dying to sit down. Do something!

URANIE. Quick, fetch a chair!

CLIMENE. Oh, Heavens!

URANIE. What's wrong?

CLIMENE. I can't stand it a minute longer!

URANIE. What's the matter?

CLIMENE. I'm feeling faint!

URANIE. Is it an attack of the vapours?

CLIMENE. No.

URANIE. Do you want me to unlace your dress?

CLIMENE. Good gracious, no! Ah!

URANIE. So what's wrong with you? When did the symptoms start?

CLIMENE. More than three hours ago. I caught them at the Palais Royal Theatre.*

URANIE. What?

CLIMENE. Yes. For my sins, I've just been to see that worthless hotchpotch of a play *The School for Wives*. I've still not recovered. It made me feel nauseous, and I expect it'll take me at least a fortnight to get over it.

ELISE. Well, fancy that! You take ill when you least expect it.

URANIE. I don't know how it is—my cousin and I must be very unlike you. We went to see the same play the day before yesterday, and came back in good form, and perfectly fit.

CLIMENE. What! So you've been to see it too?

URANIE. Yes, and we listened to it from start to finish.

CLIMENE. And didn't it send you into convulsions, darling?

URANIE. No. Thank God, I'm not as fragile as that. Actually, I think the play would be more likely to cure people than make them ill.

CLIMENE. Good gracious, I can't believe what I'm hearing! You're always making out you're so sensible, and now you say a thing like that? You think you can get away with such mad opinions? I suspect you must be starved of culture, to relish a play seasoned with such stale old clichés. In my judgement, the whole production was completely lacking in spice. The bit about *women making their babies through the ear** was in appalling taste; *custard pie** was simply revolting. And when he served up the *soup*,* I thought I was going to throw up.

ELISE. Oh, goodness, how elegantly put! I could have sworn it was a good play; but Madame's so persuasive and eloquent, and she expresses herself in such a charming way, that you have to agree with her, whatever you really think.

URANIE. Well, I'm not so accommodating, myself. And quite frankly, I think it's one of his best plays.

CLIMENE. Oh, I feel really sorry for you, hearing you say that. I can't bear to listen—you've no judgement. Tell me, how can a decent woman enjoy a play which never stops attacking our modesty, and filling our imaginations with smutty innuendo?

ELISE. I love the way you put that! I must say, Madame, you're a devastating critic! I pity poor Molière, having you for an enemy.

CLIMENE. Take my tip, darling! Revise your opinions, and don't be half-hearted about it. You'll ruin your reputation if you go about telling everybody you liked the play.

URANIE. Well, I don't see what you found in it to make you blush.

CLIMENE. Oh, dear me, everything! A decent woman couldn't watch it without being shocked. I found so much sleaze, and so many smutty bits...

URANIE. You must be more of an expert on sleaze than everyone else, then. I didn't find any, myself.

CLIMENE. Believe me, that's because you chose not to find any. God! The sleaze! It's there for all to see! Lying there, showing itself off. The most hardened voyeur would be shocked at all that nudity.

ELISE. Oh!

CLIMENE. Ha, ha, ha!

URANIE. Yes, but can you pick out one of the sleazy passages you mean?

CLIMENE. Oh, dear, do I have to?

URANIE. Yes. I want to know—let's have just one of the passages that shocked you so much.

CLIMENE. Well, what about the scene where Agnes goes on about how he took her... You know.*

URANIE. Well? What's so smutty about that?

CLIMENE. Ah!

URANIE. Come on?

CLIMENE. Ugh!

URANIE. No, tell us.

CLIMENE. I've nothing to say.

URANIE. I don't think there's any harm in it.

CLIMENE. That's just too bad.

URANIE. You mean, that's just as well. I take things as they come. I don't twist them so as to uncover things that aren't there.

CLIMENE. Our reputation as women...

URANIE. Why make such a song and dance about our reputation as women? Being more prudish than the prudes doesn't look good. It's the worst type of affectation. It's too ridiculous, the way you go on, feeling insulted at everything, taking it all the wrong way; to you, it seems, the simplest words are smutty. You're taking offence at shadows. Don't think you'll be respected for going on the way you do. On the contrary, people just get irritated by mysterious criticisms and affected posturing like yours. They look at your own behaviour and find fault with it. They enjoy discovering things to attack in what you do. For example, when we went to see the play the other day, there was a group of women in the box opposite ours. They made faces during the whole performance, and turned their heads away to hide their blushes. Everyone mocked at their behaviour; if they'd kept quiet, nobody would have said a thing. Do you know, a manservant in the audience shouted out that their ears were more virginal than all the rest of their bodies!

CLIMENE. So you want us to make believe we're blind during the play, and pretend we don't see what we see?

URANIE. You shouldn't try to see what's not there.

CLIMENE. Look, yet again, I insist: the sleaze hits you in the face.

URANIE. Well, I don't agree.

CLIMENE. What! you don't feel outraged at what Agnes says in that passage we were talking about?

URANIE. Not at all. She doesn't say a single improper word; if you want to read things into it, it's you that's being smutty, not her. All she's talking about is a ribbon that's been taken away from her.

CLIMENE. Oh, ribbon on as much as you like. But what about when she says *My*, then hesitates? That wasn't put in for nothing. That *my* makes you have the strangest fantasies. That *my* is scandalous! It's outrageous! whatever you say, you'll never be able to justify the insolence of that *my*.

ELISE. Madame's quite right, cousin. I'm on her side against that *my*. That *my* is as insolent as can be. You're wrong to try to defend that *my*.

CLIMENE. The obscenery*—it's unbearable.

ELISE. What was that word again, Madame?

CLIMENE. Obscenery, Madame.

ELISE. Oh, goodness! Obscenery. I don't know what it means, but I think it's a perfectly lovely word.

CLIMENE. You see? Your own flesh and blood is on my side.

URANIE. Oh, for Heaven's sake! It's all talk with her—she's not saying what she thinks. I wouldn't believe her, if I were you.

ELISE. Oh, that's so mean! Why make Madame suspect me? What would become of me, if she believed what you say? Oh, Madame, could you possibly think such things of me?

CLIMENE. No, of course not. I'm taking no notice of what she says. I think you're much more sincere that she claims you are.

ELISE. Ah! You're so right, Madame. Believe me, I think you're the most convincing person in the world. I agree with what you say, I'm charmed by every single word you speak.

CLIMENE. Oh dear, I'm not trying to seem affected.

ELISE. That's obvious, Madame. You're so simple and natural. It shows in your words and your tone of voice—the way you look at people, the way you walk, your clothes, your behaviour—you've an air of distinction that's quite enchanting. I've been all eyes and ears, studying you. I'm full of you. I try to ape you, and copy everything you do.

CLIMENE. You're making fun of me, Madame.

ELISE. Me? Not at all, Madame. Who could want to make fun of you?

CLIMENE. I'm not worth imitating, Madame.

ELISE. Oh, yes you are, Madame.

CLIMENE. You're flattering me, Madame.

ELISE. Oh, no I'm not, Madame.

CLIMENE. Oh, please, spare my blushes, Madame.

ELISE. I am sparing you, Madame. I'm not telling you the half of what I think, Madame.

CLIMENE. Oh, please, let's stop all this. You make me feel so embarrassed. [*To* URANIE] So, you see, it's two against one. An intelligent woman shouldn't be so stubborn.

SCENE 4

CLIMENE, URANIE, ELISE, GALOPIN, THE MARQUIS

GALOPIN [*at the door*]. Please stop there, Monsieur.

THE MARQUIS. I don't think you know who I am.

GALOPIN. Yes, I do. You're not to go in.

THE MARQUIS. Why make such a fuss, boy?

GALOPIN. Going in, when you're told not to—it isn't right.

THE MARQUIS. I want to see your mistress.

GALOPIN. I told you, she's not at home.

THE MARQUIS. But she's here, in this room.

URANIE. What's the matter?

THE MARQUIS. It's your page, Madame, playing the fool.

GALOPIN. I keep telling him you're not at home, Madame, but he will insist on coming in.

URANIE. But why tell Monsieur I'm not at home?

GALOPIN. The other day, you told me off for telling him you were in.

URANIE. Cheeky monkey! Don't believe a word he says, Monsieur, please. He's a little fool—he took you for someone else.

THE MARQUIS. I realize that, Madame. Saving your grace, I could teach him a thing or two about the upper classes.

ELISE. My cousin's much obliged to you for being so understanding.

URANIE [to GALOPIN]. Fetch a chair, you little wretch.

GALOPIN. There's a chair right here.

    [*The little page pushes the chair forward roughly, then goes out*

THE MARQUIS. Madame, your little page has no respect for my person.

ELISE. That's so wrong of him.

THE MARQUIS. What do you think? Am I paying the penalty for looking so undistinguished? Ha! ha! ha! ha!

ELISE. When he's older, he'll know how to recognize a gentleman.

THE MARQUIS. Well, ladies, what were you talking about when I interrupted you?

URANIE. The play *The School for Wives.*

THE MARQUIS. I've just been to see it.

CLIMENE. Well, Monsieur, and how did you find it?

THE MARQUIS. Totally unacceptable.

CLIMENE. Oh, good! I'm absolutely delighted!

THE MARQUIS. It was just terrible! Dash it all, I had tremendous trouble getting a ticket. I nearly suffocated in the crush round the door, and people kept treading on my toes. Just look at the state my frills and ribbons* are in, do!

ELISE. It's true—that's a punishable offence. You're quite right to condemn *The School for Wives*.

THE MARQUIS. In my opinion, it's the worst play ever written.

URANIE. Ah! there's Dorante. We were expecting him.

SCENE 5

URANIE, ELISE, CLIMENE, THE MARQUIS, DORANTE

DORANTE. Please don't move, and don't stop your conversation. I know what you're discussing. They've been talking about nothing else in Paris, for the last four days. It's been most amusing, hearing all the different verdicts. Do you know, some people have attacked the play for the very things other people admired the most.

URANIE. Monsieur le Marquis here has been saying bad things about it.

THE MARQUIS. That's true. I think it's detestable, by Jove! Detestable, as detestable as can be. What you'd call detestable.

DORANTE. Well, my dear Marquis, I find your opinion detestable.

THE MARQUIS. What, Chevalier! Are you sticking up for the play?

DORANTE. Yes, I am.

THE MARQUIS. Dash it all! I guarantee it's detestable.

DORANTE. That's not good enough. Come on, Marquis, please tell me why the play is what you say it is?

THE MARQUIS. Why it's detestable?

DORANTE. Yes.

THE MARQUIS. It's detestable, because it's detestable.

DORANTE. After that, there's nothing more to say. He's proved his point. But go on. Tell us more. Talk to us about its faults.

THE MARQUIS. How should I know? I didn't even bother to listen. But I do know that I've never seen anything so pathetic. God damn it! Dorilas was right next to me, and he agreed.

DORANTE. He's certainly a figure of authority—you've got strong support there.

THE MARQUIS. You only have to look at the bursts of laughter that keep coming from the pit.* Do you need any more proof that the play's worthless?

DORANTE. I see, Marquis. You're one of those gentlemen snobs, who sit in the best seats,* in full view of the audience, and assume that the people in the pit have no common sense. You lot would be ashamed at laughing with the pit, even at the best show in the world. The other day, I saw one of our friends sitting there, making himself look ridiculous. He listened to the whole play with a long face, as grim as could be. The more the audience laughed, the more he frowned. Every time there was a burst of merriment, he shrugged and looked contemptuously at the pit. Sometimes, he pulled a bitter face, and said out loud—'Go on then, laugh away, you groundlings!' It was like a second entertainment, the way he carried on! He generously offered himself up to the audience's gaze. Everyone agreed he gave a magnificent performance.* Look here, Marquis, it's time you, and people like you, realized that sitting in expensive seats, paying half a gold piece instead of 15 sous, doesn't buy good taste. You can misjudge a play sitting in a box, just as well as standing in the pit. In short, I'd be inclined, on the whole, to trust the pit's approval, because there are people in the pit who know the rules, and how to apply them in judging a play. And the rest judge the play the way a play should be judged, that's to say they let it speak to them. They're not prejudiced, or smugly complacent, or ridiculously touchy.

THE MARQUIS. What's this, Chevalier? You're defending the pit? God damn it! I'm delighted to hear that. I'll make sure they all know you're on their side. Ha, ha, ha, ha, ha, ha!

DORANTE. Go on, have a laugh at my expense. I believe in good sense. As for all those Marquis de Mascarilles,* I can't bear their brainstorms. It makes me mad when men forget they're gentlemen and make fools of themselves in public. I can't abide people who make their minds up, and trumpet their opinions, without knowing what they're talking about. They go to the theatre, and applaud the bad bits, but ignore the good ones. They judge paintings and music in the same way, criticizing or approving the wrong things. They pick up a few technical terms in passing, and make a point of getting them wrong, and misusing them. Yes, God damn it, gentlemen! Keep quiet if you don't know what you're talking about, for heaven's sake. Don't make yourselves ridiculous to everyone around. Just think—if you don't say a word, people may imagine you're quite clever.

THE MARQUIS. By Jove, Chevalier, that's a bit strong.

DORANTE. Good gracious, Marquis, I didn't mean you. I was talking about a dozen gentlemen who dishonour courtiers like us by their eccentric behaviour, and make ordinary people believe that we're all the same. I plan to keep on making my point. I'll tell them what I think of them every time I meet them. I'll make them see reason in the end.

THE MARQUIS. I say, Chevalier, Lysandre's quite brainy, don't you think?

DORANTE. Yes, frightfully brainy.

URANIE. You can't deny that.

THE MARQUIS. Well, ask him what he thinks of *The School for Wives*. You'll see! He'll tell you he doesn't like it.

DORANTE. Yes, well, being too clever ruins a lot of people. They shed so much light on the subject, they can't see it at all. They'd hate to agree with everyone else—they want to make up their own minds—it looks better.

URANIE. That's true. I daresay our friend's like that. He wants to be the first to hold an opinion. We're all supposed to wait respectfully, and let him decide. If anyone dares to like something before he does, he regards it as an attack on his intellect. He takes his revenge by adopting the opposite view. We're supposed to ask his opinion on anything intellectual. I'm sure that if the author had shown him the play before it was performed in public, he'd have said it was terrific.

THE MARQUIS. Well, what about the Marquise, Araminte? She's been spreading the word that it's appalling. She says she could never stand filth, and it's full of it.

DORANTE. I say it's typical of how she goes on. Some people make themselves ridiculous by trying to be too upright. She's got brains, but she's been following a bad example, copying women who realize they're ageing and losing a certain *je ne sais quoi*, so they find a way of making up for it. By their posturing and their excessive prudery, they make up for the loss of their youth and beauty, or so they hope. This particular woman takes it further than the rest—she's so clever that she finds unsavoury bits where no one else can see anything wrong. They say that she's so scrupulous that she actually deforms our language. Scarcely a single word escapes the lady's severity: she wants to cut off their heads or their tails, because they contain disgraceful syllables.

URANIE. You're crazy, Chevalier.

THE MARQUIS. In short, Chevalier, you think you're defending your play by satirizing the people who condemn it?

DORANTE. Not really; but I believe that the lady in question is wrong to be so shocked.

ELISE. Hold on, Monsieur le Chevalier. There could be others who agree with her.

DORANTE. Well, at least I know you're not one of them, and when you went to see the play...

ELISE [*indicating* CLIMENE]. That was true then, but now I've changed my mind. Madame has produced such convincing arguments that she's won me over to her side.

DORANTE [*to* CLIMENE]. Ah, Madame, I beg your pardon. If you like, I'll go back on what I said, for love of you.

CLIMENE. I don't want it to be for love of me, but for love of reason; let's face it, this play has nothing going for it, and I don't see how...

URANIE. Ah, here's Monsieur Lysidas, the writer. He's come just in time to join in the debate. Monsieur Lysidas, do take a seat over there.

SCENE 6

URANIE, ELISE, CLIMENE, THE MARQUIS, DORANTE, LYSIDAS

LYSIDAS.* I'm afraid I'm a bit late, Madame. I had to read my play at Madame la Marquise's—you know, the play I told you about. I had to stay an hour longer than I expected, to listen to everyone paying me compliments.

ELISE. When it comes to making a writer late, praise works like a charm.

URANIE. Do sit down, Monsieur Lysidas. We'll read your play after supper!

LYSIDAS. Everyone there is coming to the first night. They've promised to do their best for me.

URANIE. I can believe you. But, please, do sit down. We're in the middle of a conversation, and I'd like it to go on.

LYSIDAS. I hope you've got your box booked for the great day, Madame.

URANIE. We'll see. Let's go on with what we were talking about.

LYSIDAS. I warn you, it's almost sold out, Madame.

URANIE. That's wonderful. Anyway, you arrived just when I needed you—everyone here was against me.

ELISE [to URANIE, indicating DORANTE]. He was on your side to start with; but now he knows that Madame [indicating CLIMENE] is leading the opposition, I think you'll have to look for help elsewhere.

CLIMENE. No, no. I wouldn't want to interfere in his courtship of Madame your cousin; I'll allow his intellect to follow his heart.

DORANTE. Well, if you say I have your permission, Madame, I'll make so bold as to defend myself.

URANIE. But first, let's have Monsieur Lysidas's opinion.

LYSIDAS. What about, Madame?

URANIE. *The School for Wives.*

LYSIDAS. Ha! ha!

DORANTE. What do you think of it?

LYSIDAS. I've nothing to say on the subject. You know that we authors have to be very tactful about each other's works.

DORANTE. Oh, come on! Between ourselves, what do you think of the play?

LYSIDAS. Me, Monsieur?

DORANTE. Do come clean—give us your opinion.

LYSIDAS. I think it's very good.

DORANTE. Really?

LYSIDAS. Really. Why not? Isn't it the best play ever seen?

DORANTE. Hmm! You're a sly devil, Monsieur. You're not saying what you think.

LYSIDAS. Oh, come, come!

DORANTE. Oh yes, I know you very well. Stop pretending.

LYSIDAS. Me, Monsieur?

DORANTE. I can see perfectly well that you're saying that about the play to be polite. In your heart of hearts, you agree with the people who think the play's bad.

LYSIDAS. Ha, ha, ha!

DORANTE. Come on, admit it! The play's nothing to write home about.

LYSIDAS. It's true that the cognoscenti don't think much of it.

THE MARQUIS. God damn it, Chevalier—straight for the jugular. That'll teach you to mock. Ha, ha, ha, ha!

DORANTE. Go on, my dear Marquis. Go on!

THE MARQUIS. You see—the intellectuals are on our side.

DORANTE. I admit that Monsieur Lysidas's opinion carries weight. But if Monsieur Lysidas doesn't mind, I won't give up just for that. Since I've been bold enough to disagree with Madame [*indicating* CLIMENE], I hope he'll allow me to object to what he says too.

ELISE. What! Madame, Monsieur le Marquis, and Monsieur Lysidas are all against you, and you go on digging your heels in? Ugh! How ill mannered of you!

CLIMENE. What astonishes me is that reasonable people can take it into their heads to defend such a stupid play.

THE MARQUIS. God damn it, Madame, it's pathetic from start to finish.

DORANTE. That's easily said, Marquis. Nothing's simpler than making sweeping judgements. Nothing's safe from your earth-shattering verdicts.

THE MARQUIS. Well, dash it all! Lots of actors* went to see it, and condemned it utterly.

DORANTE. Oh, I've nothing more to say. Marquis, you're right. The actors didn't like it and we've got to believe them, of course. They're very intelligent and they don't have an axe to grind. There's nothing more to say. I give up.

CLIMENE. Give up or don't give up—I can tell you, you won't persuade me to approve of such an improper play. And I can't stand the way it attacks and satirizes women.

URANIE. Well, I wouldn't take offence, or assume that what's said in the play is meant for me. That sort of satire attacks the age we live in, and only gets at individuals on the rebound. I don't think we should take a general criticism personally. We should learn the lesson it teaches, if we can, without letting on that it applies to us.

People shouldn't feel affronted at ridiculous portraits on stage. Plays are like public mirrors, and you should never admit you can see yourself in them. If you make too much fuss when the author castigates a fault, you're tacitly admitting you share the fault yourself.

CLIMENE. In my case, I'm not concerned with my own position. My standing in society is well established, I believe. I'm not afraid people will think that those character portraits of rackety women apply to me.

ELISE. Indeed, Madame, nobody would apply them to you. Everyone knows how you behave. Nobody will be in any doubt about all that.

URANIE [*to* CLIMENE]. That's why nothing I said is to do with you, Madame. My words, like the satirical portraits in the play, are of general relevance.

CLIMENE. I don't doubt it, Madame. Anyway, don't let's dwell on all that. I don't know how you take the way our sex is insulted, at one point in the play. For my part, I'm absolutely furious. That impertinent playwright calls us 'animals'!

URANIE. But, don't you see, he puts the words into the mouth of a ridiculous character?

DORANTE. What's more, Madame, surely you know that insults mean nothing between lovers? Some people choose to love in an angry way, others to be affectionate. At such moments, one says the oddest things. What's curious is that the women for whom they're intended often take them as marks of affection.

ELISE. You can say what you like, I won't swallow all that—nor the *soup* and the *custard pie* Madame mentioned earlier.

THE MARQUIS. By Jove, yes! Custard pie! I'd chuck every egg in the basket, and more, at the custard pie. Custard pie! Egad! Custard pie!

DORANTE. So? What do you mean, 'custard pie'?

THE MARQUIS. God damn it! Custard pie, Chevalier.

DORANTE. What about it?

THE MARQUIS. Custard pie!

DORANTE. Explain yourself, do.

THE MARQUIS. Custard pie!

URANIE. It seems to me you've got to explain what you mean.

THE MARQUIS. Custard pie, Madame!

URANIE. What's wrong with that?

THE MARQUIS. Nothing at all. Custard pie!

URANIE. Oh, I give up.

ELISE. Monsieur le Marquis is quite right to shove it down your throats. I'd like Monsieur Lysidas to put in the finishing touches, in his own inimitable fashion.

LYSIDAS. It's not my way to criticize, and I'm quite indulgent about other writers' works. Monsieur le Chevalier admires this playwright, so he'll forgive me if I point out that those kind of plays are not really plays at all. There's a tremendous difference between these bits of nonsense and the beauty of serious theatre. That doesn't stop everyone from trying their hand at such things, these days. Everyone goes to see them, and great works play to horribly empty theatres, while all Paris flocks to those bits of silliness. I confess, it makes my heart bleed. It's a disgrace for France.

CLIMENE. It's true. Popular taste is strangely debased, where theatre is concerned. This century is becoming deeply sordid.

ELISE. That's another lovely expression—'deeply sordid'. Did you invent it, Madame?

URANIE. Oh, please!

ELISE. I knew it.

DORANTE. So, Monsieur Lysidas, you believe that serious verse tragedies are the only clever and beautiful works, and that comedies are stupid, and deserve no praise?

URANIE. That's not what I think. I agree that tragedy is beautiful when it's well done; but comedy's charming too, and I don't believe one is easier to write than the other.

DORANTE. That's true, Madame. If you'd said that comedy was actually harder to write, you wouldn't be far wrong. In my opinion, it's much easier to write pompously about high sentiments, accusing fortune in verse, lamenting one's destiny, and insulting the gods, than to think oneself into the ridiculous side of men, and make good theatre out of ordinary people's faults. When you're portraying a hero you can do what you like. You make your portrait up out of your head. Nobody's looking for a likeness. All you need do is follow your imagination, let it have its head. Forget realism, make your characters extraordinary. But when you portray real people, you have to draw from life. Your audience wants your portrait to be recognizable. Unless they can recognize your contemporaries, you've achieved nothing. To sum up, if you're writing a serious play, all you need do is produce something that makes sense, and is well written. But in comedy that's not enough. You have to be witty, and making decent people laugh is a daunting task.

CLIMENE. Well, I think I'm one of the decent people; but I didn't laugh once, during the whole play.

THE MARQUIS. Neither did I, by Jove!

DORANTE. In your case, Marquis, it doesn't surprise me. You didn't find any of your clever puns in it.

LYSIDAS. But what one does find is no better, Monsieur. And in my judgement, all the jokes fall rather flat.

DORANTE. They didn't think so at the court!...

LYSIDAS. Ah, Monsieur!... The court!...

DORANTE. Out with it. Monsieur Lysidas. I know that you're trying to say that the court doesn't know about such things. When your words fall flat, you writers always take refuge in such complaints. You say this century is unjust, that courtiers are ignorant. Let me tell you, if you please, Monsieur Lysidas, that courtiers are as perspicacious as anyone else. Wearing a lace collar* and a feather in your hat doesn't make you stupider than a fellow in a short wig and drab doublet. The greatest test for all your plays is the verdict of the court; if you want to succeed, you should aim to please the court. Nowhere else are judgements so well founded. Apart from the fact that there are many scholars amongst the courtiers, they have their own brand of intelligence, based on simple good sense, and on their experience of society. There's no comparison. Their judgements are more subtle than the pedants', for all those gentlemen's fossilized knowledge.

URANIE. That's true. You've only got to spend some time at court to realize that there's so much going on there, you can keep up to date by just keeping your eyes open. In particular, you learn to distinguish between good and bad jokes.

DORANTE. I agree that there are some ridiculous people at court. Everyone knows I'm the first to attack them. But, frankly, there are plenty of them among professional men of letters; fair enough, we mock at a few of the marquis, but I think there's much more to mock in writers. It would be amusing to make a play out of their scholarly grimaces and their ridiculous refinements, their vicious habit of putting character assassinations into their works. They're hungry for praise, and hypocritical in their speech. They make and break reputations, and form cliques to attack their rivals, and defend their allies. They fight wars of words, battling it out in prose and verse.

LYSIDAS. I must say, Monsieur Molière is lucky to have such an enthusiastic defender. But let's get to the point. The question is, is his play any good? I undertake to demonstrate that it's full of glaring flaws.

URANIE. It's very odd how you poets all condemn the plays that everybody flocks to see. You only admire the ones nobody goes to. You loathe the popular ones with an invincible hatred, and you're unbelievably admiring of the others.

DORANTE. That's because it's noble to stand up for the underdog.

URANIE. But please, Monsieur Lysidas, tell us about these flaws. I didn't notice any.

LYSIDAS. If you knew your Aristotle and Horace,* Madame, you'd see at once that the play offends against all the rules of art.

URANIE. I confess that I'm not well acquainted with those gentlemen's work, and I don't know the rules of the art.

DORANTE. You writers make me laugh with your rules: you make people look small if they don't know them, and you knock the rest of us silly with them—it happens every day. To hear you talk, you'd think that the rules of dramatic art were the greatest mysteries in the world. And yet they're nothing but a few simple observations, based on common sense, on what can prevent such writings from giving pleasure. With that same common sense that inspired those remarks in the first place, you can come to the same conclusions nowadays, quite simply, without the help of Horace and Aristotle. I wonder—isn't the greatest rule of all that you must give pleasure to the public? And if a play has done that, hasn't it followed the right path? How can a whole audience be mistaken about such things? Isn't a person the best judge of his own enjoyment?

URANIE. I've noticed one thing about all those gentlemen: the people who go on most about the rules, and know them best, write plays that nobody enjoys.

DORANTE. Yes, Madame, and that's what proves that one shouldn't waste time on complicated arguments like theirs. I mean, if the plays that obey the rules are flops, and the plays that are triumphs don't obey the rules, then it must follow that the rules are no good. Those writers want to tangle the public in a web of subtleties. Let's reject all that, and consider nothing but the effect the play has on us. We should let ourselves go, and enjoy the things that give us that gut feeling of satisfaction. We shouldn't keep looking for reasons for spoiling our own enjoyment.

URANIE. Personally, when I go to see a play, I only think about whether it got through to me; if I enjoy it, I don't ask myself if I was wrong, or if, according to Aristotle's rules, I ought not to be laughing.

DORANTE. It's just like someone finding a sauce delicious, but then deciding to judge its quality by the rules of the cookery book.*

URANIE. I agree. I'm astonished at the way some people try to get so sophisticated about things that we ought to be reacting to spontaneously.

DORANTE. You're right, Madame, to find all all this sophistication rather peculiar. If we lived by it, we couldn't go on believing in ourselves. Our own senses would be completely enslaved. We wouldn't dare find anything good, not even food and drink, without permission from the distinguished experts.

LYSIDAS. So, Monsieur, to sum up your argument, your one point is that the public liked *The School for Wives*. You don't care if it obeys the rules, provided...

DORANTE. Hold on, Monsieur Lysidas. I won't let you get away with that. It's true that I say that the great art is to please the public; as this play pleased the people it was written for, I think that's all it needs, and nothing else matters. But that's not all. I'm prepared to argue that the play doesn't offend against any of the rules you've mentioned. For my sins, I've studied them as much as anyone, and I could easily demonstrate that it probably sticks to the rules more than any other play we have.

ELISE. Fight our corner, Monsieur Lysidas! If you back down, we're lost.

LYSIDAS. What, Monsieur! The protasis, the epitasis, and the peripeteia?

DORANTE. Oh, come on, Monsieur Lysidas! Don't bore us rigid with your technical terms. Do us a favour, don't try to seem so learned. Give us a speech in normal language; talk to us in a way we can understand. Do you really believe that a Greek term gives weight to your argument? Don't you think it would do just as well if you said the introduction of the subject instead of the protasis, the intrigue instead of the epitasis, and the denouement instead of the peripeteia?

LYSIDAS. Well, they're the technical terms of our art. It's considered the thing to employ them. But since those words offend your ears, I'll adopt a different tone, and I'll ask you to give a clear answer to three or four things I'm going to say. How can we accept a play which offends against the very essence of the theatre? For a play is a dramatic poem, and drama comes from a Greek word for action: this shows that the nature of a poem of that kind consists in action. Now in this particular play, there's no action. It's all made up of speeches by Agnes or Horace.

THE MARQUIS. Aha, Chevalier!

CLIMENE. That's a very perspicacious comment, which goes into the subtleties of the situation.

LYSIDAS. What could be more unfunny, or, to put it bluntly, more crude, than those bits of dialogue where the audience always laughs, particularly that gag about making babies through the ear?

CLIMENE. That's right.

ELISE. Aha!

LYSIDAS. The scene with the two servants in the house, now. Isn't it boring, much too long, and very out of place?

THE MARQUIS. Oh, that's so true.

CLIMENE. Absolutely.

ELISE. He's hit the nail on the head.

LYSIDAS. Doesn't Arnolphe give his money to Horace much too freely? And, since he's a figure of fun throughout the play, should he have been made to do the decent thing like that?

THE MARQUIS. Very good! Another brilliant point.

CLIMENE. Admirable!

ELISE. Marvellous!

LYSIDAS. As for the sermon and the Maxims of Marriage, aren't they ridiculous? Don't they offend against the respect we owe our sacraments?

THE MARQUIS. Oh, well said!

CLIMENE. That's what I like to hear!

ELISE. You couldn't have put it better!

LYSIDAS. Lastly, what about Monsieur de la Souche himself? He's supposed to be intelligent, he's taken seriously in many places. Doesn't he sink too low when he's so comic and so over the top in Act V, in the passage when he explains to Agnes how passionately he loves her, rolling his eyes extravagantly, sighing like an idiot, and weeping sentimental tears that make everyone laugh?

THE MARQUIS. Gad, that was stunning!

CLIMENE. A miracle!

ELISE. Long live Monsieur Lysidas!

LYSIDAS. I'm leaving aside a host of other criticisms, so as not to go on too long.

THE MARQUIS. By Jove! Chevalier, you're done for!

DORANTE. We'll see about that.

THE MARQUIS. You've met your match, old man!

DORANTE. Perhaps.

THE MARQUIS. Go on, reply! Speech! Speech! Speech!

DORANTE. With pleasure. I...

THE MARQUIS. Come on! Give us your answer, do!

DORANTE. Let me get a word in edgeways. If...

THE MARQUIS. By gosh, I defy you to give him an answer.

DORANTE. I bet you do, if you keep on interrupting.

CLIMENE. Oh, please, let's hear what he's got to say.

DORANTE. First, it isn't true to say that the whole play is made up of speeches. Quite a lot of action happens on stage, and the speeches themselves are used to further the action, so they become part of the plot. Particularly as the speeches are all made unknowingly to the character concerned, so that he keeps being thrown into confusion, which makes the audience laugh. Every time he's told something new, he takes whatever measures he can to protect himself, since he lives in permanent fear of disaster.

URANIE. *The School for Wives* is full of characters confiding in each other, and that's one of its best features. It's about an intelligent man, who's told what's going on by the innocent girl he loves, and the foolish boy who's his rival. Even so, he can't escape his fate. I think that's one of the strengths of the play.

THE MARQUIS. Nonsense, nonsense!

CLIMENE. What a feeble response!

ELISE. I don't think much of your arguments.

DORANTE. As for the line about making babies through the ear, the joke's at Arnolphe's expense. The author didn't put it in as a witticism in its own right, it's there to bring out the character. It shows up his eccentricity, because he reports a trivial, silly remark made by Agnes as though it was the finest thing in the world. It makes him bubble over with mirth.

THE MARQUIS. That's not a good answer.

CLIMENE. It's not satisfactory.

ELISE. You haven't told us anything.

DORANTE. As for the money he gives away so freely: to start with, the letter from his best friend is enough of a guarantee. Then, it's not impossible for a person to be ridiculous in some respects, and decent in others. And as for the scene with Alain and Georgette in the house, which some people find long and dull, it certainly has a purpose: just as Arnolphe was caught out while he was away by the complete innocence of the girl he loves, so when he comes home he's kept waiting by the door because of the ignorance of his servants. It's so that he should be punished repeatedly by the very precautions he had taken to protect himself.

THE MARQUIS. Those points are worthless!

CLIMENE. You're missing the mark!

ELISE. That's pathetic!

DORANTE. As for the moral speech that you call the 'sermon', I can tell you for a fact that genuinely pious people have heard it without being shocked, as you say they are. And the author is justified in using the terms 'hell' and 'boiling cauldrons' by the eccentricity of Arnolphe, and the innocence of the girl he's talking to. As for the passionate outburst in Act V, people have said it's over the top, and too comic. But I'd like to know if it's not a satirical comment on lovers. Don't ordinary respectable people, at moments like that, do certain things...?

THE MARQUIS. Look here, Chevalier, you'd best be quiet.

DORANTE. Very well. But think! if we look at the way we behave, when we're really in love...

THE MARQUIS. I don't want to listen to this.

DORANTE. No, do listen. When you're carried away by passion...

THE MARQUIS [*singing*]. Tra, la, la, la, la, la, la, la, la, la, la.

DORANTE. What?

THE MARQUIS. Tra, la, la, la, la, la, la, la, la, la, la.

DORANTE. I don't know if...

THE MARQUIS. Tra, la, la, la, la, la, la, la, la, la, la.

URANIE. It seems to me...

THE MARQUIS. Tra, la, la, la, la, la, la, la, la, la, la.

URANIE. This debate's most entertaining. I think we could turn it into a short play. It would fit in quite well at the end of *The School for Wives*.

DORANTE. You're right.

THE MARQUIS. Gad, Chevalier, what a part you'd play in it! You'd look pretty silly.

DORANTE. That's true, Marquis.

CLIMENE. I'd like to see it done, provided the whole thing was written down exactly as it happened.

ELISE. I'd be happy to play my own character.

LYSIDAS. I wouldn't refuse to play mine, I believe.

URANIE. Since everyone's willing, Chevalier, why don't you note it all down, and give it to Molière, to turn into a play? After all, you do know him.

CLIMENE. I'm sure he wouldn't dream of it. The lines would scarcely do him credit.

URANIE. Not at all—I know what he's like. He doesn't mind if people attack his plays, as long as they attract the audiences.

DORANTE. Yes, but how would he end this play? We can't have a wedding, or a recognition scene, and I can't see how we could end the debate.

URANIE. We'll have to think of some happening to bring it about.

SCENE 7

GALOPIN, LYSIDAS, DORANTE, THE MARQUIS, CLIMENE, ELISE,
URANIE

GALOPIN. Madame, dinner is served.

DORANTE. Ah, that's just the ending we were looking for, we couldn't have dreamed up anything more natural. They'll have a lively, outspoken debate on both sides, just as we've been doing, and nobody will give way. A little page-boy will come in to say dinner is served, and they'll all go off to eat.

URANIE. Let's leave it at that. I couldn't think of a better way to end the play.

THE END

THE IMPROMPTU AT
VERSAILLES

1663

CHARACTERS

MOLIÈRE,* a ridiculous marquis
BRÉCOURT, a man of quality
LA GRANGE, a ridiculous marquis
DU CROISY, a poet
LA THORILLIÈRE,* an importunate marquis
BÉJART,* an official
MADEMOISELLE* DU PARC, an affected marquise
MADEMOISELLE BÉJART, a prude
MADEMOISELLE DE BRIE, a discreet coquette
MADEMOISELLE MOLIÈRE, a wit and a tease
MADEMOISELLE DU CROISY, a simpering menace
MADEMOISELLE HERVÉ, an affected servant

The scene is set in Versailles, in the theatre

SCENE 1

MOLIÈRE [*alone, speaking to his fellow actors, off stage*]. Come along, ladies and gentlemen. What are you playing at, taking so long? Will you come here, all of you? To hell with the lot of them! Hey there, Monsieur Brécourt!

BRÉCOURT [*off stage*]. What is it?

MOLIÈRE. Monsieur La Grange!

LA GRANGE [*off stage*]. What's the matter?

MOLIÈRE. Monsieur du Croisy!

DU CROISY [*off stage*]. What do you want?

MOLIÈRE. Mademoiselle du Parc!

MADEMOISELLE DU PARC [*off stage*]. What do you want?

MOLIÈRE. Mademoiselle Béjart!

MADEMOISELLE BÉJART [*off stage*]. Yes, what?

MOLIÈRE. Mademoiselle de Brie!

MADEMOISELLE DE BRIE [*off stage*]. Uh-uh?

MOLIÈRE. Mademoiselle du Croisy!

MADEMOISELLE DU CROISY [*off stage*]. What is it now?

MOLIÈRE. Mademoiselle Hervé!

MADEMOISELLE HERVÉ [*off stage*]. Coming, coming!

MOLIÈRE. All these people are driving me crazy, I swear.

[*Enter* BRÉCOURT, LA GRANGE, DU CROISY

Hell's teeth, gentlemen! Do you want to drive me mad today?

BRÉCOURT. What do you want us to do? We haven't learnt our

parts, and it's you who's driving us mad, making us perform under these conditions.

MOLIÈRE. Oh. it's impossible to get actors to do anything!

[*Enter Mesdemoiselles* BÉJART, DU PARC, DE BRIE, MOLIÈRE, DU CROISY, *and* HERVÉ

MADEMOISELLE BÉJART. Well, here we are! What do you think you're going to do?

MADEMOISELLE DU PARC. What's in your mind?

MADEMOISELLE DE BRIE. What's all this about?

MOLIÈRE. Look, please, do come quickly. We're all in costume, and the King won't be here for a couple of hours. So let's make use of the time to rehearse our play, and work out how to perform it.

LA GRANGE. How can we perform it when we don't know it?

MADEMOISELLE DU PARC. As for me, I'm telling you I can't remember a single word my character speaks.

MADEMOISELLE DE BRIE. I know for sure I'll be needing the prompter from start to finish.

MADEMOISELLE BÉJART. As for me, I'm getting ready to perform with my script in my hand.

MADEMOISELLE MOLIÈRE. Me too.

MADEMOISELLE HERVÉ. Personally, I haven't much to say.

MADEMOISELLE DU CROISY. Me neither. But even so, I'm quite likely to miss my cues.

DU CROISY. I'd give a lot to be out of this.

BRÉCOURT. I'd rather be horsewhipped than go through with it, I'm telling you.

MOLIÈRE. What a hopeless bunch—when all you've got to do is play a simple part! What would you do, if you were in my shoes?

MADEMOISELLE BÉJART. What, you? No need to feel sorry for you. You wrote the play, so you won't forget your lines.

MOLIÈRE. Do you think forgetting my lines is all I've got to worry about? Don't you realize, I'm the one who carries the can for the success or failure of the play? Do you think it a mere nothing, putting on a comic play before an audience like this? What do you think it's like, trying to make important people laugh, the sort of people who fill you with respect, and only laugh when they feel like it? Don't you think any writer would be terrified at such an ordeal? How much do you think I wouldn't give to be out of this?

MADEMOISELLE BÉJART. If you were really so terrified, you'd have been more careful. You'd never have agreed to put on the play in eight days.

MOLIÈRE. Well, what was I to do? It was by royal command.

MADEMOISELLE BÉJART. What were you to do? Respectfully refuse, explaining that it was impossible at such short notice. In your shoes, anyone else would have been more careful of his reputation. He'd have taken care not to commit himself. Where will you be, if the whole thing's a flop, I'd like to know? Don't you think your enemies will take advantage?

MADEMOISELLE DE BRIE. That's right. You should have excused yourself respectfully before the King, or asked for more time.

MOLIÈRE. Look, Mademoiselle, prompt obedience is what pleases kings. They're not happy when you put obstacles in their path. They appreciate things at the time they want them; if you try to defer their enjoyment, it spoils it for them completely. They don't want to have to wait for their pleasure. They like things best when there's been less preparation. When we do what they ask, we shouldn't think of ourselves: we're here to give them pleasure. When they order us to do something, it's up to us to take advantage of the fact that they want it. It's better to do their bidding badly, than to put it off; we may be ashamed at having been inadequate, but at least we can take credit for being quick to obey their orders. But let's get on with the rehearsal.

MADEMOISELLE BÉJART. How do you think we can get on with it, when we don't even know our lines?

MOLIÈRE. I'm telling you, you will know them. Even if you're not word perfect, couldn't you use your brains? It's a prose play, and you know what it's about.

MADEMOISELLE BÉJART. Well, thanks a bundle. Prose is even worse than verse.

MADEMOISELLE MOLIÈRE. You know what? You should have written a play for yourself to perform, all by yourself.

MOLIÈRE. Be quiet. You may be my wife, but you're an idiot.

MADEMOISELLE MOLIÈRE. Thank you so much, dear husband. You see how it is? People change when they marry. A year and a half ago, you wouldn't have said that!*

MOLIÈRE. Oh, please be quiet!

MADEMOISELLE MOLIÈRE. It's really very odd. A simple ceremony removes all our attractions. A suitor and a husband look at the same person in very different ways.

MOLIÈRE. Must you keep on and on?

MADEMOISELLE MOLIÈRE. I'm telling you, if I wrote a play, that would be my subject. I'd defend decent women against a lot of accusations. I'd make husbands aware of the difference between their rudeness and the suitors' civil talk.

MOLIÈRE. Oh, stop going on about it. Now's not the moment to chat. We've got other things to do.

MADEMOISELLE BÉJART. They asked you to produce something on the way you've been attacked. So why didn't you write that play about actors you've been talking about for so long? You've got all the material there, and it's absolutely relevant. What's more, they've been trying to show you up, so you could have given them tit for tat—they've laid themselves wide open. You'd have painted a much more faithful portrait of them than they've done of you. If you show an actor in a comic role, you aren't really portraying the man himself, just imitating the character he's playing. You're using the same traits and mannerisms that he employs in creating the different ridiculous characters he copies from nature. But if you imitate an actor playing a serious role, you're picking out defects that are genuinely his. In a tragic role, an actor should cut out the ridiculous gestures and tones of voice that make him recognizable.

MOLIÈRE. That's true; but I've my reasons for not doing it. Between ourselves, I didn't think it was worth it. And it would have taken too long to work the idea out. They perform on the same days as us,* so I've only been to see them three or four times since we've been in Paris.* I only picked up the most blatantly obvious aspects of their way of performing. I'd have had to study them more closely to produce really lifelike portraits.

MADEMOISELLE DU PARC. I recognized some of them when you told us about them.

MADEMOISELLE DE BRIE. I've not heard about all this.

MOLIÈRE. It's just a passing idea I had. I let it drop—it was just a bit of nonsense, a joke. Probably no one would have laughed at it.

MADEMOISELLE DE BRIE. Tell me about it, since you've told all the others.

MOLIÈRE. We haven't time just now.

MADEMOISELLE DE BRIE. Just a few words.

MOLIÈRE. I thought of writing a play about a poet (I'd have played the part myself). He'd have gone to see a troupe of actors, just back from the country, to offer them a play. He'd say: 'Do you have any actors and actresses who can do justice to my work? My play is...?' 'What, monsieur?' the actors would reply. 'Both our male and female actors were considered quite acceptable, when we were on tour.' 'Which of you plays the King?' 'This actor sometimes takes it on.' 'What? That good-looking young man?* Are you joking? You have to have a vast, outsize King, a King, egad, with a really good gut to him, a King of enormous girth. He's got to fill the throne, good and proper. A fine thing to have a King with a good figure! Well, that's a black mark for a start. But let's hear him recite a dozen lines?' At that, the actor would say a few of the King's lines in Corneille's *Nicomède*:*

'Do you know what, Araspe? He's served me far too well;
By building on my power...'*

He'd speak the lines as naturally as possible. And the poet would say: 'What? Is that what you call reciting? You must be joking. You have to recite the line with the proper emphasis. Listen to this' [*and he imitates that excellent actor from the Hôtel de Bourgogne company, Montfleury*]:*

'Do you know what, Araspe...?'

Do you see the way I'm standing? Mind you take note. You see, you have to stress the end of the speech. That's how you get the audience going, and drive them wild.' 'But, Monsieur,' the actor would answer, 'I think that a king, having a private conversation with his Captain of the Guard, would use a more ordinary tone of voice, not shriek like a man possessed.' 'You don't know what you're talking about. Just try speaking the lines the way you do, you'll see. Nobody will say "Ah"! Now let's see the love scene.' So an actor and an actress play a scene together. They choose the one between Camille and Curiace:*

'My dearest, must you go? This fatal honour, it
Delights you at the cost of all our happiness?'
'Alas, I have no choice...' etc.

They'd perform it as the other actor did, as naturally as they could. And the poet would say at once: 'You've got to be joking! This is hopeless. Here's how you should speak the lines' [*imitating Mademoiselle Beauchâteau, an actress from the Hôtel de Bourgogne company*]:

'My dearest, must you go?... etc.
No. I know you too well...' etc.

Don't you find that seems natural, isn't it passionate? You should admire the way she keeps on smiling, even when suffering the most terrible afflictions.' Well, anyway, that's the idea. The poet would have run through all the actors and actresses, one after the other.

MADEMOISELLE DE BRIE. I find that idea quite amusing. I recognized some of those actors, the moment you started speaking. Do go on, please.

MOLIÈRE [*imitating another actor, Beauchâteau, in the role of Le Cid*].

'Pierced to the depth of my heart',* etc...

And what about this one—would you recognise him doing Pompée in Corneille's *Sertorius* [*imitating another actor, Hauteroche*]?

'The enmity that reigns between our camps
Does not mean we forget our honour's due'*... etc.

MADEMOISELLE DE BRIE. I think I know who it is.

MOLIÈRE. What about this one? [*imitates de Villiers, another actor*]:

'My Lord, Polybe is dead',* etc...

MADEMOISELLE DE BRIE. Yes, I know who it is. But I think one or two of them might be difficult to do.

MOLIÈRE. You know, every single one of them has characteristics you can take off. I'd have to study them carefully. But, look, you're making me waste precious time. For Heaven's sake, let's think of our own problems. Don't let's spend time chatting. [*To* LA GRANGE] You, there, concentrate. You and I are going to have to play two marquis.

MADEMOISELLE MOLIÈRE. Oh, your everlasting marquis!

MOLIÈRE. Yes, your everlasting marquis. Who the devil do you want us to choose for a comic part in a play? These days, the marquis is the funny man of the theatre. You know how, in old plays, it was always the farcical servant that made the audience laugh? Well, nowadays, there always has to be a ridiculous marquis to keep the audience amused.

MADEMOISELLE BÉJART. That's true. We couldn't do without him.

MOLIÈRE. As for you, Mademoiselle...

MADEMOISELLE DU PARC. Yes, as for me, I'm going to make a mess of my character. I don't know why you've cast me in this absurdly affected part.

MOLIÈRE. Oh, heavens, Mademoiselle, you said the same when I cast you in *The School for Wives Criticized*.* But you were very good, and everyone agreed you couldn't have been better. Believe me, this will be just the same. You'll play the part better than you think.

MADEMOISELLE DU PARC. How can that be? I'm the least affected person in the world.

MOLIÈRE. That's true. Which proves what a good actress you are, since you can play a character who's so unlike you. I'd like you all to think yourself into your parts, and imagine you're the character you're playing.

[*To* DU CROISY] You're playing the poet. Fill yourself full of your character. Put on that pedantic air that never leaves you, not even in high society. Make sure your voice sounds self-important. Pronounce your words carefully, making sure every syllable is clear. Pay attention to the spelling of the words, and speak them exactly as they are written.

[*To* BRÉCOURT] You have a straight part. You're a courtier, and a decent man. It's the same sort of part as you played in *The School for Wives Criticized*.* I mean, you must behave sensibly, speak naturally, and gesticulate as little as possible.

[*To* LA GRANGE] As for you, I've nothing to say to you.

[*To* MADEMOISELLE BÉJART] You play one of those women who think that if they don't have lovers, they can do whatever else they like. They always take refuge in prudishness, look down on everyone, and insist that everyone else's good points mean nothing, in comparison to their pathetic honour—when, in actual fact, no one could care less. Always keep your character in mind, and don't forget to screw up your face.

[*To* MADEMOISELLE DE BRIE] You're playing one of those women who think they're the most virtuous creatures in the world, provided they keep up appearances. They think there's no sin without scandal. They try to pretend that their current affairs are conducted on a purely friendly footing. What they call friends, others call lovers. Mind you enter into the role.

[*To* MADEMOISELLE MOLIÈRE] You're playing the same part as in *The School for Wives Criticized*.* I've nothing to say to you, or to Mademoiselle du Parc.

[*To* MADEMOISELLE DU CROISY] You're playing one of those women who have nothing but good to say about others. They slip in a few poisonous words in passing about every one. They'd hate it if they let anyone get away with praising their fellow men. I'm sure you'll play the part to perfection.

[*To* MADEMOISELLE HERVÉ] As for you, you're the *précieuse*'s lady's maid. She keeps joining in the conversation, and does her best to copy her mistress's language. I'm describing your characters to you, so you can really enter into the roles. Now let's start the rehearsal. We'll see how it goes. Oh, no! Here comes a bore— typical! That's all we need!

SCENE 2

LA THORILLIÈRE, MOLIÈRE, *etc.*

LA THORILLIÈRE. Oh, hello, Monsieur Molière.

MOLIÈRE. Delighted to see you, Monsieur. [*Aside*] Oh, curse the fellow!

LA THORILLIÈRE. How are you?

MOLIÈRE. Very well, thanks. [*To the actresses*] Now, ladies, don't...

LA THORILLIÈRE. I've just been out and about, and I've been saying great things about you.

MOLIÈRE. I'm much obliged. [*Aside*] Go to hell! [*To the actors*] Now, mind you take care to...

LA THORILLIÈRE. Are you performing a new play today?

MOLIÈRE. Yes, Monsieur. [*To the actors*] Look, mind you remember...

LA THORILLIÈRE. Did the King commission it?

MOLIÈRE. Yes, Monsieur. [*To the actors*] I want you to bear in mind...

LA THORILLIÈRE. What's it called?

MOLIÈRE. Yes, Monsieur.

LA THORILLIÈRE. I said, what's it called?

MOLIÈRE. Oh, I don't honestly know. [*To the actresses*] This is very important, you must...

LA THORILLIÈRE. What will your costumes be like?

MOLIÈRE. As you see. [*To the actors*] And, please...

LA THORILLIÈRE. When will you start?

MOLIÈRE. When the King arrives. [*Aside*] Blast him, and his questions!

LA THORILLIÈRE. When do you think that will be?

MOLIÈRE. I'll be damned if I know, Monsieur.

LA THORILLIÈRE. Don't you know...

MOLIÈRE. Look here, Monsieur, I'm the most ignorant man in the world. I don't know the answers to any of your questions, I promise you. [*Aside*] He's driving me nuts! What a brute—he comes along and starts calmly asking questions. He couldn't care less if we've got other things to do.

LA THORILLIÈRE. How do you do, ladies?

MOLIÈRE. Look at that—he's off on another tack.

LA THORILLIÈRE [*to* MADEMOISELLE DU CROISY]. You're looking like an angel. [*Looking at* MADEMOISELLE HERVÉ] Are you both performing today?

MADEMOISELLE DU CROISY. Yes, Monsieur.

LA THORILLIÈRE. Without you in it, the play wouldn't be worth much.

MOLIÈRE [*aside to actresses*]. Can't you get rid of that man for me?

MADEMOISELLE DE BRIE [*to* LA THORILLIÈRE]. Monsieur, we've got to rehearse some scenes.

LA THORILLIÈRE. Oh, I say! I don't want to be a nuisance. Just carry on.

MADEMOISELLE DE BRIE. But...

LA THORILLIÈRE. No, no, I'd be most upset if you thought I was cramping your style. Carry on, don't mind me.

MADEMOISELLE DE BRIE. Yes, but...

LA THORILLIÈRE. I don't stand on ceremony, I tell you. You can rehearse as much as you like.

MOLIÈRE. Monsieur, the ladies can't bring themselves to tell you they'd rather be alone during the rehearsal.

LA THORILLIÈRE. Why? It won't harm me in the least.

MOLIÈRE. It's the way they always do it, Monsieur. Besides, you'll enjoy it more if you don't know what to expect.

LA THORILLIÈRE. Oh, very well. I'll go off and tell everyone you're ready to start.

MOLIÈRE. Not at all, Monsieur. There's no need to rush things.

[*Exit* LA THORILLIÈRE]

SCENE 3

MOLIÈRE, LA GRANGE, *etc.*

MOLIÈRE. Oh, the world's packed full of nuisances! Come on, let's start. The first scene is in the King's antechamber. Try and picture it—it's a source of constant entertainment. It's a good setting—you can bring in all the characters you like, even the women I want to include. [*To* LA GRANGE] Remember to make your entrance from over there, like I told you. You must put on an aristocratic air, be combing your wig and humming a little tune as you make your entrance: 'La, la, la, la, la, la!' The others, move to the side. Two marquis need a lot of room. They're not the kind of men to squeeze their persons into a small space. [*To* LA GRANGE] Go on, begin.

LA GRANGE. 'Good day, Marquis.'*

MOLIÈRE. No, damn it, that's not the right tone of voice for a marquis. You must be more hoity-toity. Those gentlemen tend to put on peculiar voices, so as not to sound like ordinary people. 'Good day, Marquis'. Say it again.

LA GRANGE. 'Good day, Marquis.'

MOLIÈRE. 'Ah, Marquis! Your servant, sir.'

LA GRANGE. 'What are you doing here?'

MOLIÈRE. 'Gad, can't you see? I'm waiting for these gentlemen to unblock the door, so that I can make my presence known.'

LA GRANGE. 'By Jove, what a crush! I don't plan to rub shoulders with that crowd. I'd rather go in last.'

MOLIÈRE. 'I can see at least twenty people who've got no hope of getting in. That doesn't stop them crowding round the door, and blocking all the approaches.'

LA GRANGE. 'Let's shout our names to the usher, and he can call us in.'

MOLIÈRE. 'That's all very well for you. But it won't do for me—I don't want Molière to put me in one of his plays.'

LA GRANGE. 'Yes, but, Marquis, I think it's you he was taking off in *The School for Wives Criticized*.'

MOLIÈRE. 'Me? Charming! It's you, to the life.'

LA GRANGE. 'Oh, really? Decent of you to lend me your character.'

MOLIÈRE. 'Gad, it's good of you to give it me, when it belongs to you.'

LA GRANGE [*laughing*]. 'Ha, ha, ha! How amusing!'

MOLIÈRE [*laughing*]. 'Ha, ha, ha! How farcical!'

LA GRANGE. 'What! Are you really insisting you're not the inspiration for the Marquis in *The School for Wives Criticized*?'

MOLIÈRE. 'No, you're right, it's me. "Detestable, by Jove! Detestable! Custard pie!"* It's me, it's me, I promise you it's me.'

LA GRANGE. 'Gad, yes, it's you! You've no cause to mock. Let's bet on it, if you like. We'll see which of us is right.'

MOLIÈRE. 'What do you want to bet this time?'

LA GRANGE. 'I bet you a hundred pistoles* that it's you.'

MOLIÈRE. 'And I bet you a hundred pistoles that it's you.'

LA GRANGE. 'A hundred pistoles, ready money?'

MOLIÈRE. 'Yes, ready money. Ninety pistoles that Amyntas owes me, and ten pistoles in cash.'

LA GRANGE. 'You're on.'

MOLIÈRE. 'Agreed.'

LA GRANGE. 'Your money's at risk.'

MOLIÈRE. 'Yours isn't safe.'

LA GRANGE. 'Who'll decide between us?'

SCENE 4

MOLIÈRE, BRÉCOURT, LA GRANGE, *etc.*

MOLIÈRE [*to* BRÉCOURT]. 'Here's a man who'll be the arbiter. Chevalier!'

BRÉCOURT. 'What?'

MOLIÈRE. Oh, no! The other one's talking like a marquis now! Didn't I tell you that your character has to speak in a natural voice?

BRÉCOURT. Yes, you did.

MOLIÈRE. Well, do it then. 'Chevalier!'

BRÉCOURT. 'What?'

MOLIÈRE. 'Can you help us decide on a bet we've had?'

BRÉCOURT. 'What was it?'

MOLIÈRE. 'We were arguing about who was the Marquis in Molière's *The School for Wives Criticized*: he's bet it's me, and I've bet it's him.'

BRÉCOURT. 'My judgement is, it's neither the one nor the other of you. You're both crazy to want to apply such things to yourselves. I heard Molière complaining about it only the other day. He was talking to some people who were saying the same as you. He was insisting that nothing annoyed him more than being accused of targeting individuals in his character portraits. He says his aim is to show up human behaviour, without attacking individuals. All his characters come out of his head. They're figments of his imagination, with fantastic touches to keep the audience happy. He wouldn't dream of including any real portraits. The one thing that could put him off the theatre is being accused of creating characters modelled on real people. It's constantly happening, and his enemies have been encouraging people to believe it, so as to do him a bad turn with people he certainly didn't have in mind. What he says makes sense. Why on earth decide that an actor's gesticulations and speeches are modelled on a real person? Why try to cause trouble for Molière, by spreading the word that he's put so-and-so in his play, when the character's mannerisms could apply to hundreds of people? Comedy is about showing up the defects of men in general, and, more particularly, the men of our century. So Molière couldn't write a play without there being some parallels in real life. If he's going to be accused of targeting all the people who have the flaws he's writing about, he might as well stop writing plays.'

MOLIÈRE. 'I say, Chevalier, you're desperate to justify Molière. And to spare the feelings of our friend here.'

LA GRANGE. 'Not at all. It's you he's sparing. I think we'd better find another arbiter.'

MOLIÈRE. 'Very well. But, look here, Chevalier, don't you think your Molière is played out, and won't be able to find any more subjects to...'

BRÉCOURT. 'No more subjects? We'll give him plenty of subjects, old man. We're not about to become sensible, and learn wisdom from what his characters say and do.'

MOLIÈRE. Wait a minute. You want to say all that bit more emphatically. Listen, this is how I want it spoken: 'No more subjects? We'll give him plenty of subjects, old man. We're not about to become sensible, and learn wisdom, from what he says and does. Do you believe that, in his theatre, he's exhausted the topic of man's ridiculous side? Even without going outside the court, can't you see at least twenty types of character that he hasn't used yet? For instance, couldn't he write about people who strike up intense friendships, and then think it's clever to tear each other to shreds behind each other's backs? And what about those over-the-top sycophants, the insipid admirers, whose praise has no bite, and whose flattery is so sickly sweet it revolts everyone around? What about all those appalling fair-weather friends, who love you when things are going your way, who admire you when you're prosperous, and humiliate you in your misfortune? What about the people who are never happy at court, those useless hangers-on, those interminable nuisances? All they've ever done is keep on bothering the King, and then they think they're entitled to a reward, just for having pestered him for ten years! And how about the people who are equally polite to everybody, and parade their good manners all over the place? They run up to everyone they see to embrace them, and everybody's their best friend: "Your humble servant, Monsieur." "I'm at your service, Monsieur." "I'm your man, my dear fellow." "Consider me your greatest friend, Monsieur." "I'm delighted to embrace you, Monsieur." "Oh, Monsieur, I didn't see you. Do me the favour of relying on me. I'm absolutely yours to command. There's nobody I respect more. I honour you more than anybody else. I beg you to believe me. I implore you not to doubt me." "Your servant, sir." "Your humble servant." Come on, Marquis! Molière's got more than enough subjects. The ones he's touched on so far are a mere nothing, compared to the ones that are left.' That's more or less how you should speak that speech.

BRÉCOURT. OK, I get it.

MOLIÈRE. Carry on, then.

BRÉCOURT. 'Here come Climene and Elise.'

MOLIÈRE [*to* MESDEMOISELLES DU PARC *and* MOLIÈRE]. This is where the two of you come in. [*To* MADEMOISELLE DU PARC] You, make sure you walk with a wiggle of the hips, and make affected gestures. I know it's hard for you, but there you are. Sometimes you have to force yourself.

MADEMOISELLE MOLIÈRE. 'Why, Madame, I recognized you miles away! You've such an air about you—it couldn't have been anyone else.'

MADEMOISELLE DU PARC. 'You see, I'm waiting for someone to come out. I want to see him on a matter of business.'

MADEMOISELLE MOLIÈRE. 'Me too.'

MOLIÈRE. Here are some boxes, ladies. You can pretend they're chairs.

MADEMOISELLE DU PARC. 'Do sit down, Madame, please.'

MADEMOISELLE MOLIÈRE. 'After you, Madame.'

MOLIÈRE. That's fine. After an exchange of politenesses in dumb show, everyone sits down, and you perform seated, except for the marquis, who keep on sitting down, then getting up in the heat of the moment. 'Gad, Chevalier, you ought to give your lace frills* some medicine.'

BRÉCOURT. 'What for?'

MOLIÈRE. 'They're not looking at all good.'

BRÉCOURT. 'Very funny, I must say.'

MADEMOISELLE MOLIÈRE. 'Good gracious, Madame, how dazzling your complexion is, and your lips are amazingly red!'

MADEMOISELLE DU PARC. 'Oh, please, Madame! Don't look at me. I'm looking ghastly today.'

MADEMOISELLE MOLIÈRE. 'Do lift your veil, just a bit.'

MADEMOISELLE DU PARC. 'Ugh! I look simply awful, I tell you. I even frighten myself.'

MADEMOISELLE MOLIÈRE. 'You're so beautiful!'

MADEMOISELLE DU PARC. 'Not at all.'

MADEMOISELLE MOLIÈRE. 'Let's see.'

MADEMOISELLE DU PARC. 'Oh, please! Do stop it!'

MADEMOISELLE MOLIÈRE. 'Oh, do, please!'

MADEMOISELLE DU PARC. 'No, for Heaven's sake!'

MADEMOISELLE MOLIÈRE. 'Come on!'

MADEMOISELLE DU PARC. 'This is so embarrassing.'

MADEMOISELLE MOLIÈRE. 'Just for a second.'

MADEMOISELLE DU PARC. 'Oh!...'

MADEMOISELLE MOLIÈRE. 'You're going to have to show yourself. You can't deprive us of the pleasure of seeing you.'

MADEMOISELLE DU PARC. 'Goodness, how peculiar you are! When you want something, you insist on having your way.'

MADEMOISELLE MOLIÈRE. 'Oh, Madame, you needn't be afraid to show yourself in broad daylight, I promise you. People are so spiteful, saying you try to improve on nature!* I can really tell them what's what, now I've seen for myself.'

MADEMOISELLE DU PARC. 'Oh, dear! I don't really know what's meant by improving on nature. But where are those ladies going?'

SCENE 5

MADEMOISELLE DE BRIE, MADEMOISELLE DU PARC, *etc.*

MADEMOISELLE DE BRIE. 'Do you want to hear some tremendous news, ladies? I must tell it you in passing. Monsieur Lysidas here has just told us that there's been a play written attacking Molière, and it's going to be performed by the King's troupe.'*

MOLIÈRE. 'That's right. They tried to read it to me. It was written by someone called Br... Brou... Brossaut.'*.

DU CROISY. 'The name on the posters is Boursault, Monsieur. But between ourselves, lots of people have collaborated on the play, and we can expect great things. All us writers and actors look on Molière as our greatest enemy. So we all got together to do him a bad turn. We all contributed to his portrait; but we wouldn't have dreamt of putting our names to it. If the whole of the literary establishment got together to destroy him, it would make him look too important in the eyes of the world. We wanted to make his defeat even more humiliating, so we chose an unknown writer, with no reputation whatsoever.'

MADEMOISELLE DU PARC. 'I must confess, I'm absolutely delighted at the news.'

MOLIÈRE. 'Me too! Damn it, he'll have a taste of his own medicine. He's going to cop it, by Jove.'

MADEMOISELLE DU PARC. 'That'll teach him to mock at everything. I mean! The impertinent fellow doesn't believe that women can be brilliant! He criticizes all our refinements of speech. He wants us to use nothing but ordinary language.'

MADEMOISELLE DE BRIE. 'The point about language isn't important. But he criticizes all our relationships, even the innocent ones. The way he goes on, you'd think it was a crime to be admired.'

MADEMOISELLE DU CROISY. 'It's unbearable. We women can't get away with anything any more. Why can't he leave our husbands in peace, not keep opening their eyes and making them take notice of things they wouldn't have seen otherwise?'

MADEMOISELLE BÉJART. 'Never mind all that; but he even mocks at decent women. He makes wicked jokes about them, and calls them "devil-women, full of virtue".'*

MADEMOISELLE MOLIÈRE. 'Impertinence! Let's hope he's thoroughly punished.'

DU CROISY. 'We've got to give our support when the play's performed, Madame. The actors...'

MADEMOISELLE DU PARC. 'Tell them they needn't worry. I guarantee the play will be a success—I'll stake my reputation on it.'

MADEMOISELLE MOLIÈRE. 'Quite right, Madame. Too many people have an interest in believing the play is good. I mean, surely all the people who think that Molière has attacked them in his satires will take the opportunity of being avenged on him, by applauding the play.'

BRÉCOURT [ironically]. 'Indeed. And as for me, I'll answer for twelve marquis, six précieuses, twenty coquettes, and thirty cuckolds. They'll all be there to applaud.'

MADEMOISELLE MOLIÈRE. 'Quite right. Why make a point of offending all those people, specially the cuckolds? They're all quite charming.'

MOLIÈRE. 'Gad! He's going to be thoroughly flattened, him and his plays, so I've been told. All the actors and writers, both great and small, are absolutely furious with him.'

MADEMOISELLE MOLIÈRE. 'Serve him right. Why does he write those ghastly plays that the whole of Paris flocks to see? And why does he paint such lifelike portraits that everyone recognizes themselves? Why doesn't he write plays like Monsieur Lysidas? Then nobody would be against him, and all the other writers would have something good to say about him. It's true that not many people go to see Monsieur Lysidas's plays; but even so they're very well written, nobody attacks them, and everyone that goes to see them is dying to approve of them.'

DU CROISY. 'That's true. My great advantage is that I don't make enemies, and all my works are admired by the cognoscenti.'

MADEMOISELLE MOLIÈRE. 'You're right to be pleased with yourself. That's worth more than all the public applause and all the money that Molière earns with his plays. Who cares if nobody comes to see your plays, as long as all your learned colleagues approve?'

LA GRANGE. 'So, when are they going to perform this play, *The Painter's Portrait*?'

DU CROISY. 'I don't know; but I'm getting ready to take my place in the front row, and shout: "This is absolutely brilliant!"'

MOLIÈRE. 'Gad! Me too!'

LA GRANGE. 'Me too, by Jove!'

MADEMOISELLE DU PARC. 'Well, I'm putting myself out for this play. I've organized a group to shout their approval, and put paid to any negative criticism. It's the least we can do, giving our support to the man who's working to protect our interests.'

MADEMOISELLE MOLIÈRE. 'Oh, well said!'

MADEMOISELLE DE BRIE. 'We've all got to do the same.'

MADEMOISELLE BÉJART. 'Definitely.'

MADEMOISELLE DU CROISY. 'I agree.'

MADEMOISELLE HERVÉ. 'Let's have no mercy on this fellow, who will insist on imitating people.'

MOLIÈRE. 'By God, Chevalier, my friend, that Molière of yours had better go and hide himself!'

BRÉCOURT. 'What, him? You know what, Marquis? He's planning to go to see the play, to have a good laugh at the way he's been portrayed.'

MOLIÈRE. 'By Jove, he'll be laughing on the other side of his face, then.'

BRÉCOURT. 'Maybe he'll find more to laugh at than you think. I've seen the play. All the best ideas in it are actually cribbed from Molière, so I shouldn't think he'll mind if people enjoy it. As for the passages which attempt to blacken his name, nobody will think much of them, unless I'm much mistaken. And as for all the people they've tried to get together to protest that Molière's por-traits are too lifelike, it's all rather a poor show—they're ridicu-lous to attack him for that. It's the first time I've heard that a playwright is to blame for making his characters too convincing.'

LA GRANGE. 'The actors tell me they're expecting him to retaliate, and then he'll see...'

BRÉCOURT. 'What, him retaliate? I must say, I think he'd be mad to bother to reply to all their invective. Everybody knows what their motive is. The most effective answer would be to write a play that would be as successful as all his others. That would be the best way to take revenge. I know what they're like: I promise you, a new play that takes away their audiences would make them angrier than all the satires he could compose against their persons.'

MOLIÈRE. 'But, Chevalier...'

MADEMOISELLE BÉJART. Do you mind if I just interrupt the rehearsal for a moment? [*To* MOLIÈRE] Do you know what? If I were in your shoes, I'd have done things differently. Everyone's expecting you to mount a vigorous defence. And after the things that I gather they said about you in that play, you had every right to say what you liked about them in reply, and you shouldn't have spared any of them.

MOLIÈRE. It makes me mad to hear you say things like that. You women, you're all the same. You want me to lash out at them immediately, follow their example, and burst into insults and invective. That would satisfy my sense of honour! That would really upset them! Can't you see that they're ready and waiting for that sort of response? When they were debating whether to put on *The Painter's Portrait*, and wondering if I would retaliate, what do you bet that some of them said: 'Let him insult us as much as he likes, as long as we make some money'? Do you believe they're ready to feel shame? What sort of revenge would it be, if I gave them what they were hoping to get?

MADEMOISELLE DE BRIE. But they complained bitterly about a few words you said about them in *The School for Wives Criticized** and *The Ridiculous Précieuses*.*

MOLIÈRE. That's true. Those few words are highly offensive; they're quite right to quote them. No, really, that's not the point. The real harm I did them was being lucky enough to please the public more than they would have liked. Everything they've done since we came to Paris has made it quite clear what upsets them. Let's just let them get on with it; I don't think I need worry about their plotting. If they criticize my plays, so much the better. I hope I never write plays that they do like. That would be a very bad thing for me.

MADEMOISELLE DE BRIE. But it can't be much fun seeing your work torn to shreds.

MOLIÈRE. What do I care? Didn't I get everything I wanted from my play? I was lucky—it appealed to the distinguished audience I was particularly eager to please. Don't you think I'm right to be happy with how it turned out? Can't you see that their attacks have come too late? It's out of my hands at this point. If people attack a successful play, they're attacking the audience who liked it, for their lack of judgement, not the art of the man who wrote the play, don't you see?

MADEMOISELLE DE BRIE. Well, if I were you, I'd lampoon that pathetic little playwright, for taking it upon himself to write attacks on people who don't spare him a thought.

MOLIÈRE. You're crazy. A fine subject to keep the court amused, that Monsieur Boursault! I'd like to know how one could clean him up enough to make him presentable. If I mocked at him on stage, I'm not sure he'd be fortunate enough to make the audience laugh. He doesn't deserve the honour of being performed before such a distinguished gathering, though he'd like nothing better. He's been attacking me with gusto—he thinks it's a way of getting himself known. The man's got nothing to lose; the actors set him up against me, to get me mixed up in a stupid conflict. They're hoping to use him as a device, to distract me from the other works I want to write. But you lot, you're so naive, you fall into the trap. Anyway, I plan to make a public statement. I don't aim to reply to all their criticisms and counter-criticisms.* They can attack my play as much as they like, that's fine by me. They can take it over, turn it inside out like a piece of clothing, and put it on in their theatre, in an attempt to profit from its appeal to the public, and my share of success; I don't mind. They need the money, and I'm happy to contribute to their living expenses, as long as they keep to what I can decently allow them to use. There are limits, though, and some things don't strike either the audience, or the target of their satire, as funny. I'll willingly make them a present of my plays, my looks, my gestures, my words, and the way I speak them on stage. They can do and say what they like with them, if it does them any good. I don't mind, and if the public enjoys it, I'll be delighted. But if I let them do all that, then they should do me a favour, and leave the rest alone. They shouldn't touch on some of the things I hear they've been attacking me for in their plays.* I plan to put this politely to the gentleman who's taken it upon himself to be their playwright. That's the only answer I'm prepared to give them.

MADEMOISELLE BÉJART. But look here...

MOLIÈRE. No, you look here, all this is driving me wild. Don't let's talk about it any more. We're letting ourselves get distracted, making speeches instead of rehearsing our play. Where were we? I don't remember.

MADEMOISELLE DE BRIE. We'd got to the bit where...

MOLIÈRE. Oh, no! What's that noise? It must be the King arriving,

I'm sure of it. I can see we won't have time to go any further. That's what comes of wasting time. Oh, well. You'll just have to do your best with the end of the play.

MADEMOISELLE BÉJART. Oh, God, I'm petrified! I can't play my part unless I rehearse the whole play.

MOLIÈRE. What? You can't play your part?

MADEMOISELLE BÉJART. No.

MADEMOISELLE DU PARC. I can't do mine either.

MADEMOISELLE DE BRIE. Me neither.

MADEMOISELLE MOLIÈRE. Nor me.

MADEMOISELLE HERVÉ. Nor me.

MADEMOISELLE DU CROISY. Nor me.

MOLIÈRE. So what do you think you're going to do? Are you all making fun of me?

SCENE 6

MOLIÈRE, BÉJART, *etc.*

BÉJART. Gentlemen, I've been sent to tell you that the King's arrived. He's waiting for you to start.

MOLIÈRE. Oh, Monsieur, I'm having such problems. Right now, I'm absolutely desperate. These women here are in a state. They're insisting they need to rehearse their roles before they go on. Please, please, let us have just a bit longer. I know how good the King is, he realizes how rushed we've been. [*To the actresses*] Please, try to get a grip on yourselves. Show some spirit, please!

MADEMOISELLE DU PARC. You ought to go and make your excuses.

MOLIÈRE. What do you mean, make my excuses?

SCENE 7

MOLIÈRE, MADEMOISELLE BÉJART, *etc.*, AN OFFICIAL

AN OFFICIAL. Gentlemen, start the play!

MOLIÈRE. Just a minute, Monsieur. This whole thing is going to drive me mad, and...

SCENE 8

MOLIÈRE, MADEMOISELLE BÉJART, *etc.*, A SECOND OFFICIAL

THE SECOND OFFICIAL. Gentlemen, start the play!

MOLIÈRE. In a minute, Monsieur. [*To his friends*] What do you mean? Do you want to disgrace me?...

SCENE 9

MOLIÈRE, MADEMOISELLE BÉJART, *etc.*, A THIRD OFFICIAL

THE THIRD OFFICIAL. Gentlemen, start the play!

MOLIÈRE. Yes, Monsieur, just coming! Why must people come butting in, telling us to start the play, when the King didn't give the order!

SCENE 10

MOLIÈRE, MADEMOISELLE BÉJART, *etc.*, A FOURTH OFFICIAL

THE FOURTH OFFICIAL. Gentlemen, start the play!

MOLIÈRE. Yes, Monsieur, we're starting. [*To his friends*] So, what now? Are you going to humiliate me?...

SCENE 11

BÉJART, MOLIÈRE, *etc.*

MOLIÈRE. Monsieur, you've come to tell us to get started, but...

BÉJART. No, gentlemen, I've come to tell you that the King's been informed of your predicament. He's doing you a special favour, allowing you to put off performing your new play till another day. For today, he'll be satisfied with whatever you feel ready to perform.

MOLIÈRE. Oh, Monsieur, you've given me back my life! How gracious of the King to allow us the time to rehearse the play he wanted to see. Let's go and thank him for showing us such kindness.

THE END

TARTUFFE

1664

CHARACTERS

ORGON,* a rich bourgeois
ELMIRE,* his wife
MADAME PERNELLE,* his mother
DAMIS, his son
MARIANE,* his daughter
CLEANTE, his brother-in-law
TARTUFFE,* a religious hypocrite
LAURENT, his servant
DORINE,* Mariane's maid
FLIPOTE, Mme Pernelle's servant
MONSIEUR LOYAL, a bailiff
THE KING'S OFFICER

The scene is set in Paris, in Orgon's house

ACT I

SCENE 1

MADAME PERNELLE, ELMIRE, DAMIS, DORINE, MARIANE,
CLEANTE, FLIPOTE

MADAME PERNELLE. Come on, come on, I've got to get away,
Flipote.*

ELMIRE. Hold on! I can't keep up, you're off at such a trot.

MADAME PERNELLE. Now daughter-in-law, stop there. Go back,
and leave me be.
I don't need you to make a silly fuss of me.

ELMIRE. A mother-in-law deserves respect, for that's her due.
But, mother, why rush off so fast? What's bitten you?

MADAME PERNELLE. There's such a carry-on in here. Why should
I stay?
Not one of you will listen to a word I say.
I'm not at all impressed with how you run this place.
I reason with you, you defy me to my face.   10
You don't respect me: each one says what he believes.
You jabber all at once. It's like a den of thieves.*

DORINE. If...

MADAME PERNELLE. As for you, my girl, you're just a lady's maid,
But too impertinent and cheeky, I'm afraid.
You butt in endlessly, and treat us to your views.

DAMIS. But...

MADAME PERNELLE. You're a blithering idiot. I can't excuse
Your folly, though you are my grandson. Yes, I've told
Your father several times you're getting much too bold.
You're turning into such a terrible bad lot,
I know you'll make big trouble for my son, that's what.   20

MARIANE. I think...

MADAME PERNELLE. And as for you, his sister, you're discreet.
   You don't speak out of turn, you seem so good and sweet—
   But still waters run deep—you know what people say—
   They'd watch your secret lifestyle, if I had my way.

ELMIRE. But, mother...

MADAME PERNELLE. As for you, my dear daughter-in-law,
   The way you lead your life is something I deplore.
   You ought to set a good example to the rest,
   And their late mother always acted for the best.*   *Elmire Second wife*
   You squander money, and it fills me with distress
   To see you in your finery, like some princess.   30
   A wife should try to please her husband, not her beaux.
   She doesn't need to look so elegant, you know.   *Madame Pernelle religious*

CLEANTE. But, after all, Madame...

MADAME PERNELLE.   Yes, you're her brother, Sir,
   I do admire you, and there's no one I prefer.
   But if I were her husband, that's to say my son,
   I'd ask you, please, to keep away from everyone.
   Your views on life are reckless. Yes, they make me choke!
   I don't think your advice is right for decent folk.
   I've spoken very frankly, but that's how I am—
   I always speak my mind. I don't believe in sham.   40

DAMIS. Your friend, Monsieur Tartuffe, must be your greatest fan...

MADAME PERNELLE. Try listening to him, for he's a worthy man.
   It drives me wild with fury every time I hear
   A silly fool like you attack him with a sneer.

DAMIS. You think that I'll allow this shameless hypocrite
   To rule the household like a tyrant, is that it?
   We're not to be allowed the slightest merriment
   Unless Monsieur has deigned to give us his consent?

DORINE. If we believe the maxims that he likes to spout,
   Then everything we do's a crime, as it turns out.   50
   He keeps an eye on us, and constantly finds fault.

MADAME PERNELLE. He's right to do so, he's a fine man, worth his
   salt.

He plans to show you all the way to Heaven above,
And my son should persuade you he deserves your love.

DAMIS. I don't care how much you and Father try to tell
Me what to feel, you won't get me to wish him well.
I'll be true to myself by saying what I think:
The way he carries on drives me beyond the brink.
I'll have to settle things with that flat-footed toad—*
I can't control myself. Watch out, when I explode!   60

DORINE. It's shocking when a total stranger so contrives
To worm his way so cunningly into our lives.
When he turned up, he didn't have a pair of shoes;
His outfit wasn't worth a measly couple of sous.
But now it's plain the fellow doesn't know his place.
He lords it over all of us. It's a disgrace.

MADAME PERNELLE. Oh, Lawks! When he gives you advice, it's so
    devout!
It might improve things here if you would hear him out.

DORINE. You tell us he's a saint, in fact, you're sure of it.
Believe me, though, the fellow's just a hypocrite.   70

MADAME PERNELLE. How you run on!

DORINE.   His servant Laurent's just as bad.
I wouldn't trust the master, wouldn't trust his lad.

MADAME PERNELLE. I can't vouch for the servant, I don't know
    him well,
But Tartuffe is a man of honour. I can tell
That you detest the man and long to see him fall
Because of the home truths he tells you, one and all.
It's Heaven's benefit he's interested in,
And when he's up in arms, he's only fighting sin.

DORINE. But why is it that recently he's seemed depressed,
And gets all grumpy, if we ever have a guest?   80
How can a visitor fill Heaven with disgust,
And make the fellow shout about it fit to bust?
Between ourselves, I know what's causing his alarm:
He's jealous! Yes, he's got his eye upon Madame.

MADAME PERNELLE. Be quiet, girl! You be more careful what you
    say.
  I've watched your social life: it fills me with dismay.
  The chaos in the house, the noise that I deplore,
  And all the carriages lined up outside your door,
  The troops of rowdy servants, all up to no good,
  Make you notorious throughout the neighbourhood.   90
  You say it's innocent, it's nothing, just a fling—
  But people have been talking, and that's not the thing.

CLEANTE. Do you think you can stop the gossip, then, Madame?
  Life wouldn't be worth living if we feared the harm
  Of wagging tongues so much. It really is the end
  If there's an outcry when we entertain a friend.
  If we listened to them, and dropped our old friends flat,
  Do you think that society would stop its chat?
  When gossips get to work, why, nobody is safe.
  It's best to take no notice. If it makes you chafe,   100
  You learn to live your life ignoring the 'on-dits',
  And leave the busybodies saying what they please.

DORINE. Who *are* these gossips, then? Don't tell me, I can guess.
  Our neighbour Daphne and her tiny husband, yes?
  The people whose behaviour's most ridiculous
  Will always be the first to dish the dirt on us.
  They never miss a trick, jump to conclusions when
  They ferret out some vague relationship, and then
  They spread the gossip round. It's all a load of fun.
  They alter all the facts, convincing everyone—   110
  Or so they hope. Misrepresenting what we do,
  They think their own behaviour will seem better too.
  They say we're like them, but the whole thing's a mirage:
  We cover their intrigues, we act as camouflage,
  They want some fellow sufferers to share the blame:
  They're in disgrace, but we're much worse—so they proclaim.

MADAME PERNELLE. Go on, then. Talk away, till you're blue in the
    face.
  A decent woman like Orante, now. She's a case
  In point. She lives a godly life in every way.
  She finds *your* way of life quite shocking, so they say.   120

DORINE. Oh, that's quite true. The woman's worthy of respect!
　　She leads a holy life, she's quite without defect;
　　But age has brought her to her saintly attitude,
　　And it's because she's lost her looks that she's a prude.
　　As long as she was able to attract the men,
　　She took advantage and enjoyed herself; but then
　　She realized her looks were gone, her eyes less bright,
　　And gave up men before they dropped her. She's so right!
　　You cover up your fading charms with virtue's veil,
　　And hide your weaknesses the moment you grow stale!   130
　　That's what it's like if you're an elderly coquette.
　　It's hard to bear when all the gentlemen forget
　　Your charms. Cast on one side, in dreary solitude,
　　Your last resort is to become a full-time prude.
　　These upright women are excessively severe.
　　They judge us harshly, and their disapproval's clear.
　　They cast aspersions on the people all around
　　Because they're jealous, not through godliness, I've found.
　　They hate to see us happy, eagerly destroy
　　The pleasures that they're too decrepit to enjoy.   140

MADAME PERNELLE. Now, daughter-in-law, I see you thrive on
　　fairy tales.
　　In your house, it appears, the lady here regales
　　The company with chat while we stand idly by.
　　But now at last my turn has come to preachify.
　　I tell you that my son is right, without a doubt,
　　To give a home to someone holy and devout.
　　Our house was in a shambles, but then Heaven sent
　　Him here to end your sin and make you all repent.
　　Oh, hear ye him, for your salvation is at stake!
　　He's trying to put right each terrible mistake: 150
　　Your busy social life, which you regard as fun,
　　Is all manipulated by the Evil One.
　　The conversation never runs on piety—
　　It's frivolous chit-chat in your society.
　　Malicious gossip, running down your friends is rife:
　　You never spare your neighbour, nor your neighbour's wife.
　　We don't know where to look, we decent, honest folk,

And your unruly carry-on has to provoke.
The conversation runs a thousand different ways,
All jabbering together. As our preacher says,   160
It sounds exactly like the Tower of Babylon,
For everyone joins in, and you all babble on.*
I'll tell you why the preacher made that comment, where...

> [*Notices that* CLEANTE *is smiling*

Now look at Monsieur, smirking in the corner, there!
That's right, take up with fools, keep going, sneer away,
Although... Daughter-in-law, I've nothing more to say.
I'm losing patience. Don't think you can pacify
Me now. I won't be coming back so soon. Goodbye.

> [*Gives a slap to* FLIPOTE

Come on, you! Hurry up! Stop gawping, and come here!
Hell's teeth! I'll wake you up! I'll slap you round the ear!   170
Get on, you slut!*

SCENE 2

CLEANTE, DORINE

CLEANTE.   I don't think that I'll show her out:
  It would be rather dangerous, for the old trout
  Might lecture me again...

DORINE. (*maia*)   Oh, really? It's a shame
  She's gone. If she could hear you call her by that name,
  She'd go all hoity-toity on you; out of pique,
  She'd say she isn't old, and you've a blooming cheek!

CLEANTE. You saw: the slightest comment earned us a reproof:
  She's obviously besotted with her dear Tartuffe.

DORINE. I tell you, Sir, her son is even more perverse.
  When you set eyes on him, you'll see that he's much worse.   180
  [In times of civil war, he showed what he could do:*]
  He did his duty by the King, and saw it through.
  But he's been like a brainwashed moon-calf since he first

Took up with that Tartuffe. Now things are at their worst.
He calls him 'brother', loves him better than his life,   *obsessed w/ Tartuffe*
A thousand times more dear than husband, child, or wife.
He tells him all his secrets; lets him govern all
His actions like a wise director. He's in thrall
To him, he cherishes, embraces him. It's like
A lover doting on his mistress, if you like.   190
At meals, he sits him in the place of honour, then
Rejoices when the fellow eats enough for ten.
We have to give him all the choicest bits to chew,
And if he burps, our master cries out: 'God bless you!'

[*This is a servant speaking**

He's mad about him. He's his hero, he's his king.
He worships every word, quotes him on everything.   *gullible*
His slightest actions are described as miracles,
And all his speeches are religious oracles.
The fellow knows he's found a dupe he can exploit.
He has a thousand clever tricks: he's most adroit.   200
He does him out of money, knows just how to ask,
And still feels free to take the rest of us to task.
Then there's that stuck-up idiot, his servant, who
Thinks that he's every right to tell us what to do.
He comes to lecture us, and glares with burning eyes,
Then: 'Throw away those ribbons, patches, rouge!' he cries.
The other day, the monster found a hanky, took   *vanity*
It off and tore it—it was in a holy book.*
He said it was a sin for which we must repent
To mix God's holy word with devil's ornament.   210

SCENE 3

ELMIRE, MARIANE, DAMIS, DORINE, CLEANTE

ELMIRE. You're lucky that you stayed behind. She's such a bore!
   She gave another lecture, standing at the door.
   My husband's here. Don't want to catch him unawares:
   I think I'd rather go and wait for him upstairs.

CLEANTE. I've very little time, I've really got to go.
   I'll wait down here, and leave him when I've said hello.

DAMIS. Look, could you touch upon my sister's marriage plan?
   I'm terrified that our Tartuffe has put a ban
   Upon the project. Is he making Father change
   His mind? You know how much I'm longing to arrange   220
   This marriage. It's Valere my sister loves, and he
   Lives with his pretty sister. She's the one for me!
   So if...

DORINE. He's coming!

SCENE 4

ORGON, CLEANTE, DORINE

ORGON.   Ah! I'm glad to find you here.

CLEANTE. How was the country? Barren, at this time of year?
   At any rate, I'm glad you're back. Now I must go.

ORGON. Dorine... Brother-in-law, wait there a bit. I know
   That you'll excuse me. I must see how things have been
   At home. I'll put my mind at rest and ask Dorine.
   How has it been here in the two days I've been gone?
   Is everybody well, and what's been going on?   230

DORINE. Two days ago, Madame was taken very ill.
   She had a fever, and she's got a headache still.

ORGON. And Tartuffe?

DORINE.   What, Tartuffe? He's well, without a doubt,
   With rosy cheeks and scarlet lips, all sleek and stout.*

ORGON. Poor fellow!*

DORINE.   Then that night she went right off her food—
   She tried to eat a little bit. It was no good.
   Her head hurt dreadfully. She found it an ordeal.

ORGON. And Tartuffe?

DORINE.   Sat in front of her and had his meal,
  Devoutly ate two partridges washed down with wine,
  Then finished off with half a leg of lamb minced fine.   240

ORGON. Poor fellow!

DORINE.   Her condition lasted through the night.
  She lay there suffering until the morning's light.
  Her bouts of fever stopped what sleep she tried to take,
  And someone had to sit with her until daybreak.

ORGON. And Tartuffe?   *only cares about Tartuffe*

DORINE.   Feeling tired and pleasantly well fed,
  He left the table, and went straight upstairs to bed.
  He snuggled in all cosily, and straightaway   *Just being lazy*
  Fell sound asleep, and didn't wake till it was day.

ORGON. Poor fellow!

DORINE.   In the end, we got her to agree
  To let us call the doctor. When he bled her, she*   250
  Felt better right away, the moment it was done.

ORGON. And Tartuffe?

DORINE.   He recovered, not to be outdone;
  To fortify his soul against the devil's harm,
  Replacing all the blood just taken from Madame,
  He finished off his meal with four big cups of wine.   *gluttony*

ORGON. Poor fellow!

DORINE.   Now the two of them are feeling fine,
  And I'll go off and find Madame, so I can tell
  Her how relieved you seemed that she is fit and well.

SCENE 5

CLEANTE, ORGON

CLEANTE. Well, brother, she was laughing at you to your face.*
  Now, don't be cross, but I believe she's got a case.   260
  In fact, to be quite frank, I think the girl is right.

I never thought I'd ever witness such a sight:
Did he use magic to persuade you to forget
Important things, and love a person you've just met?
You've spent a fortune rescuing him from despair,
And now, it seems, you want...

ORGON.   Brother-in-law, stop there!
You don't know anything about him. Stop your chat.

CLEANTE. All right, so I don't know him, I'll allow you that.
But if I'm to find out what kind of man he is...

ORGON. Oh, if you knew him well, you'd be in ecstasies!   270
You'd never stop adoring him once you began.
He is a man... who... er... in short, a man... a man.   *worshiping man*
If you sat at his feet, he'd bring you peace, for sure;
The world would seem to you a great heap of manure.*
I've learnt from him, the truth is clearer in my eyes.
He's taught me to reject the things I used to prize.
The people that I thought I loved, I now deny,
And I could watch my mother, children, wife all die,
And, shall I tell you what? I just couldn't care less.*

CLEANTE. What warmth, my brother, what compassion you   280
express!

ORGON. I wish you'd seen how it turned out when first we met!
Like me, you'd have been drawn to him from the outset.
He came to church, and every day I saw that he
Fell on his knees and bowed his head in front of me.
The congregation as a whole became aware
Of how much ardour he would pour into his prayer.
He heaved great heavy sighs, and waved his arms around,
And often he'd bend very low and kiss the ground.
When I went out, he'd always hurry on before
To offer me some holy water by the door.   290
He has a servant, who's under his influence,
He's told me of his station, and his indigence.
I gave him money; with becoming modesty,
He always tried to give some of it back to me.
'No, it's too much', said he, 'Oh, it's too much by half.
I don't deserve your sympathy on my behalf.'

doesn't mean it

When I refused to take it back, he would ensure,
In front of me, that it was given to the poor.
At last I was inspired by Heaven to take him in.
Since that day, we've all prospered through his discipline.   300
He watches everything, my honour is his life,
And he's become inseparable from my wife: *right....*
He tells me if young fellows give her the glad eye,
The man's a lot more jealous and concerned than I.
But you wouldn't believe the ardour of his zeal:
The sin that any trivial action can reveal
Disturbs him. A mere nothing shocks him to the core.
The other day, he said that he had to deplore
The fact that, when at prayer, he chanced to catch a flea,
And having caught it, killed it, much too angrily.   310

CLEANTE. Good Lord! What's this I hear? Have you gone raving
      mad?
   Or was that speech a joke, and have I just been had?
   You must be teasing me. So, what does all that mean?

ORGON. Ugh! Brother, that's the language of the libertine.
   You must work hard to keep your spirit free of crimes—
   Or else, as I've explained to you a dozen times,
   You may end up in dreadful trouble, very soon.

CLEANTE. It's typical of people like you to impugn
   The attitudes of others. Just because I've seen
   What you can't see, you choose to call me libertine.   320
   You say I've no respect for any sacred thing
   Because I find your empty cant embarrassing.
   You won't get me worked up, I take it in good part:
   I know what I believe, and God sees in my heart.*
   A man who rules the rest by putting on such airs
   Can be a hypocrite for all his fervent prayers.
   When battle's joined, and men of honour come to fight,
   The quiet men are brave, the boasters may take fright;
   So truly pious men, whom people must admire,
   Will not make such a song and dance about hell-fire.   330
   Oh, Heavens! Can't you see there's a distinction
   Between hypocrisy and true devotion?

You want the two of them to share a single space;
You can't see one's a mask, the other a true face.
You mix up artifice with real sincerity,   *trying 2*
And try to take appearance for reality,   *talk sense into*
Respecting empty phantoms more than flesh and blood,   *Orgon*
And bogus coinage more than currency that's good!
My fellow human beings are the strangest crew:
They can't be moderate and calm in what they do.   340
So, rational behaviour's not what they expect;
They set it on one side, and show it no respect.
They're all out to exaggerate and maximize,
They manage to destroy the noblest enterprise—
In passing, brother-in-law, I say this in your ear.

ORGON. I daresay you're a doctor we should all revere:
You know the lot; in short, you're the embodiment
Of holy wisdom, and of true enlightenment.   *sarcastic*
Yes, you're an oracle, a Cato of our time.*
Compared with us poor foolish dolts, Sir, you're sublime.   350

CLEANTE. No, brother, no! I'm not a doctor to revere,
And all man's earthly wisdom isn't lodged up here.
No, all my learning can be summed up in a word:
I can tell truth from falsehood, see through what's absurd.
Of all my heroes, I find certain men stand out,
And I admire them: men who seem truly devout.
There's nothing nobler, nothing worthier, I feel,
Than holy fervour, genuine religious zeal.
But then, by contrast, nothing is more odious
Than all the trappings of belief that's dubious,   360
Those charlatans whose fervent piety's for show,
Who sacrilegiously pretend to mop and mow,
And make a mockery, with cool impertinence,
Of everything that we should hold in reverence,
Who show off their beliefs like some grotesque parade,
Who buy and sell devotion like a kind of trade,
Who strive for all the dignities that they can earn
And wink, nod, make affected gestures in return.
Those men are wildly eager to receive their pay:
They rush to make their fortunes, following God's way.   370

They drip with holy unction, yet they can be bought,
Extol the joys of solitude, but love the court.
They reconcile their pious notions with their vice,
They're spiteful, hasty, insincere, and cold as ice.
If they want to destroy a man, they boldly claim
That it's God's will that he's brought low, and put to shame.
They're dangerous because their anger doesn't show:
They make use of religious faith to bring us low.
They're much admired for their beliefs, and so they try
To smite us with the sword of faith and let us die.   380
There are a lot too many of this two-faced crew,
But it's not difficult to tell if faith is true.
We all know men who burn with real religious fire;
They set us an example we must all admire.
Just look at Ariston, just look at Periandre,
Oronte, Alcidamas, Polydore or Clitandre.*
Nobody grudges them the credit they deserve,
But they don't make such a pretence of holy verve,
And they're not overbearing in their piety.
As well as their belief, they show some charity,   390
And they don't criticize what other people do.
They see all that as arrogance, and sinful too.
They leave the others to show off. Instead, they try
To teach us by example, not to preachify.
They don't like to believe the wickedness they see,
But have a tendency to say it just can't be.
They don't indulge in intrigues, never like to plot.
Instead, they try to make the best of what they've got.
They never will attack a sinner viciously—
For it's the sin they criticize, exclusively.   400
Their zeal isn't excessive, and it never seems
The interests of God have pushed them to extremes.
These are my heroes. They're the men I think are great.
And they're the men whom I would want to imitate.
To tell the truth, your fellow's not like them, I feel.
You're acting in good faith when you promote his zeal,
But I think that you're dazzled by a bogus light.

ORGON. Monsieur my brother-in-law, must you go on all night?

CLEANTE. But...

ORGON.   I'm your humble servant.

                                    [ORGON *makes to exit*

CLEANTE.   Don't rush off yet. Bear
    With me. Let's change the subject. You know that Valere,   410
    With your consent, wants to become your son-in-law?

ORGON. Yes.

CLEANTE.   You've a date fixed for the happy day, what's more.

ORGON. That's true.

CLEANTE.   So why're you putting off the wedding, then?

ORGON. I couldn't say.

CLEANTE.   Perhaps you've changed your mind again?

ORGON. Could be.

CLEANTE.   So do you plan to go back on your word?

ORGON. I haven't said so.

CLEANTE.   Look—from everything I've heard,
    I think you ought to keep the promises you've made.

ORGON. It all depends.

CLEANTE.   Why has the marriage been delayed?
    I'm here because Valere asked me to speak to you.

ORGON. The Lord be praised!   420

CLEANTE.   Yes, but, meanwhile, what must we do?

ORGON. Oh, anything you like!

CLEANTE.   Yes, but it's time we knew
    What your intentions are. So what are they?

ORGON.   To do
    What Heaven ordains.

CLEANTE.   But can't you let us know what's what?
    You gave Valere your word. Will you keep it, or not?

ORGON. Goodbye.

[*Exit* ORGON

CLEANTE.   Oh, dear! Their happiness is under threat.
I'd better warn them that their plans may be upset.

ACT II

SCENE 1

ORGON, MARIANE

ORGON. Ah, Mariane.

MARIANE.   Yes, Father?

ORGON.   Quick. Come here. We must
  Have a few words in private.

MARIANE.   What's the matter?

ORGON [*looking into a little side room*].   Just
  Hang on. I've got to check that no one's listening
  Next door. The walls are thin, one can hear everything.   430
  Oh, good, nobody there. Now, Mariane, I find
  That you have always shown a gentle cast of mind,
  Dear girl! I've always been quite fond of you, you know.

MARIANE. I'm grateful, and I realize how much I owe.

ORGON. That's well said, daughter. But, if you propose to earn
  My love, do as you're told. That must be your concern.

MARIANE. Of course I will. I always try to do my best.

ORGON. That's very good. Now, do you like Tartuffe, our guest?

MARIANE. What, me?

ORGON.   Yes, you. Come on—be careful what you say.

MARIANE. Oh, dear! You tell me what you want, and I'll obey.   440

ORGON. Ah, that's well said. Now, can you say this after me?
  He's full of merit, and as holy as can be;
  Your young heart has been touched, your love for him is true,
  You'll take him as the husband that I've picked for you.
  Well?

                              [MARIANE *recoils in surprise*

MARIANE.   Well?

ORGON.   So?

MARIANE.   What's that?

ORGON.   What?

MARIANE.   Has there been some mistake?

ORGON. What?

MARIANE.   Who was it you said you wanted me to take?
And who has touched me, whom do I love tenderly,
And want him as the husband that you've picked for me?

ORGON. Tartuffe.

MARIANE.   But that's not true, I'm sure you realize.
Why do you want me to tell you a pack of lies?   450

ORGON. The thing is, though, you see, I want it to be true,
And doing what I say should be enough for you.

MARIANE. But, Father, you...

ORGON.   Look, I've resolved, most earnestly,
To link Tartuffe through marriage to our family.
You're going to marry him, and I've made up my mind,
And when you tie the knot, I...

SCENE 2

ORGON, MARIANE, DORINE

ORGON.   Now, what's this I find?
You're desperate to know what's going on, eh, Miss,
And so that's why you come to spy on us like this?

DORINE. I've got to tell you there's a rumour going round—
Some accident it seems has got it off the ground—   460
That there's a marriage planned. Yes, that's the news I got,
But I replied, the story was a load of rot.

ORGON. It seems incredible to you, then?

DORINE.   So much so,
    That if you told it me yourself, I'd just say 'No!'

ORGON. I'll tell you what, I'll prove it to you at a stroke.

DORINE. Get on with you! You're telling us a silly joke.

ORGON. I'm telling you what's going to happen, shortly too.

DORINE. What rubbish!

ORGON [to MARIANE].   Daughter, I'm not making fun of you.

DORINE. Oh, get away, Monsieur!—Don't you believe a word.
    He's joking.   470

ORGON.   But I tell you...

DORINE.   Now, don't be absurd:
    We won't believe you.

ORGON.   In the end, you'll drive me mad!

DORINE. All right, so we believe you then, and it's too bad.
    What, Monsieur, though you look respectable and wise,
    And though you've got a beard of most substantial size,*
    We see you're mad enough...

ORGON.   Do you know what, my dear?
    You've been allowed too many liberties round here.
    You ought to know your place, here in the family.

DORINE. Calm down, Sir, and let's talk this over quietly.
    Have you gone off your head to hit on such a plan?
    Your daughter wouldn't suit this type of holy man—   470
    He's likely to have many other fish to fry.
    And anyway, what good would it do to ally
    Yourself to him? You've plenty money. Do you need
    A pauper son-in-law?

ORGON.   Be quiet, now. Indeed,
    The fact that he has nothing means we must respect
    His poverty. It's honest, not some odd defect.
    It should raise him so high, the noblest must seem low,
    Since after all he let his own possessions go,

He looked on money as a liability,
And concentrated only on eternity.
But I can step in now, provide the wherewithal   490
To sort out his affairs, and give him back his all.
He does have ancient rights, I'll help him if I can;
Although he's lost his money, he's a gentleman.

DORINE. Yes, so he always says, he's full of vanity,
   Which doesn't quite fit in with all that piety.
   A man who leads a godly life, and has real worth,
   Should try not to show off about his noble birth;
   And true humility and true devotion
   Don't go so well with arrogant ambition.   500
   So why?... But you're annoyed. Let's not discuss his pride,
   But talk about the man, and leave his birth aside.
   Will you give her to him without a qualm, Monsieur,
   And let a man like him control a girl like her?
   Shouldn't you ask yourself whether it's quite the thing,
   And wonder what results this union may bring?
   I can't see any girl remaining pure and chaste
   When married to a man who isn't to her taste;
   I say she won't agree to lead a decent life
   Unless she likes the man who takes her for his wife.   510
   The husbands who end up with horns, and deep in shame
   At what their wives have done, should often take the blame:
   For it may be out of the question to stay true
   If you've been married to a man who's not for you.
   If you should give your daughter to a man she hates,
   You'll be to blame for all her subsequent mistakes.
   Just think how dangerous your plan may prove to be!

ORGON. It's up to her to tell me what to do. I see.

DORINE. Yes, you'd be well advised to learn from what I say.

ORGON. Now, daughter, can we stop wasting time in this way?   520
   As I'm your father, I'll make sure that you're content.
   I'm well aware I'd given Valere my consent,
   But he frequents the gaming houses, he's been seen,
   And I suspect he's something of a libertine.
   He doesn't often go to church, I know that's true.

DORINE. D'you think he should get there at the same time as you,
   Like some people who go there only to be seen?

ORGON. I didn't ask for your opinion, Miss Dorine.

[*To* MARIANE

He's such a holy man; God hears his every prayer,
That in itself is riches far beyond compare.   530
This marriage will exceed your most ardent desire;
Your life will be such bliss, your hearts will be on fire.
Together you'll both live in faithful harmony,
Two sweet young doves who love each other's company.
There'll never be a moment when you disagree,
And you'll do everything you want with him, you'll see.

DORINE. Her? What she'll do for him is cuckold him a bit.

ORGON. Ugh! What a thing to say!

DORINE.   He's got the looks for it.
   I say he won't escape, for that's his destiny,
   However virtuous your daughter tries to be.   540

ORGON. Will you stop interrupting, giving yourself airs,
   And poking your nose into other folk's affairs?

DORINE. It's for your own good, Monsieur, I'm not out to tease.

[*Every time he turns away to speak to his daughter, she interrupts him*

ORGON. Well, we don't need your help. Keep quiet, if you please!

DORINE. But I feel so concerned...

ORGON.   I don't need you to care!

DORINE. Whatever you say, I shall not give up, so there!

ORGON. Harrumph!

DORINE.   Your honour matters to me. I can't stand
   The thought that you're a laughing stock, you understand.

ORGON. Will you be quiet!

DORINE.   It goes against my conscience
   To let you set up such a bad misalliance.   550

ORGON. Shut up, you little devil! This is an outrage!*

DORINE. What's this? a pious man, to fly in such a rage?

ORGON. Your comments are so stupid, frankly I feel stung,
I won't say it again. You've got to hold your tongue.

DORINE. Well, you can't stop me thinking, but I won't speak out.

ORGON. You can think all you like, but take care not to flout
Me with a single word.

[*Turns to* MARIANE

I'm sure that you'll be glad
To know I've pondered every detail.

DORINE.   I'll go mad
If I can't speak!

[*She stops talking when he turns towards her*

ORGON.   He knows that it isn't his place
To be a ladies' man...   560

DORINE.   Him with his pretty face!

ORGON. So even if you find you don't appreciate
His other gifts...

[*He crosses his arms and looks at* DORINE

DORINE.   You'll have her in a fine old state!
If I were in her shoes, led to the sacrifice,
The man who married me would pay a hefty price,
And straight after the wedding day I'd make him see
A wife can always be avenged, take it from me.

ORGON. You disobey me, though I told you what to do.

DORINE. Eh, what? There's nothing wrong, I'm not talking to you.

ORGON. So what're you doing, then?

DORINE.   I'm talking to myself.

ORGON. Good grief! What insolence! She'll have to watch   570
herself;

She could do with a taste of the flat of my hand.

> [*He gets ready to slap her; but every time he looks at her,*
> DORINE *stands rigid without speaking*

Now, daughter, you'll agree, I'm sure you understand...
You'll take this husband... I expect you to obey...

> [*To* DORINE

Why aren't you talking?

DORINE.   To myself? What can I say?

ORGON. Come on, one little word.

DORINE.   Not in the mood for it.

ORGON. Come on, I'm waiting here.

DORINE.   I'm not a stupid twit!

ORGON. So, daughter, to sum up, you must do as you're told,
And fit in with my plans without being cajoled.

DORINE [*running out*]. I'd never let them fob me off with such a
creep!

> [ORGON *tries to slap* DORINE *and misses*

ORGON. Ha! Daughter, that's a dreadful harpy that you keep!   580
If this goes on much longer, I'll commit some sin—
I've got to stop—you see the rage she's put me in.
Her insolent remarks are more than I can bear.
I've got to go outside and breathe some good fresh air!

SCENE 3

DORINE, MARIANE

DORINE. So, tell me now, have you forgotten how to speak?
And must I play your part because you've got so weak?
How could you let him plan a project that's absurd,
And not object to it, not with a single word?

MARIANE. He's so inflexible, so what else can I do?

DORINE. Do what it takes to stop the danger threatening you! 590

MARIANE. Well, what?

DORINE.　　　　　　　Tell him you can't love on another's whim;
That marrying must be for you and not for him;
Since you're the person who's the object of this deal,
It's not to him but you the husband must appeal.
Tell him, if he finds Tartuffe so magnificent,
To marry him himself—there's no impediment.

MARIANE. A father can control his daughter, I confess.*
I can't hold out—it takes more strength than I possess.

DORINE. Let's sort this out. Valere is keen to tie the knot:
So, tell me now, do you love him, or do you not? 600

MARIANE. Oh, God! You're so unfair towards my love, Dorine!
How can you ask me such a question, when you've seen
How passionately in love I am, and when you've heard
Me tell you so a thousand times? It's too absurd.

DORINE. And how am I supposed to know if what you say
Is what you mean, and if you really love him, pray?

MARIANE. Don't talk like that, Dorine. You know you've got me
　　wrong:
I never hid my feelings from you—they're too strong.

DORINE. Ah! So you love him then?

MARIANE.　　　　　　　　　Oh, yes, of course I do.

DORINE. And what about Valere, he feels the same as you? 610

MARIANE. Yes, I believe so.

DORINE.　　　　　　　And the two of you are keen
To marry one another?

MARIANE.　　　　　　Yes, that's right, Dorine.

DORINE. And if you marry someone else, what'll you do?

MARIANE. I'll kill myself if I'm compelled to be untrue.

DORINE. Oh, very good! A fine solution to your plight!
  The best thing is to die, that'll put matters right!
  Your remedy's magnificent! Ugh! I can't bear
  To hear that sort of talk, it drives me to despair.

MARIANE. You're in such a bad mood: why must you criticize?
  I'm so unhappy, but you just won't sympathize.   620

DORINE. No, I don't sympathize with people who talk rot,
  And go to pieces when a crisis comes, that's what!

MARIANE. What can I do? The truth is that I'm far too shy.

DORINE. When you're in love, you should stand firm, or at least try.

MARIANE. You know I love Valere. I tried to make a stand—
  But surely it's still up to him to win my hand?

DORINE. The problem is, your father's gone quite mad. We know
  He's so obsessed with his Tartuffe, he plans to go
  Against the marriage to Valere that was agreed—
  So is all that your lover's fault? Oh, no, indeed!   630

MARIANE. But if I make a scene, and tell him I'm resolved,
  Then don't you think it looks as if I'm too involved?
  He's worth it, but I fear that all this honesty
  Might cast a blight upon my maiden modesty.
  I surely can't blurt out my love to everyone...

DORINE. No, no, of course not! Carry on as you've begun.
  You want to marry Monsieur Tartuffe. I'd be wrong
  To try to put you off, your longing is so strong.
  What reason could I have for combating this match,
  When in himself your suitor is a perfect catch?   640
  Monsieur Tartuffe! Oh, oh! He's such good qualities,
  And when you get beyond the first formalities,
  You'll find he doesn't wipe his nose upon his sleeve;*
  It'll be bliss to be his woman, I believe.
  I tell you, in society he's got a name.
  He's handsome, he's well known back home from where he came;
  He's got such nice red cheeks, and such fine scarlet ears,*
  And when you marry him, you'll be content for years.

MARIANE. Oh, God!...

DORINE.   Think how your heart will overflow with joy,
  When you become the wife of such a pretty boy!   650

MARIANE. Oh, Dorine, please be quiet! What awful things you say!
  I've got to stop this marriage. Help me find a way.
  I'll do my bit—I'm ready to do anything.

DORINE. A girl obeys her father's wish in everything,
  No matter if he picks a monkey for her groom.
  You've got a glowing future now, forget the gloom.
  He'll take you to his home town in a public coach:*
  The relatives will all rush out as you approach,
  And you'll have such a fine time in their company.
  They'll introduce you to their high society,   660
  And take you off to meet their citizens of mark,
  Madame the bailiff's wife, the wife of the town clerk,
  Who graciously will let you sit upon a stool.*
  When there's the carnival, you'll savour to the full*
  The ball, the orchestra, some fiddles, say, that scrape,
  Perhaps a puppet-show, or a performing ape!*
  That is, if your dear husband...

MARIANE.   Oh, you'll make me die!
  I need you to give me advice, not speechify.

DORINE. Your servant, Madam.

MARIANE.   Oh, Dorine, I beg of you!

DORINE. No. For your punishment, this business must go   670
  through.

MARIANE. Dear, sweet Dorine...

DORINE.   No.

MARIANE.   I'm committed, there's no doubt...

DORINE. No. Tartuffe is your man, you're going to try him out.

MARIANE. You know that I was always ready to confide
  My feelings to you...

this is very funny

DORINE.   <u>No. You'll be Tartuffified.</u>

MARIANE. Oh, very well then. Since I see that you don't care
What happens to me, leave me here to my despair.
My grief will help me out, I won't lament in vain,
For I know of a remedy for all my pain.

[*Attempts to exit*

DORINE. All right, come back! I won't be angry any more.
I'm sorry for you. Let's forget what's gone before.   680

MARIANE. You see, Dorine, if Father buries me alive
By marrying me off, I know I won't survive.

DORINE. Don't fret about it. We'll get round this one, I swear,
I've got my methods... Oh, here's your young man, Valere.

SCENE 4

VALERE, MARIANE, DORINE

VALERE. Madame, I've just been told some unexpected news.
I'm sure you're overjoyed: I'd like to hear your views.

MARIANE. What's that?

VALERE.   You're promised to Tartuffe.

MARIANE.   It must be said
My father's got some such idea into his head.

VALERE. Your father, then, Madame...

MARIANE.   Seems to have changed his mind.
He's just explained it all, the new plan's been outlined.   690

VALERE. What, can you mean it?

MARIANE.   Yes, I'm very serious.
He says that such a marriage will be glorious.

VALERE. And what's the answer that you're planning to supply,
Madame?

MARIANE.   I just don't know.

VALERE.   That seems a fair reply—
You just don't know?

MARIANE.   No.

VALERE.   No?

MARIANE.   Well, what do you advise?

VALERE. I think that to accept the marriage would be wise.

MARIANE. You want me to accept?

VALERE.   Yes.

MARIANE.   Really?

VALERE.   Yes, that's right.
It's a most worthy match, your future will be bright.

MARIANE. Well, Sir, I may pursue the course you advocate.

VALERE. It's good advice, and you should go along with it.   700

MARIANE. You seem to recommend it with a cheerful heart.

VALERE. And when I gave it, you received it in good part.

MARIANE. I'll do as you suggest to make you happy, Sir.

DORINE [*aside*]. Let's see what comes of this. They're making quite
a stir.

VALERE. So that's how much you care? And you were being untrue
When you...

MARIANE.   Oh, don't! Let's leave that out, I beg of you:
You told me to my face you thought that I must take
The man they want to tie me to—there's no mistake;
And now I'm telling you your wisdom will suffice,
Now that you've given me such excellent advice.   710

VALERE. Don't justify yourself and blame it all on me—
For you'd already made your mind up, I can see;
And I must say your argument, though quite absurd,
Gives you a good excuse for not keeping your word.

MARIANE. You're right. Yes. That's well said.

VALERE.   I see now. It's quite clear
You never really cared that much for me, I fear.

MARIANE. Oh, dear! It's up to you to think just what you choose.

VALERE. That's right. It's up to me. You think you can ill–use
A man, but I can do it too. You wait and see!
I know someone who'll be delighted to have me.   720

MARIANE. I'm sure you're right, and everybody knows you're quite
A catch.

VALERE.   Let's drop all that: my virtues don't excite
Your interest. It seems that they're inadequate.
I know a girl whose heart is more compassionate.
You throw me out: she'll welcome me with open arms,
And, with her help, I'm sure I'll soon forget your charms.

MARIANE. You'll find it easy. I can see your change of heart
Won't take even the smallest effort on your part.

VALERE. I'm going to make that effort, you'll be satisfied.
I've been abandoned. It's a question of my pride—   730
Yes, I'll try to forget, on that you can depend,
And if I don't succeed, at least I can pretend.
The most degrading thing a man can do's reveal
He loves a girl who dropped him flat without appeal.

MARIANE. Yes, that's quite true. You're right. That's how it seems
to me.

VALERE. Of course I am, and everybody will agree.
And, after all, can you expect my love to last
Intact in every way, as it was in the past?
I've got to see you locked in someone else's arms,
So shouldn't I move on at once, and have no qualms?   740

MARIANE. Oh, yes. I long for you to go and break your vow—
I wish you'd hurry up. Go on, then, do it now.

VALERE. You long for it?

MARIANE.   Yes.

VALERE.   You've insulted me enough.
I'll go and do it now. This is your last rebuff.

        [*He makes as though to exit, but keeps coming back*

MARIANE. Oh, good!

VALERE.   Just bear in mind you'll have to take the blame
For this—it was your fault, yes, you and your new flame.

MARIANE. Yes.

VALERE.   If I try to find a cure for my distress,
I'm following your example.

MARIANE.   My example. Yes.

VALERE. There's nothing more to say, so I'll make my retreat.

MARIANE. That's good.   750

VALERE.   This is the last time that we'll ever meet.

MARIANE. That's just as well.

        [VALERE *makes to exit, but turns back when he reaches the door*

VALERE.   Eh?

MARIANE.   What?

VALERE.   Did you call me just now?

MARIANE. Me? No—you're dreaming.

VALERE.   Then I'll go, if you'll allow.
Goodbye, Madame.

MARIANE.   Goodbye, Monsieur.

DORINE.   You're mad, I find.
What's all this folly? You've completely lost your mind.
I let you quarrel, watched the whole scenario,
To get a clear idea of how far you'd both go.
Now then, Monsieur Valere.

        [*She grabs him by the arm, and* VALERE *puts on a show of resistance*

VALERE.   What do you want, Dorine?

DORINE. Come here.

VALERE.   No, I'm too hurt. Don't try to intervene.
    I'm doing as she says—there's no cause for dispute.

DORINE. No, stop!   760

VALERE.   Certainly not, for I'm quite resolute.

DORINE. Huh!

MARIANE.   It's because I'm here he's going, I believe.
    The best thing I can do is turn my back, and leave.

DORINE [*leaving* VALERE *and running to* MARIANE]. Now she's off.
    Don't rush off like that!

MARIANE.   Let go.

DORINE.   Come here!

MARIANE. No, no, I'm going now. Don't try to interfere.

VALERE. It's clear that she's disgusted at the sight of me.
    The best thing I can do is go, and leave her be.

DORINE [*leaves* MARIANE *and runs to* VALERE]. You won't behave
    like this, I won't allow you to!
    Just stop this nonsense now, and come here, both of you!

                              [*She draws them towards each other*

VALERE. What do you want to do?

MARIANE.   Why? What's all this about?

DORINE. To bring you both together, sort your problems out.   770

                              [*To* VALERE

    Why pick a quarrel, then? Have you gone off your head?

VALERE. No, but, look here, you heard the awful things she said.

DORINE [*to* MARIANE]. And were you mad, to lose control so
    stupidly?

MARIANE. Well, you saw how it was, and what he said to me.

DORINE [*to* VALERE]. You are a pair of idiots. Her one concern
    Is to stay free for you. She told me so.

[*To* MARIANE

Your turn—
He loves no one but you, he wants you for his wife,
And if that isn't true, I'll answer with my life.

MARIANE. Then why did he see fit to give me that advice?

VALERE. And why ask for my views on such a sacrifice?   780

DORINE. You're mad. Give me your hands now. Come along, don't
pause.

[*To* VALERE

Come on, you.

VALERE [*giving his hand to* DORINE]. Why d'you want my hand?

DORINE [*to* MARIANE].   That's right. Now yours.

MARIANE [*giving her hand as well*]. But what's the point?

DORINE.   Come, that's enough of these goodbyes.
You love each other much more than you realize.

VALERE [*to* MARIANE]. Now, don't go through the motions so
reluctantly
And try to look at folk a little pleasantly.

[MARIANE *turns to look at* VALERE *and gives a little smile*

DORINE. Take it from me, these youthful lovers are quite mad!

VALERE. Now, surely you must see why I was feeling bad,
And doesn't it strike you that you were most unkind
To tell me the bad news as though you didn't mind?   790

MARIANE. Well, what about you? Weren't you a bit unfair?

DORINE. Let's talk about all that when we've got time to spare.
The marriage must be stopped—I'm sure you see that too.

MARIANE. So tell us quickly, then: what have we got to do?

DORINE. We'll think of plenty clever tricks, take it as read.
It's so much nonsense, and your father's off his head.
But for the moment, I think you must make believe

You go along with all his schemes. We must achieve
Our aim. To start with, if he tries to force your hand,
You'll find a way to hold things up a little, and   800
We'll manage to gain time, and win through in the end.
One time you can fall ill, at least you can pretend:
Your so-called illness will produce a long delay.
Or else you can make out it's an unlucky day—
Because you saw a funeral procession pass,
Or dreamed of muddy water, broke a looking glass.
There's one important fact that must mean our success:
They can't do it by force—you still have to say 'yes'.
But first we must make sure, if we hope to succeed,
That no one sees you here. I'm sure we're all agreed.   810

[*To* VALERE

Now go off quickly, and drum up your friends' support:
We must make sure your marriage happens as it ought.
And we'll go off to find your brother, and confide
In him, and get your stepmother in on our side.
Goodbye.

VALERE [*to* MARIANE]. We've got a fight on our hands. I'll be true,
For all my hopes of happiness are here, with you.

MARIANE [*to* VALERE]. And I can't answer for my father, but I swear
That I will marry nobody except Valere.

VALERE [*to* MARIANE]. How happy I am! Even if they make us
    drop...

DORINE. Young lovers! Honestly, they don't know when to   820
    stop.
Just go away!

VALERE [*takes a step, then turns back*]. One thing...

DORINE.   Stop chattering, I say!

    [*Takes them both by the shoulder and pushes them away*

You go this way, and you had better go that way.

ACT III

SCENE 1

DAMIS, DORINE

(504)

DAMIS. May lightning strike me down, and kill me on the spot!
    Let everybody call me blithering idiot!
    No, nothing can control me when I lose my grip.
    I feel it coming on—I'm bursting to let rip!

DORINE. Oh, do try to control your temper just a bit,
    For all your father did was simply mention it.
    Not all our plans come off, and there's many a slip—
    Or so the saying goes—betwixt the cup and lip.   830

DAMIS. I've got to stop that stinker's monkey-tricks today!
    I think I'll have a few words with him right away.

DORINE. Do calm down! Let's see what your stepmother can do.
    Just let her deal with him, and with your father too.
    She seems to have some influence over Tartuffe:
    He listens to her, and I guess he's not aloof.
    It's my belief the fellow's rather sweet on her.
    If that were true, what fun! I wish to God it were!
    But anyway, she's sent for him, to help you out.
    She'll touch upon the wedding, see what he's about,   840
    Discover his true feelings, make quite sure he knows
    He'll complicate his cosy lifestyle if he goes
    On hoping he can get his way in this affair.
    His valet says he can't be seen, as he's at prayer,
    But he'll be finished shortly, then he should appear—
    So, please, just go away. I'll wait for him right here.

DAMIS. No, when they meet, I want to be there, listening.

DORINE. No, no! Leave them alone!

DAMIS.   I won't say anything.

DORINE. You're joking! You—you're always going to extremes,

And that's the quickest way to ruin all our schemes.   850
Get out!

DAMIS.   No. I can watch without losing my cool.

DORINE. You can't. He's coming now. Quick, get away, you fool!

SCENE 2

TARTUFFE, LAURENT, DORINE

TARTUFFE [*noticing* DORINE]. My hairshirt and my scourge—
Laurent, put them away,
And pray for Heaven's light upon you day by day.*
If anyone should ask, I'll be in prison, where   *probably not*
I'm taking alms, to give the prisoners a share.

DORINE [*aside*]. Oh, how pretentious! What a prig! How insincere!

TARTUFFE. What do you want?

DORINE.   To say...

TARTUFFE [*pulling a handkerchief from his pocket*]. Oh, gracious
Lord! Oh, dear!
Please take this handkerchief before you talk to me.

DORINE. What's that?   860

TARTUFFE.   Cover your bosom, I don't want to see.
The soul can be disturbed by such a wanton sight;
I wouldn't want to have ideas if they're not right.

DORINE. Well, dear me! How temptation seems to turn you on!
Very outspoken One glimpse of flesh, and all your self-control is gone.
I don't know how it is that you're so very hot,
But I'm not quite so quick to covet what you've got.
Me, I could see you standing bare from head to toe,
And all your naked flesh would never tempt me so.

TARTUFFE. Now speak to me a bit more modestly, I pray,
Or I'll have no alternative but go away.   870

DORINE. No, no, I'll be the one to go. I came to call
  For you. I have a message for you, and that's all.
  Madame is shortly coming down to talk to you;
  She hopes that you will grant her a brief interview.

TARTUFFE. Alas! With all my heart.

DORINE [*aside*].   That's cheered him up! I'll lay
  A bet that in that quarter, things are as I say.

TARTUFFE. Will she be coming soon?

DORINE.   I think that I can hear
  Her now. Yes, I was right. I'll leave you with her here.

SCENE 3

TARTUFFE, ELMIRE

TARTUFFE. May gracious Heaven grant you true spiritual wealth,
  And bring your body and your soul abundant health!   880
  May all your days be blest! These are the true desires
  Of quite the humblest mortal Heaven's grace inspires.

ELMIRE. Thanks for that pious wish. You really are too kind.
  We'll be more comfortable sitting down, you'll find.

TARTUFFE. Now, have you quite recovered from your illness, pray?

ELMIRE. My fever came down quickly, I feel well today.

TARTUFFE. I've little merit, and my prayers are much too base
  To bring about this evidence of Heaven's grace—
  But every prayer I made to him who reigns supreme
  Had your full convalescence as its only theme.   890

ELMIRE. You didn't need to take such trouble, show such zeal.

TARTUFFE. Well, your good health is dear to me. I truly feel
  I'd give mine to help you in your infirmity.

ELMIRE. Oh, what a fine display of Christian charity!
  I owe you something for your kindness, now, that's true.

false modesty

TARTUFFE. But you deserve much more than I can do for you.

ELMIRE. I've got a secret, and I'd like to sound you out.
 I must say that I'm glad that nobody's about.

TARTUFFE. I too am very glad, I too feel no regret.
 Madame, I'm so delighted with our tête-à-tête.   900
 To be alone with you has been my ardent plea,
 Which till now Heaven never has accorded me.

ELMIRE. I'd like a quiet word with you. Can I appeal
 To you to be quite frank, and tell me how you feel?

TARTUFFE. The one grace I implore, for you must know the whole,
 Is humbly to expose to you my naked soul,
 To swear to you that all that public fuss I made
 When, drawn by your attractions, your admirers paid
 Their visits, was not due to hatred of you, nay
 'Twas more a holy zeal which carried me away,   910
 Disinterested urge...

ELMIRE.   I take it like that too.
 You want to save my soul, that governs what you do.

TARTUFFE [*squeezing her fingers*]. Oh, yes, indeed, Madame. The
 ardour that I feel...

ELMIRE. Ouch! Don't squeeze me so hard!

TARTUFFE.   It's through excess of zeal.
 I never could harm you deliberately, and
 In fact, I'd much prefer...

        [*He puts his hand on her knee*

ELMIRE.   Monsieur, what's this? Your hand...

TARTUFFE. I'm just touching your gown: the fabric is so rich. *Pervert*

ELMIRE. Well, please let go of me, I'm rather ticklish.

  [*She pushes back her chair, and* TARTUFFE *pushes his forward*

TARTUFFE. Oh, goodness, what fine lace! It's really marvellous!
 This new embroidery is quite miraculous.   920
 They never used to do this kind of thing so well.

ELMIRE. That's so, but I think we should stick to business. Tell
  Me, is it true my husband plans to break his word,
  And give his daughter's hand to you? That's what I've heard.

TARTUFFE. He's mentioned it; but, to reveal my true desires,
  That's not the happiness to which my soul aspires.
  A much more marvellous attraction conquers me,
  Felicity for which I long most ardently.

ELMIRE. You don't give in to earthly passions like the rest.

TARTUFFE. A heart that's made of stone does not beat in my   930
  breast.

ELMIRE. You care for Heaven alone, love God for all you're worth.
  Your interest is fixed by nothing on this earth.

TARTUFFE. The passion for eternal beauty which I feel
  Does not mean that my earthly passions are less real.
  Our senses can be charmed—to us it may be given
  To look on perfect beauty as a gift from Heaven.*
  In Heaven, a woman's beauty strikes an answering chord—
  But you are the most wonderful work of the Lord.
  He's taken such great pains over your countenance,
  That all hearts must be won by such magnificence.   940
  You perfect creature, every time I look at you
  I see Divine Creation shining forth anew.
  When I see you my heart with passion overflows—
  You are a portrait for which God himself did pose.
  I fought this secret love, I thought I was undone—
  I feared that I was tempted by the Evil One.
  I even thought it best to shun your lovely eyes,
  For fear they might prevent me winning Heaven's prize.
  But then, exquisite creature, I saw it would prove
  That there was nothing sinful in my ardent love,   950
  And I could reconcile it with my modesty,
  And so I gave way to my feelings totally.
  I do admit that it is somewhat staggering
  To dare to make my heart a holy offering.
  My dearest wish is that you will be well disposed,
  That my infirmities will never be exposed.
  In you are all my hopes, my wealth, my quietude:

On you rests my despair or my beatitude.
It all depends on you, and I can't rest until
I'm happy if you wish, or wretched if you will.   960

ELMIRE. Well! That's a declaration not to be despised!
You know, to tell the truth, I am a bit surprised:
It seems to me that you should fight your instincts more,
And think what you are doing carefully, before
You say such things. You're so devout, I think you can...

watch it

TARTUFFE. Although I am devout, I am no less a man.*
When we are faced with heavenly beauty such as yours,
Our hearts are smitten straightaway, we cannot pause.
I know that what I say sounds strange coming from me,
But then, Madame, I am no angel, as you see;   970
Perhaps my declaration does put me to shame,
But then, your own bewitching beauty is to blame.
The moment that I saw your lovely looks, I knew
That I had lost my heart—its queen had to be you.
Your heavenly gaze, that glows like light ineffable,
Made all resistance from my heart impossible.
I fasted, prayed, and wept, but nothing I could do
Could overcome the charms that I could see in you.

trying 2 quit her

My looks, my sighs, told you my feelings were sincere;
But now I can speak out, I'll make them still more clear.   980
If you look kindly on me, as I humbly crave,
And pity my distress, since I'm your abject slave,
If your kind eyes can gaze on me without a frown,
And, pitying my dismal plight, deign to look down,
O marvel most delectable, you'll always be
An object of unique devotion to me.
Your honour runs no risk if you give me your heart:
You needn't fear the least exposure on my part.
Those courtiers, ladies' men whom women can't resist,
Talk all the time—no juicy gossip can be missed.   990
They boast of how their love affairs are getting on.
If you give in to them, it's commented upon.
You can't rely on them, their tongues are volatile;
The altar where they sacrifice they soon defile.
But men like us burn with a fire that's more discreet.

Your secret's safe with us. We never will repeat
What's happened, for our reputation matters so,
That those we love are kept quite safe from every foe.
You'll find, if you accept the heart I offer here,
A love that's scandal-free, and pleasure without fear.   1000

ELMIRE. I've listened to your rhetoric, and what I hear
Has put your case. Yes, your position's very clear.
Doesn't it worry you that I might feel I ought
To tell my husband all about your paying court
To me? If I tell him about this interview,
Might it affect the way that he feels about you?

TARTUFFE. I know that you're so full of Christian charity,
That you'll see fit to pardon my temerity.
Yes, you'll excuse the human weakness that I show,
Which brought about this outburst. Though you're hurt, I   1010
    know,
Consider your good looks, and try to bear in mind
That I'm a man of flesh and blood, and far from blind.

ELMIRE. Another woman might perhaps decide to treat
You differently, but I intend to be discreet.
Yes, I'll make sure my husband doesn't get to learn
Of this, but let me ask a favour in return:
First, promise me your firm support in our affair,
I mean the marriage of Mariane and Valere.
Don't use the unjust power you've won as a pretence
To help you to get rich at other folks' expense.   1020
And...

SCENE 4

DAMIS, ELMIRE, TARTUFFE

DAMIS [*emerging from the little room where he was hiding*]. No,
    Madame, stop there! The world must learn of this.
I've been hiding in here, and so I didn't miss
A thing. It seems that Heaven's goodness brought me here
To catch him out before he tries to interfere.

The way's wide open now for me to pay him back:
He's been in charge for long enough. Watch me attack
The fellow! Call my father! He must know the whole.
The man makes love to you. He has a scoundrel's soul.

ELMIRE. No, Damis, it's enough for him to mend his ways.
If he learns to deserve my pardon, he repays   1030
My trust. Don't interfere, I've given him my word.
I don't like it when there's a fuss. It's too absurd—
You certainly ought not to raise your father's fears:
This sort of thing should never reach a husband's ears.

DAMIS. Well, you may have your reasons for the things you do,
And I'll do things my way: I've got my reasons too.
You want to spare the man—is this some kind of joke?
He's insolent and proud, he makes me want to choke.
He's triumphed for too long, and made me mad with rage,
Brought chaos to this house, and been free to rampage.   1040
The hypocrite has caught my father in his snare,
Brought ruin to my hopes, and those of poor Valere
For far too long. It's time my father knew it all.
Thanks be to God, I now see how Tartuffe will fall.
Oh, I'm so grateful for this opportunity—
To give it up like that would be absurdity.
It will be courting punishment if I allow
This chance to pass me by, or fail to act right now.

ELMIRE. Damis...

DAMIS.   Leave me alone. I'll do the thing my way.
I've never felt so happy as I do today.   1050
It's no use making speeches, trying to prevent
Me taking my revenge, for that's now my intent.
I'm going to do it now, I'm quite unstoppable—
And here's the very man to make it possible.

SCENE 5

ORGON, DAMIS, TARTUFFE, ELMIRE

DAMIS. I've got a treat for you. It's time that you got wise
To what's been going on. You'll see—what a surprise!
Monsieur here has made sure your kindness is repaid.
He's shown us his appreciation of your aid:
He's just revealed the secret of his tenderness—
He's aiming to dishonour you, and nothing less.   1060
I came upon him and Madame, and overheard
Him telling her his love—seduction, in a word.
Her instinct was to keep things quiet and discreet,
And not expose the evils of the man's deceit.
But I don't want to pander to his impudence,
And keep you in the dark, condoning his offence.

ELMIRE. Well, I believe a husband needs his peace of mind,
And telling tales is not advisable, I find.
We don't need men to save our honour, take the lead.
We know how to defend ourselves, that's all we need.   1070
That's how I feel, and you'd have seen it my way too,
Damis, if I had any influence on you.

                                                              [*Exit* ELMIRE

SCENE 6

ORGON, DAMIS, TARTUFFE

ORGON. Oh, Heavens, is it true? Eh? What's all this I hear?

TARTUFFE. Yes, brother, I'm a guilty, wicked man, I fear,*
A miserable, evil sinner, of no worth,
The greatest scoundrel that has ever walked the earth.
My life is soiled with filth and rubbish at all times:
It's like a heap of garbage, piled high with my crimes.
I see that Heaven plans a punishment for me,
And has in mind to mortify me thoroughly.   1080

Whatever I'm accused of, let it be allowed:
I won't defend myself—I couldn't be so proud.
Believe what you are told by him, oh, feel no doubt,
Yes, treat me like a criminal, and throw me out.
I'll cringe with shame, dear brother. Such will be my lot—
You know that I'll deserve much worse than I'll have got.

ORGON [*to* DAMIS]. You scoundrel! Do you dare to tell such dreadful
    lies,
And soil his purity? You must apologize!

DAMIS. What! you believe this rubbish just like all the rest,
And let the hypocrite...   1090

ORGON.   Shut up, you little pest!

TARTUFFE. Oh, let him say his piece, and don't try to find fault
With him. You should believe the things he says. You ought
To try to be detached and not to favour me.
You don't know what I'm capable of, do you see?
Do you trust in appearances? D'you think you should?
Because of what you see, do you believe I'm good?
No, no, I'm telling you, I know you've been deceived,
And I'm not what you think, I'm not to be believed.
The whole world has decided I'm exemplary:
The real truth is, I am a worthless nobody.   1100

                                   [*To* DAMIS

Yes, my dear son, go on, call me a perjurer,
A sinner, infamous, a thief, a murderer;
Use every insult, find disgusting names to call
Me now, I won't object, for I've deserved them all.
Down on my knees I'll take the blows, for now's the time
To pay the price in shame for my past life of crime.

ORGON [*to* TARTUFFE]. Ah, brother, it's too much.

                                   [*To* DAMIS

                       Well, does it wring your heart,
You traitor?

DAMIS.   Can't you see the fellow's playing a part?

ORGON. Be quiet, scum!

[*To* TARTUFFE

Now, brother, get up, for me, please!

[*To* DAMIS

You scoundrel!   1110

DAMIS.   Can he?...

ORGON.   Just be quiet!

DAMIS.   I'm livid! He's...

ORGON. If you say one more word, I swear I'll break your arm.

TARTUFFE. Dear brother, in God's name, you must try to stay
    calm.
  I'd rather suffer agonies, let my heart break,
  Than let him bear the slightest scratch for my poor sake.

ORGON [*to* DAMIS]. You villain!

TARTUFFE.   Leave him be, my friend. Down on my knees,
  I beg for mercy for him.

ORGON.   Oh, please get up! Please!

[*To* DAMIS

You monster, look!

DAMIS.   So...

ORGON.   Quiet!

DAMIS.   What?

ORGON.   Don't dare reply!
  I know you've got your knife in him, I can guess why.
  You all detest him, I can see that the whole pack,
  Wife, children, servants, all, have joined in the attack.   1120
  You'll stop at nothing, and you're using all your guile
  To get rid of this holy martyr you revile.
  The more you try to have him thrown out on his ear,
  The more I will insist on keeping him right here.

I mean to give my daughter to him for his bride,
And so I'll utterly confound my family's pride.

DAMIS. Can you force her to marry him without a fight?

ORGON. Yes! Just to make you mad, I'll see it's done tonight.
Ah! I defy you all. You'll see—I'll make you learn
I'm going to be obeyed. I'm master now—my turn!   1130
Take back the things you've said, it's your turn to say 'please'.
So beg his pardon quickly. Now! Down on your knees!

DAMIS. What, me apologize? He's lying, acting dumb...

ORGON. What's that, you're holding back? Insulting him, you
    scum?
Quick, where's my stick?*

[*To* TARTUFFE

        Let go, let me get at the lout!

[*To* DAMIS

You, leave my house at once! Go on now! Out! Get out!
And don't you ever dare to show your face again!

DAMIS. All right, I'm leaving, but...

ORGON.   Out! or I'll go insane!
I'm cutting you out of my will, you're so perverse;
But I've one final gift to you—a father's curse!   1140

SCENE 7

ORGON, TARTUFFE

ORGON. How could he hurt a holy man? The boy's insane!

TARTUFFE. I pray to Heaven to pardon him for causing pain.

[*To* ORGON

If you knew how I feel—he's tried to compromise
Me, blacken my good name in my dear brother's eyes...

ORGON. Alas!

TARTUFFE.   The mere thought of such base ingratitude—
My soul's in agony at his harsh attitude...
The horror that I feel... My heart's too full to cry...
Oh, I can't speak, I think I may be going to die.

ORGON [*running in tears to the door through which he chased*
   DAMIS]. You brute! What held me back? Oh, why did I
   delay?
I should have knocked you down, not let you get away!   1150
Control yourself, dear brother, don't be so upset.

TARTUFFE. You see, you see by what confusion we're beset.
I just bring trouble to this house—here's one more blow.
I think, dear brother, that it's time for me to go.

ORGON. What's that? You must be joking, brother.

TARTUFFE.   I can see
They hate me, they don't want you to believe in me.

ORGON. I'm on your side—do you think that I'll hear them out?

TARTUFFE. But they'll keep on attacking me, I'm in no doubt;
Right now, you know for sure I'm guilty of no crime,
You may listen to what they say, another time.   1160

ORGON. Oh, never, brother, no!

TARTUFFE.   Your wife will gain control:
A woman can deceive a loving husband's soul.

ORGON. No, no...

TARTUFFE.   Now, brother, let me quickly slip away—
Then they'll give up, and not attack me in this way.

ORGON. No, you'll stay here with me—my whole life is at stake.

TARTUFFE. Well, then, to mortify myself I undertake—
But if you'd let me...

ORGON.   Ah!

TARTUFFE.   All right, let's say no more.
I realize my next task must be to explore
The ways of making sure that we don't give offence:

My honour and my love guide me in recompense   1170
To promise I will never set eyes on your wife.

ORGON. No, no, you'll never leave her side, upon my life!
My greatest joy on earth is making people squirm:
You'll see her all the time, I promise, I'll stand firm.
Yes, I'll defy them all, I'll show them, and I swear
That I'll adopt you as my one and only heir.
It'll be quite official, and I'll do it now,
And soon with all my worldly goods I'll you endow.*
My future son-in-law, my dear and honest friend,
Means more to me than wife and children, in the end.   1180
Will you accept the deed of gift I'm offering?

TARTUFFE. May Heaven's will be done, in this and everything!

ORGON. Poor fellow! Let's draw up the deed just as I've said.
This'll confound their envy. May it strike them dead!

ACT IV

SCENE 1

CLEANTE, TARTUFFE

CLEANTE. Yes, people have been talking, I've heard all their
    views:
  Your reputation's suffered greatly at this news.
  I'm very glad, Monsieur, that I ran into you,
  To tell you how I feel in a brief word or two.
  Let's not investigate the cause of this outburst.
  For argument's sake, say that I believe the worst: 1190
  So let's assume Damis was wrong when he defied
  You, and his accusations were unjustified.
  Couldn't you take the situation in good part,
  With Christian charity, not with a vengeful heart?
  They quarrelled over you. Was it right to allow
  The man to throw his son out, straight after a row?
  I tell you yet again, I'm going to be frank,
  The whole world is outraged: they know they've you to thank.
  You'll try to patch things up, if you want my advice.
  Before you let this run its course, you must think twice.   1200
  Do sacrifice your anger to the Holy One,
  And try to reconcile the father with his son.

TARTUFFE. Alas! With all my heart, I'd do it if I could;
  I feel no bitterness, let that be understood.
  I don't blame him at all, I pardon him the whole;
  I long to serve the boy, Monsieur, with all my soul.
  But no, I can't, it's not in Heaven's interests, so
  If he should come back home, then I would have to go.
  For after what he did, which was quite infamous,
  For us to meet together would be scandalous.   1210
  To start with, Heaven knows what people would assume—
  They'd think I had ulterior motives, and presume
  That I felt guilty, so decided to conceal
  My guilt with a pretence of charitable zeal,

That I'm afraid of him, and it will be supposed
I want to buy his silence, keep him well disposed.

CLEANTE. I find all these excuses thoroughly far-fetched.
And I'm afraid, Monsieur, your arguments are stretched
Beyond their limit. Why take on Heaven's concerns,
To make sure every guilty man gets his returns?   1220
God has no need of us, for he knows what to do.
Remember, we are told to pardon people who
Have wronged us. Don't judge others as mere mortals may,
If you intend to follow God's exalted way.
You say people will talk. The gossip won't mislead,
And everyone will see you're doing a good deed.
We should stand back, and do what Heaven may ordain.
We shouldn't clutter up our minds with things profane.

TARTUFFE. I do forgive him in my heart, as I have said.
I've proved that my behaviour's always Heaven-led.   1230
But now, after the shocking things he did today,
I just can't live with him—it wouldn't be God's way.

CLEANTE. But, Sir, is it God's way for you to pay such heed
To his impulsive father, letting him proceed
To make this deed of gift, and should you underwrite
A gift to which, let's face it, Sir, you've got no right?

TARTUFFE. It will be obvious to those who know me best:
This isn't the result of my self-interest.
I'm never blinded by the meretricious charms
Of worldly wealth—I'd really rather live off alms.   1240
If I agree I'm going to let this father make
Me a donation which I then consent to take,
The reason is, in truth, that I've begun to fear
His wealth may fall into the wrong hands around here.
There may be someone who, if he becomes the heir,
Will make immoral use of money that's his share,
Far from devoting all of it, as I now plan,
To God's eternal glory, and the good of Man.

CLEANTE. Hmm... I don't think that you should be so
scrupulous:

Your fears could make the rightful heir feel querulous.   1250
Don't take this burden on yourself, leave it to him,
Let him enjoy his wealth, or lose it, on a whim.
Believe me, better let the money be misused.
You're not a cheat, so you don't want to be accused
Of standing back, and not opposing Orgon's scheme.
Oh, where's your sense of shame? And where's your self-esteem?
And how can holy dogma make out that it's fair
To steal a legacy, and rob a rightful heir?
If Heaven's made you feel that it's impossible
To live with young Damis, since he's unspeakable,   1260
Well, shouldn't you now beat a dignified retreat
And leave this house? And wouldn't that be more discreet
Than, flying in the face of justice, to allow
The only son to be thrown out of doors, right now?
I say, it looks as if you're making very free,
Monsieur...

TARTUFFE.   Monsieur, the time's exactly half past three.
I must attend to pious duties, I perceive—*
So you'll excuse me if I quickly take my leave.

CLEANTE. Oh!

SCENE 2

ELMIRE, MARIANE, DORINE, CLEANTE

DORINE.   Help us with Miss Mariane, Sir! She can't bear
It, and she's gone to pieces. She's in such despair!   1270
The wedding contract has been drawn up for tonight.
She keeps on breaking down, she's in a dreadful fright.
Help us to work on him, I see him coming now.
We must try everything, including force. Somehow,
We'll make him drop this plan that's ruining us all.

SCENE 3

ORGON, ELMIRE, MARIANE, CLEANTE, DORINE

ORGON. Ah! I'm delighted to find all of you on call.

[*To* MARIANE

what This contract here's designed to fill you full of beans.
I think you'll know by now exactly what it means.

MARIANE. Oh, father, in the name of God, who knows my pain,
I'm begging you to stop. I can't go on... the strain...   1280
Please, father, think again. Oh, don't give me away,
And don't oblige me to obey you in this way,
And don't reduce me, by this cruel thing you do,
To blaming Heaven for the duty I owe you.
You gave me life in hope of finding happiness.
Please, don't condemn me to a life of wretchedness.
I thought you'd let me marry. If you now refuse,
And won't allow me to live with the man I choose,
At least be good enough, I beg you on my knees,
To save me from the hell of this new marriage. Please,   1290
Father, don't drive me to the last extremity:
Don't crush me with the force of your authority.

ORGON [*feeling himself weakening*]. Come on, my heart, stand firm.
No human weakness, now.

MARIANE. I don't care if you love him best, you can endow
Him with your property, it's all the same to me,
And you can also give mine to him, willingly.*
I give up all my claim to it as from today.
But, please, at least stop short of giving me away:
And, please, let me retreat into a convent, where
I'll live the last remaining days I have to spare.   1300

ORGON. So that's the way things are: she wants to be a nun
Because I put a stop to her romantic fun!
Get up! The more you feel your husband leaves you cold,
The better you will be for doing as you're told.

So let this marriage serve to mortify your flesh,
And don't come whingeing back to bother me afresh.

DORINE. But what...

ORGON.   Mind your own business. Don't make yourself heard,
For I forbid you to pronounce a single word.

CLEANTE. Perhaps a few words of good counsel would suffice...

ORGON. The whole world benefits from all your good advice.   1310
I've listened to you, and you're sensible, I find;
But I'll go my own way this time, if you don't mind.

ELMIRE [*to* ORGON]. I can't believe my eyes, I don't know what to
    say,
Your wilful blindness must have carried you away.
You're blinkered and obsessed, your prejudice is strong,
If, after all that's happened, you're so sure we're wrong.

ORGON. Your humble servant. I'll believe what I can see.
You're partial to my son, that's how it looks to me,
You tried to back him up; you helped him to conceal
His trick on the poor fellow, chose not to reveal   1320
The truth. But you remained so calm I doubted you:
You would have seemed much more upset if it were true.

ELMIRE. If someone makes a gallant declaration, must
A woman prove she's angry by her loud disgust?
And is the only way to deal with such events
To make a fuss, all flashing eyes and wild laments?
For my part, I just laugh when men try such a ploy—
For making scenes is something that I don't enjoy.
It's better to stay cool and calm at every stage.
I'm not one of those prudes who flies into a rage,   1330
Who backs her honour up by fighting tooth and nail,
And lets her temper flare at every passing male.
May God preserve me from that same high moral tone!
I'm no she-devil, and I won't throw the first stone.
I think that a refusal, measured but still cold,
Will easily put off a man who's over-bold.

ORGON. Well, I know how it was, and I won't be deceived.

ELMIRE. I tell you, I'm amazed. This has to be believed!
Now, what would you think if I showed the thing to you,
And made you see for sure that what we say is true?   1340

ORGON. Showed me?

ELMIRE.   Yes, showed you.

ORGON.   Rubbish!

ELMIRE.   If I find a way
Of showing you the truth of this, as broad as day?

ORGON. What taradiddles!

ELMIRE.   Men! Look here, let me be heard:
Don't think I'm asking you to take me at my word.
But just suppose that, from a hiding place right here,
I showed you everything, made sure that you could hear,
What would you have to say about your worthy man?

ORGON. Well, I'd say... I'd say nothing, for your clever plan
Can never work.

ELMIRE.   All this has gone on far too long,
And I've had quite enough of hearing that I'm wrong.   1350
Before we take another step, I'll go ahead
And make you witness everything that I've just said.

ORGON. All right, then, I agree. Let's see what you can do,
Let's see you demonstrate that what you say is true.

ELMIRE. You, go and fetch him here.

DORINE.   He's got a cunning mind:
He won't allow himself to be surprised, you'll find.

ELMIRE. Don't worry, men in love are easy to deceive:
They won't see through the things they're anxious to believe.
Just get him down.

                    [*To* CLEANTE and MARIANE

              You two had better go away.

SCENE 4

ELMIRE, ORGON

ELMIRE. Let's draw that table up. Climb under it, I say.   1360

ORGON. What's that?

ELMIRE.   Look, it's essential, and you've got to hide.

ORGON. But why under the table?

ELMIRE.   Just let me decide.
I've got a plan worked out, as you will shortly see.
Just get down under there. Come on, you did agree,
And mind you're careful that you can't be seen or heard.

ORGON. I must say, I was tolerant to give my word.
It makes me wonder how you'll wriggle out of this.

ELMIRE. You'll see—I'll justify the need for artifice.

[*To* ORGON, *under the table*

I may seem rather odd, you may be mystified,
But it's important that you don't feel horrified.   1370
Whatever I may say has got to be allowed:
I've got to demonstrate the truth, as I have vowed.
I'll butter him up now: I see it as my task
To get the hypocrite to put aside his mask.
I'll flatter him till he abandons all pretence,
And make him give free rein to his impertinence.
All this is for your benefit; I'll catch him out,
Pretending to encourage him till there's no doubt.
But then I'll stop the minute that you're satisfied,
And things will only go as far as you decide.   1380
It's up to you to stop his passion, call his bluff,
When you decide that things have gone quite far enough.
So spare my feelings, don't expose me more than you
Need to convince yourself that what I say is true.
I leave it up to you—you're master in this place,*
And... Here he is! Keep down! Don't move! Don't show your face!

SCENE 5

TARTUFFE, ELMIRE, ORGON *under the table.*

TARTUFFE. You want to talk to me, I understand, in here?

ELMIRE. Yes, here, in confidence—I need to bend your ear.
Before I start, though, could you kindly shut the door,
And check there's no one listening in the corridor.   1390
We want no more surprises, like what happened when
We talked last time, we can't go through all that again.
I've never been so shocked—it really made me quake.
That boy Damis! I was in terror for your sake.
I made great efforts then, you saw how hard I tried
To make him change his mind, and keep him pacified.
It's true that I was very anxious and confused:
I didn't think to lie when you stood there, accused.
But thanks to God, things turned out for the best, I'm sure,
For now we find ourselves a good deal more secure.   1400
My husband's feelings for you are extremely warm;
His admiration for you soon dispelled the storm.
He wants to flout public opinion, seemingly,
And says we must be seen together constantly.
And so, as it turns out, I've got no cause to fear
At being closeted alone with you, in here.
It means I can speak frankly, not prevaricate—
Perhaps I've been too eager to reciprocate.

TARTUFFE. I find your language hard to understand, I own,
Madame. Last time, you took a very different tone.*   1410

ELMIRE. If what I said to you last time could make you smart,
How little you must understand a woman's heart!
I see you've no idea what we are trying to say
When we defend ourselves in such a lukewarm way.
At moments such as that, our modesty will fight
Against our tender feelings, so that we take fright.
However strongly love has set our hearts aflame,
We never can confess without a sense of shame.
We start by fighting love, but make it obvious

We're more than ready to give in without much fuss— 1420
Our words deny our heart—our honour is at stake;
If you believe us then, you're making a mistake.
This confidence I'm making you is very free;
I'm not allowing for a woman's modesty.
But since I'm being open, would I have declared
That Damis should keep quiet, unless I really cared?
D'you think that I'd have taken it in such good part,
And heard you out, when you were offering your heart?
D'you think that I'd have been quite so amenable
If I found that same offer disagreeable? 1430
And when I said it was essential you renounced
Your marriage, on the very day it was announced,
I spoke out strongly then: wasn't the puzzle solved?
And wasn't it quite obvious I was involved,
That seeing you engaged had filled me with distress:
I needed your whole heart, I couldn't do with less?

TARTUFFE. Ah! There's no doubt at all, Madame, it's very sweet
To hear a voice that one adores gently entreat:
My heart runs over at your honeyed eloquence.
I melt with rapture at each beauteous utterance. 1440
To please you gives me joy of utmost magnitude.
Your words have filled my heart with sweet beatitude.
But that same heart now begs to take the liberty
Of doubting—just a bit—its own felicity.
I could see in your words an honest stratagem
To stop my marriage, which I know that you condemn;
And if I may express myself quite openly,
I won't believe your tender words implicitly
Unless you back them up, let me have something more,
And grant me some small favours that I'm longing for. 1450
In that way you would fill my soul with constant trust.
And I'd accept your charming favours—that seems just.

ELMIRE [*coughing to attract* ORGON's *attention*]. What, Monsieur?
      Why the hurry? Must you move so fast,
And use my favours up? Don't you want them to last?
It cost me dear to tell you what I feel for you;
But now it seems it's not enough, there's more to do.

The only way I'll satisfy you, so you say,
Is if I first agree to going the whole way?

TARTUFFE. The less that we deserve, the more we dare to hope.
Just talking's not enough, our feelings need more scope.   1460
A glorious destiny may lie ahead, we guess
At it, but first we need to try it, I confess.
I know I don't deserve such perfect happiness,
I doubt that my temerity's met with success.
My heart will not believe without the proof it needs—
And so, Madame, you must back up your words with deeds.

ELMIRE. Your love is such a tyrant, Sir, I feel abused.
I don't know what to think, I'm thoroughly confused.
Your passion takes control of hearts that it desires.
It's very brutal in the things that it requires.   1470
What? Is there no escape? Must you pursue me still?
And can't there be a pause before you have your will?
Can it be right to be so firm in your commands,
And to insist remorselessly on your demands?
You've found my weakness, which you ought to disregard—
Yet you're exploiting me, you're pressing me too hard.

TARTUFFE. But if you view my homage with a kindly eye,
Why don't you let me have the proof for which I sigh?

ELMIRE. But how can I agree to do the thing you ask,
Without the God you speak of taking me to task?   1480

TARTUFFE. If Heaven's the only obstacle to my desire,
I'll easily dispense with that, if you require.
Don't let it hold you back from doing what you please.

ELMIRE. But Heaven's ordinances fill me with unease!

TARTUFFE. Oh, I'll help you to dissipate your foolish fear,
For I know what to do when scruples interfere—
It's true that certain pleasures are denied to man,

[*This is a scoundrel speaking**

But we have ways of getting round this austere ban.
Depending on your needs, we know how to persuade,

We know how qualms of conscience are to be allayed,   1490
And, as we tell a sinner when he's sore distressed,
No matter what he did, he acted for the best.*
Madame, I'll teach you all these secrets. Then you'll see
That all you need to do is put your trust in me.
If you give in to me, and show me what you dare,
I'll undertake to mastermind this whole affair.

[ELMIRE *coughs*

Oh, what a cough, Madame.

ELMIRE.   Yes, it's quite merciless.

TARTUFFE. Perhaps you'd care to try a piece of liquorice?

ELMIRE. I've got a frightful cold—there's little likelihood
That all your liquorice would do it any good.   1500

TARTUFFE. Oh, what a pity!

ELMIRE.   Yes, it's worse than I can say.

TARTUFFE. Well, anyway, your scruple's easy to allay.
You can be sure your secret life won't be disclosed:
No wickedness exists until it's been exposed.
It's public outcry gives a crime its origin,
And if you sin in silence, then it's not a sin.

ELMIRE [*coughing again*]. Well, now at last I see I must give in to
    you,
There's no alternative, and it's what I must do,
For nothing short of that, I've clearly understood,
Can satisfy you that I'm really yours for good.   1510
I'm quite upset that this is how it has to be:
I'm taking this first daring step unwillingly.
But since you're so determined that I must do this,
And since you won't relent, I see I'm powerless.
You say you really must have more convincing proof—
So I must force myself not to remain aloof.
If by agreeing I'm committing an offence,
Then blame yourself: you forced me to this violence,
And nobody can say that I deserve the blame.

TARTUFFE. Yes, leave it all to me, Madame, it's all the same...   1520

ELMIRE. But first, open the door a little, not too wide—
And have a look in case my husband is outside.

TARTUFFE. There's much less need to fear him than you might
suppose.
Between ourselves, that man can be led by the nose.
He's pleased as Punch we're having meetings such as these—
And I've made sure he won't believe the things he sees.

ELMIRE. Well, never mind, it's better to be satisfied—
So kindly make quite sure, and take a look outside.

SCENE 6

ORGON, ELMIRE

ORGON [*coming out from under the table*]. Oh!... Gosh! You're right!
Oh dear! What an appalling creep!
I can't get over it, I'm struck all of a heap!   1530

ELMIRE. What's this? You must be joking. Don't come out just yet.
You haven't had enough, so hurry up and get
Under the table. Hear him to the end, make sure
You're not assuming things. You need to be secure.

ORGON. He's wickedness itself, a devil out of hell!

ELMIRE. Don't take things quite so lightly, wait for proof as well.
Before you act, make sure the evidence is strong:
Don't be in such a hurry! What if you were wrong?

[*She pushes* ORGON *behind her*

SCENE 7

TARTUFFE, ELMIRE, ORGON

TARTUFFE. So now the time has come. My rapture is profound,
Madame. I've been outside, and had a good look round.   1540
There's nobody about, and, oh! I'm all on fire...

ORGON [*interrupting*]. Hold on, before surrendering to your desire.
  Your promises of love have come out much too pat.
  Ah, ah! An honest man, to hoodwink me like that!
  It's scarcely fighting sin, the way you planned your life,
  As husband to my girl, and lover to my wife!
  For ages I could not believe that this was real,
  I kept on hoping that you would amend your spiel.
  But no—I've heard you out, and I've had quite enough.
  I need no other proof, it's time to call your bluff.   1550

ELMIRE [*to* TARTUFFE]. You know, I'd really rather not have done all
    this.
  Too bad there had to be so much unpleasantness.

TARTUFFE. What? Can you really think?...

ORGON.   Oh, stop fooling about.
  I've had enough of this. It's high time you got out.

TARTUFFE. No, listen to my plan...

ORGON.   There's nothing to discuss.
  Get out of here, and do it quick. Don't make a fuss

TARTUFFE. No, you get out. Go on. You're not the master here.
  This house belongs to me, as everyone will hear.
  I've had enough. It's time to make you understand.
  Don't try your dirty tricks on me—it's underhand.   1560
  You thought you could insult me, didn't realize
  That I can punish you, and cut you down to size.
  Now God will be avenged, and you will soon repent
  The folly that led you to say it's time I went.

SCENE 8

ELMIRE, ORGON

ELMIRE. What's he going on about? And what did all that mean?

ORGON. This is no laughing matter. I should have foreseen...

ELMIRE. What?

ORGON.   Well, from what he said I see I've been at fault.
The deed of gift gives me no reason to exult.

ELMIRE. What deed of gift?

ORGON.   You see, it's all been signed and sealed.
There's something else that worries me, which I've   1570
concealed.

ELMIRE. What's that?

ORGON.   I'll tell you soon. But first, we'd better race
Upstairs and see if my deed box is in its place.

ACT V

SCENE 1

CLEANTE. Where are you going?

ORGON.   Oh, I don't know.

CLEANTE.   Seems to me
  We ought to start by talking to the family
  To work out what to do in our predicament.

ORGON. The deed box fills me with a grim presentiment.
  It's worse than all the rest—I'm sick with misery.

CLEANTE. This deed box—does it hold a major mystery?

ORGON. My friend Argas had problems. He was in despair.
  He brought it here in secret, left it in my care.   1580
  Before he fled, he put his trust in me, explained
  That I must guard it, for the papers it contained
  Were vital, since his life and goods were both at stake.*

CLEANTE. So why let them out of your hands? What a mistake!

ORGON. Because I thought I ought to keep my conscience clear:
  I went straight to my traitor, whispered in his ear.
  When he heard all, he easily made me believe
  That it would be much better if I were to leave
  The deed box in his care, for then I could deny
  That I was keeping it, without having to lie.*   1590
  My conscience would be clear, it was the thing to do.
  I wouldn't have to swear something that wasn't true.

CLEANTE. Your situation's grim, as far as I can tell.
  This secret that he knows, the deed of gift as well,
  Both these steps that you took, if I may be quite frank,
  Were very rash—you only have yourself to thank.
  With such advantages he could do you great harm.

He has a hold on you that fills me with alarm.
To have confronted him was very ill advised.
Much better to stay cool—you should have realized.   1600

ORGON. What, when he used his faith, his power to console,
To hide his two-faced treachery, his evil soul?
The day I took him in, he was quite destitute...
That's it, I'm giving up on men of good repute:
I'll hate them worse than all things in the universe.
I plan to be a devil to them, if not worse.

CLEANTE. Why must you always let things carry you away?
You're never calm, you're fighting battles every day.
You don't let reason govern you, or so it seems,
And your idea of sense is going to extremes.   1610
You see how wrong you were, and now you realize
That this false hypocrite threw dust into your eyes.
But if you want to right this wrong, why do you need
To make a worse mistake, and one which must exceed
The first? And why must you so stubbornly confuse
All decent folk with one foul scoundrel, and accuse
The lot? Because one trickster shows his zealotry,
And dupes you with his ostentatious bigotry,
You're now convinced that everyone is just the same,
And people nowadays believe only in name.   1620
It's true that libertines provide such instances,
But virtue too exists; don't trust appearances.
There's no need to assume all men deserve respect;
By meeting decent people, you'll grow circumspect.
Don't honour crude impostors, careful how you tread,
But don't insult the real believers in their stead.
If you must be excessive, think of it my way:
Far better be too cautious, eh? That's what I say.

SCENE 2

DAMIS, ORGON, CLEANTE

DAMIS. What, Father, is it true? The scoundrel's threatened you?
Do I hear he forgets your kindness to him, too?   1630

Your treatment of him didn't move him in the least:
He's turned against you, like a savage, cruel beast?

ORGON. My boy, it's true. I'm wretched—look, I'm close to tears.

DAMIS. I'll deal with this: I'm going to cut off both his ears.
One mustn't give in to his insolence, you know.
Leave it to me, I'll liberate you with one blow.
I'll knock him out—that way, he's easy to destroy.

CLEANTE. Now, frankly, you are going wild, just like a boy.
Do show some self-control, don't go over the top.
We live in modern times: the King will put a stop   1640
To people who use violence to get their way.

SCENE 3

MADAME PERNELLE, MARIANE, ELMIRE, ORGON, DAMIS,
DORINE, CLEANTE

MADAME PERNELLE. I've heard some dreadful rumours. What's
going on here, eh?

ORGON. Look, what you heard has really happened, I'm afraid.
You see how all my kind concern has been repaid.
The man was destitute, and so I took him in.
I fed and housed him, treated him like my own kin.
I showered him with favours every day; I planned
To give him all my worldly goods, my daughter's hand.
Meanwhile, this monstrous rogue, this fiend, upon my life,
Conceived the project of dishonouring my wife.   1650
Now he's not satisfied—we foiled his first attempt,
And now he holds my goodness to him in contempt,
And wants to use the weapons I put in his hand,
By trusting him too much, to bring about my end.
I've transferred all my wealth to him, and he's about
To leave me as he was when first I helped him out.

DORINE. Poor fellow!

MADAME PERNELLE.   Son, you must be wrong. I can't believe
That he could be so bad, so eager to deceive.

ORGON. What's that?

MADAME PERNELLE. You know how people envy decent folk.

ORGON. Did you hear what I said? Is this some kind of joke, 1660
 Eh, mother?

MADAME PERNELLE. This house has a sinful atmosphere,
 And everybody knows Tartuffe is hated here.

ORGON. But what has that to do with anything I've said?

MADAME PERNELLE. When you were small, I drummed these facts
 into your head:
 Good people are in danger from society,
 And decent men are envied for their piety.

ORGON. But that's nothing to do with what has just occurred!

MADAME PERNELLE. They've made up things about him, which are
 all absurd.

ORGON. I tell you that I saw it all, with my own eyes!

MADAME PERNELLE. Yes, evil gossip always grows and 1670
 multiplies.

ORGON. Goddammit, mother, will you listen, one more time?
 I saw, with my own eyes, this most outrageous crime!

MADAME PERNELLE. Ah, spiteful tongues are always dripping
 poison. Aye,
 You can't protect yourself however hard you try.

ORGON. You're talking rubbish, and it hurts me to the core.
 I say I saw him, saw him, with my own eyes saw
 Him; do you know what seeing means? And must I shout
 It in your ear a hundred times, and yell it out?

MADAME PERNELLE. Well, God knows how appearances often
 deceive.
 The things you see you ought not always to believe. 1680

ORGON. She'll drive me mad!

MADAME PERNELLE. It's human nature to suspect:
 Things may look bad, but they're misleading, I expect.

ORGON. What's that? You think it's possible I could misread
　　The act of trying to kiss my wife?

MADAME PERNELLE.　　　　　　That's right. You need
　　To have just cause before you start accusing folk.
　　Just wait and see, don't be so hasty to provoke.

ORGON. What? Dammit! How could I have been more sure than
　　that?
　　Was I supposed to wait, and watch what he was at,
　　Until...? Mother, you'll make me say some stupid thing.

MADAME PERNELLE. The trouble is, his faith is strong, his　　1690
　　soul takes wing.
　　He surely can't have done the awful things you say!
　　I can't believe it's true, I tell you straight away.

ORGON. Oh! If you weren't my mother—I've reached such a stage...
　　I don't know what I'd say!... Oh, I'm in such a rage!

DORINE. It's your come-uppance, Sir, for what you put us through:
　　You turned a deaf ear, now she won't listen to you.

CLEANTE. We're wasting precious time in pointless repartee.
　　We must plan our campaign—I'm sure you all agree—
　　Bearing in mind that he's so very dangerous.

DAMIS. You can't believe that shameless brute would threaten　　1700
　　us?

ELMIRE. For my part, I just don't believe it's possible,
　　Since everyone can see the man's contemptible.

CLEANTE. Don't bank on it. He's got some more cards up his sleeve.
　　In the world's eyes, he'll prove you're wicked, I believe.
　　I've known him and his group attack a man for less,*
　　And tie him up in knots: you'll end up in a mess.
　　I tell you once again, in view of what he knows,
　　He's not a person one should venture to expose.

ORGON. That's true, but when I heard his boastful rigmarole,
　　I couldn't stop myself, I lost my self-control.　　　　　　1710

CLEANTE. I hope with all my heart that we'll be able to
　　Work out some way to heal the breach between you two.

ELMIRE. If I had known that he was holding every card,
  I could have stopped him sooner, and been on my guard
  Against...

ORGON.   Oh, who's that now? Tell him he'd better wait.
  It's not a time for visits—I'm in such a state.

SCENE 4

MONSIEUR LOYAL, MADAME PERNELLE, ORGON, DAMIS,
MARIANE, DORINE, ELMIRE, CLEANTE

MONSIEUR LOYAL. Dear sister, greetings to you. May I seek your
  aid?
  I want to see Monsieur.

DORINE.   He's busy, I'm afraid,
  And he won't be at home to visitors today.

MONSIEUR LOYAL. I've not come to disturb his peace in any   1720
  way:
  My presence here will not displease him, I'm quite sure.
  I've got good news for him. I'm here to reassure.

DORINE. What name shall I give, Sir?

MONSIEUR LOYAL.   Just tell him, if you would,
  Monsieur Tartuffe has sent me here, for his own good.

DORINE. It's a well-spoken man, who says that he's come here
  To bring a message from Monsieur Tartuffe. It's clear,
  He says, that you'll be pleased with it.

CLEANTE.   You'd better see
  What kind of man he is, and what his news can be.

ORGON. It may be that this man's been sent to reconcile
  The two of us. How should I play it? In what style?   1730

CLEANTE. Don't let your anger show, try not to make a riot,
  And if he talks of peace, just listen and keep quiet.

MONSIEUR LOYAL. Greetings, Monsieur. May Heaven confound
  your enemies.
  I pray to God, for him to give your conscience ease.

ORGON. Oh, what a kind beginning—see, I wasn't wrong:
  I know he's here to bring about a *rapprochement*.

MONSIEUR LOYAL. Yes, I'm deeply attached to all your family.
  I was Monsieur your father's servant, formerly.

ORGON. Monsieur, I'm so ashamed—I must apologize.
  Your face is not one that I seem to recognize.   1740

MONSIEUR LOYAL. My name is Loyal, I'm a Norman—proud of
    it—
  And I'm a bailiff, which I'm happy to admit.*
  For forty years I've had the great good fortune to
  Perform my duties well, and honourably too,
  Thank God. And now, I'm here, Monsieur, saving your grace,
  About the serving of a writ upon this place...

ORGON. What's that? You've turned up here...

MONSIEUR LOYAL.   Monsieur, kindly keep calm.
  It nothing, just a warrant—meaning you no harm.
  Your family and you are ordered to clear out,
  Lock, stock, and barrel, and that's all this is about,   1750
  Without delay, make room for others, or we'll seize...

ORGON. What, must I leave my home?

MONSIEUR LOYAL.   Yes, Monsieur, if you please.
  As of today, this house—and you've had ample proof—
  Belongs most legally to good Monsieur Tartuffe.
  Yes, he's the lord and master of your property,
  By virtue of a contract which I've brought with me:
  It's duly signed and sealed, there's no cause for dispute.

DAMIS. Well, that's some impudence—I'll hand it to the brute.

MONSIEUR LOYAL. I'm not dealing with you, you're too irascible,
  But with Monsieur your Pa: he's calm and peaceable,   1760
  And he's a man of honour, knows what game to play.
  When justice must be done, he won't stand in my way.

ORGON. But...

MONSIEUR LOYAL.   Yes, Monsieur, I know you'll show me
    great respect,
  And not for all the world will you ever reject
  My writ. Yes, you're a decent sort, and will allow
  Me to perform my task, and follow orders now.

DAMIS. Monsieur, your bailiff's robe is long and black and thick.
  Don't be surprised if it makes contact with my stick.

MONSIEUR LOYAL. Just tell your son to hold his tongue or to
    withdraw,
  Monsieur, for I'd be sorry to invoke the law   1770
  And write in my report that there has been a brawl.

DORINE. This fine Monsieur Loyal is not loyal at all.

MONSIEUR LOYAL. I have the warmest feelings for all gentlemen,
  Monsieur, and chose to take on this assignment when
  I learnt you were involved, to help you all I can—
  You might have ended up with quite a different man,
  Who wasn't so committed to your interest,
  And could have thrown you out with rather too much zest.

ORGON. Could anything be worse than telling me to go,
  And leave my own home?   1780

MONSIEUR LOYAL.   Look, I'm making things go slow,
  And putting off the execution of the writ
  Until tomorrow, so you'll come to terms with it.
  I merely plan to come back here and spend the night
  With ten men—without fuss, you'll find it's quite all right.
  The only thing I ask of you is that before
  Retiring, you bring me the key to your front door.
  I'll take great care not to disturb you at your rest,
  And nothing will be done that isn't for the best.
  But then tomorrow morning, my client expects
  You to empty the premises of your effects.   1790
  My men will help you out, I chose them big and strong.
  They'll put your things outside, and it won't take them long.
  I'm giving you a very good deal, I believe.
  I'm doing the decent thing in helping you to leave,

So I must ask you to collaborate with me,
And help me get my duty done efficiently.

ORGON. And me, I wish with all my heart that I could give
A hundred crowns—all I've got left to help me live,
And in exchange I'd like the joy, not to be missed,
Of flattening this devil's fat face with my fist.   1800

CLEANTE. Drop it—don't make more trouble.

DAMIS.   But I can't hold back!
My hand itches to fetch the creep a hefty smack.

DORINE. Your back is good and broad, you know, Monsieur Loyal.
A sharp smack with a stick would do no harm at all.

MONSIEUR LOYAL. You could be punished for the spiteful things
    you say,
And women too get prosecuted every day.

CLEANTE. I think we've had enough. Let's stop all this, Monsieur.
Give us the writ and go, that's what we would prefer.

MONSIEUR LOYAL. Goodbye, then, Sirs, may Heaven take good
    care of you.

ORGON. May Heaven confound you, Sir, and your fine master   1810
    too!

SCENE 5

ORGON, MADAME PERNELLE, DAMIS, MARIANE, DORINE, ELMIRE,
CLEANTE

ORGON. Well, mother, now at last you see that I was right.
And you can judge the scoundrel by his satellite.
So now do you believe his treachery went deep?

MADAME PERNELLE. I'm discombobulated, struck all of a heap!

DORINE. You're wrong to put the blame on him and make a fuss,
For all this goes to show he's holier than us:
He loves his fellow mortals, helps them when he can.
Material possessions can corrupt a man,

So, charitably, he has planned to take away
The obstacles that stand in your salvation's way.   1820

ORGON. Be quiet: why insist on having the last word?

CLEANTE. Let's try to sort things out, we mustn't be deterred.

ELMIRE. Why not tell everyone how shameless Tartuffe's been?
The contract will be void once what he's done is seen
In its true light. I'm sure that he won't be allowed
To get away with this, if you speak it aloud.

SCENE 6

VALERE, ORGON, MADAME PERNELLE, DAMIS, MARIANE, DORINE,
ELMIRE, CLEANTE

VALERE. Monsieur, I'm very sorry, but, you see, I'm here
To bring bad news, for you're in danger, Sir, I fear.
I've got a very close and honourable friend
Who knows I care for you, on whom I can depend.   1830
As a great favour, he's prepared to violate
The secrecy that goes with all affairs of state,
And he's just let me know that something's come to light
Which means that you've no choice but hurry, and take flight.
That trickster who imposed on all of you so long
Has just gone to the King to put you in the wrong.*
He painted you as black, and gave him what you had—
A deed box with a traitor's papers. Then, from bad
To worse, said that you'd failed to do your duty, and
Had kept this guilty secret, been most underhand.   1840
That's all that I've been told, but I can guess the rest.
In short, they've ordered your immediate arrest,
And he's been given the task of helping to waylay
You here and supervise as they take you away.

CLEANTE. Yes, that's his secret weapon—that's his perfidy!
He hopes to keep his hold upon your property.

ORGON. Oh, was there ever such an animal as him?

VALERE. If you delay, the consequences may be grim.
  I've got a carriage ready, waiting at the door,
  I've brought a thousand golden crowns with me, what's   1850
    more.
  Let's waste no time, for you've been struck a mighty blow.
  The only way to ward it off is to lie low.
  I'll take you somewhere safe, and help you. As your friend,
  I'll stay with you, and see this through right till the end.

ORGON. Oh dear! If I could say how I appreciate...
  But all my grateful thank-yous will just have to wait.
  May gracious Heaven in its goodness help me through
  This ordeal, so I can find ways of thanking you.
  Goodbye. Take care, you others, not to...

CLEANTE.   Go on, run!
  Leave us behind to work out what had best be done.   1860

SCENE 7

TARTUFFE, THE OFFICER,* VALERE, ORGON, MADAME PERNELLE,
DAMIS, MARIANE, DORINE, ELMIRE, CLEANTE

TARTUFFE. Hold on, Monsieur, hold on, don't try to run away.
  You don't have far to go to find your place today.
  You're now in custody by order of the King.

ORGON. You traitor, that is quite the worst news you could bring.
  You've ruined me, you villain, with a single blow.
  Your treachery has won, you brute! You've brought me low.

TARTUFFE. Your insults won't succeed in putting me to shame—
  I know that I must suffer in God's holy name.

CLEANTE. I must confess, the fellow's very moderate.

DAMIS. The monster mentioned God at once, he couldn't   1870
    wait!

TARTUFFE. Your outbursts are no use, they mean nothing to me.
  My one concern's to do my duty properly.

MARIANE. Your reputation will be much enhanced, I'm sure.
  The task that you perform is noble as it's pure.

TARTUFFE. True, any task is noble if it's ordered by
  His Majesty, with all that great name may imply.

ORGON. Have you forgotten that it was through charity
  I took you in, you wretch, gave you prosperity?

TARTUFFE. I know you helped me, and I don't forget the rest,
  But I must act first in the King's best interest.   1880
  That sacred duty must decide my attitude:
  And in my heart it stifles any gratitude.
  His claim on me is absolute. Indeed, my life
  Is his. For him I'd give up parents, friends, and wife.

ELMIRE. Impostor!

DORINE.   How the traitor shows he doesn't fear
  To cloak his actions in the things we all revere!

CLEANTE. But if it's as you say, and you're so full of zeal,
  Obliged to do your duty, no room for appeal,
  How is it that you waited, failing to react,
  Until his wife helped him to catch you in the act?   1890
  You weren't ready to denounce your victim, till
  He had to throw you out, and you lost his goodwill.
  There's one thing I should add, along with all the rest:
  The fact that he has given you all he possessed.
  For if you planned to treat him like a criminal,
  Why did you first accept his gift? That shows some gall.

TARTUFFE. Monsieur, I've had enough of all their talk, I find.
  It's time now to obey your orders: be so kind.

THE OFFICER. Indeed, I've waited much too long. Now you
      invite
  Me to obey my orders, and, yes, you're quite right;   1900
  And therefore I must ask you to accompany
  Me straight to jail, as your reward for felony.

TARTUFFE. What, me, Monsieur?

THE OFFICER.   Yes, you.

TARTUFFE.   But why? What have I done?

THE OFFICER. It's not to you I owe an explanation.
Compose yourself, Monsieur, he'll get his just reward.
The King who rules us is the enemy of fraud,
He sees into the depths of all his subjects' hearts,
And he's never deceived by false impostors' arts.
He can tell truth from lies; his great soul is endowed
With insight; he can guess what isn't said out loud.   1910
He sees things as they are; you'll find that wicked schemes
Don't take him by surprise, or drive him to extremes.
He honours all religious men as they deserve,
But, not blinded by admiration, will observe
Their antics. He respects sincere devotion,
But holds all hypocrites in great aversion.
This man didn't succeed in leading him astray:
He recognizes traps when they're put in his way.
His brilliant mind saw through this fellow from the start,
Exposing all the hidden corners of his heart.   1920
When he accused you, then he gave himself away.
It seems a supreme irony came into play.
The King had heard about him by another name;
He was unmasked as quite an old hand at the game.
He's done a string of evil deeds—he's a real crook;
The story of his goings-on would fill a book.
The King was most outraged on your behalf, in short,
At his ingratitude; when he tried to extort
Your property, that was the limit. I was sent
To follow him and see how far the whole thing went,   1930
Observe the full extent of all his impudence,
And put things right, and then reward your innocence.
I'm to take all your papers from this traitor, who
Claims they belong to him, and give them back to you.
By royal prerogative, the King has nullified*
The document by which your property was tied
To him. And he forgives the secret wrong you did
When you helped out your outlawed friend, before he hid.
He still appreciates your former loyalty,
The wholehearted support you gave to royalty,   1940

And wishes you to know that, now you are in need,
He'll see you are repaid in full for your good deed.
A virtuous man won't lose by trusting in his might:
He may forget the wrong you do, never the right.

DORINE. Well, Heaven be praised for this!

MADAME PERNELLE.   Oh, goodness, what relief!

ELMIRE. Things have turned out all right.

MARIANE.   This quite beggars belief!

ORGON. So, traitor, now you see...

CLEANTE.   Oh, stop there, brother, do,
Don't kick him when he's down—it's not worthy of you.
Just leave the wretched fellow to endure his fate.
He feels quite bad enough—no need to remonstrate.   1950
It's better you should hope that what's been done today
Will coax his wayward heart to follow virtue's way.
May he reform his life, and lead a better one.
Let's hope the King won't force harsh justice to be done.
Meanwhile, I think you should go to him, if you please,
And give thanks for his goodness to you, on your knees.

ORGON. Yes, that's well said. Let's take the opportunity
To give our thanks for all his generosity.
And when we have accomplished that first duty, we
Have one more thing to do, which means a lot to me.   1960
We must reward Valere, give him my daughter's hand:
There never was a truer friend in all the land.

THE END

THE MISANTHROPE

1666

CHARACTERS

ALCESTE,* in love with Celimene
PHILINTE,* friend to Alceste
ORONTE,* in love with Celimene
CELIMENE,* a young widow
ELIANTE,* cousin to Celimene
ACASTE,* a marquis, in love with Celimene
CLITANDRE,* a marquis, in love with Celimene
ARSINOË,* friend to Celimene
BASQUE, servant to Celimene
CAPTAIN OF THE GUARD
DUBOIS,* servant to ALCESTE

*The setting is a room in Paris**

ACT I

SCENE 1

ALCESTE, PHILINTE

PHILINTE. Oh, what's the matter? What's wrong now?

ALCESTE.   Leave me alone.
  Go away.

PHILINTE.   But why must you adopt this angry tone?...

ALCESTE. Oh, leave me here, I said. Go, run away and hide.

PHILINTE. Alceste, don't lose your temper. Listen, then decide.

ALCESTE. I want to lose my temper, and to make a stand.

PHILINTE. I find your angry rantings hard to understand.
  Although we're still good friends, I really must insist...

ALCESTE. What? Me, your friend? Why don't you cross me off your
      list?
  It's true I've always made a show of liking you;
  But now I've witnessed your behaviour, we're through.   10
  I tell you, I don't want your friendship any more—
  I hate you, now I know you're rotten to the core.

PHILINTE. You seem to have decided I'm the one to blame...

ALCESTE. That's right. Why don't you crawl away and die of
      shame?
  I'm telling you, there's no excuse for what you've done—
  Your antics must seem scandalous to everyone.
  You met a man, you treated him as your best friend,
  You were all over him, you hugged him without end,*
  You said he mattered to you, swore by Heaven above
  That what you felt for him was liking, even love.   20
  I asked you for the fellow's name, when he had gone,
  And you scarcely remembered who he was—come on!
  No sooner had he turned his back on you, I swear,

You spoke of him to me, as if you didn't care.
Good grief! The way you carry on is a disgrace.
You worthless coward, must you really be so base?
If I had done what you've just done, do you know what
I'd do? I'd go and hang myself, right on the spot.

PHILINTE. Come on, it's not a hanging matter, so don't tease.
I beg leave to appeal against my sentence, please.   30
It's time you showed some mercy. Don't be quite so hard.
What, make me hang myself for that? What a charade!

ALCESTE. Oh, very funny! That was typical of you.

PHILINTE. But, seriously, what am I supposed to do?

ALCESTE. You should be honourable, honest, without art,
And everything you say should come straight from the heart.

PHILINTE. But when a stranger rushes up and hugs you tight,
You have to hug him back—it seems only polite;
You can't keep him at arm's length, you must play the game,
And if he swears you're his best friend, you do the same.   40

ALCESTE. No. Your hypocrisy disgusts me, and that's flat.
You fashionable types, you all behave like that.
I tell you, I can't stand the phoney posturing
Of men who claim they like you more than anything,
And fling their arms around you, kiss you on the cheek,
Insist that they adore you, every time they speak.
They've perfect manners, and they all obey the rules,
But decent men are treated on a par with fools.
Look, I mean, what's the point of someone kissing you,
And swearing he appreciates and loves you too,   50
Proclaiming to the world that you're the only one,
Then rushing off to do the same to everyone?
No. If a man who has the slightest self-respect
Is faced with such hypocrisy, he must object.
For very little's added to our sense of worth
If we're the same as all the others on this earth.
If you respect a man, believing he's the best,
Don't put him on an equal footing with the rest.
Now you're no different from the other fellows, so,

Damn it, you're not the sort of man I want to know.   60
I can't value a friend who puts himself about,
And doesn't see why merit should be singled out.
I want to be distinguished from the rest, you see:
The friend of all humanity's no friend to me.

PHILINTE. But, in polite society, you have to do
Your bit, or people won't think very well of you.

ALCESTE. Nonsense! I say, the time has come to make a stand
Against these hypocrites. I want them to be banned.
I want us to be proper men, and when we meet,
To show our secret, inner thoughts, without deceit.   70
We must speak from the heart, lay bare our sentiments,
Not hide the truth with empty, formal compliments.

PHILINTE. It won't work. There are times when total frankness
    would
Be idiotic, totally misunderstood.
And sometimes, even if we find it an ordeal,
It's better to suppress the truth of what we feel.
Truth can be inappropriate; most people shrink
From telling everyone precisely what they think.
What if we know someone we hate, or find uncouth—
Are we supposed to tell the whole, unvarnished truth?   80

ALCESTE. Yes.

PHILINTE.   What, you want to go to poor old Emilie,
And tell her she's too old to dress so prettily—
With all that make-up, she looks like a painted whore?

ALCESTE. That's right.

PHILINTE.   Should we tell Dorilas he's a great bore?
The courtiers hate the way he shows off endlessly,
And boasts about his courage, and his pedigree.

ALCESTE. We should.

PHILINTE.   You must be joking.

ALCESTE.   Joking? Not at all.
I tell you, we must spare nobody, great or small.

My eyes are never spared, at court or in the town:
I'm always having to see sights that make me frown.   90
It puts me in a rage, to see what I detest:
The way men treat each other makes me so depressed.
Hypocrisy is everywhere, and flattery,
And crude self-interest, and even treachery.
I've had enough. Mankind's an absolute disgrace.
I'll make a stand, alone against the human race.

PHILINTE. Your grim philosophy is too morose by half.
Your fits of black depression simply make me laugh.
It strikes me we resemble, in a curious way,
The brothers in *The School for Husbands*, Molière's play,*   100
Who...

ALCESTE.   Good God! Some comparison. Please, let that drop.

PHILINTE. Fine. Let's be serious. I'm asking you to stop
This madness. You won't change the world with what you do,
And since this frankness seems to have such charms for you,
I tell *you*, frankly, you've become so querulous,
That, nowadays, the world finds you ridiculous.
You turn your nose up, claim our modern manners shock,
But everyone around thinks you're a laughing stock.

ALCESTE. Well, good, damn it! Yes, good! I ask for nothing more.
I'm quite delighted, that's what I've been hoping for.   110
Since everyone I know seems hateful in my eyes,
I'd be disgusted, if they thought that I was wise.

PHILINTE. Why blame the human race? You're eaten up with hate.

ALCESTE. It overwhelms me totally—I'm desperate.

PHILINTE. You say you loathe us all, without exception, and
There's not a single human being you can stand?
Can't you imagine any situation when...?

ALCESTE. No. My disgust is general. I hate all men—
Hate some of them because they are an evil crew,
And others for condoning what the villains do,   120
Instead of treating them with loathing and contempt,
As they deserve. They might at least make an attempt*

To judge that fellow who's no better than he ought,
I mean the filthy beast who's taken me to court:
His wickedness shines out behind his bland façade,
And everybody knows his manner's a charade.
He sighs and rolls his eyes, and mouths his platitudes,
But no one's taken in, save idiots or prudes.
Confound him! He's got his flat foot in every door.*
He gets on in the world by dirty tricks, what's more.   130
He does so well, living off his ill-gotten gains,
Ironically, he's rewarded for his pains—
He has some sort of title, which he likes to use,
But all his posturing can't alter people's views.
Call him confounded liar, no one will object;
Say he's a fraud, and nobody will contradict.
Yet, with his smirking face, he gets himself received
In the best circles, though his hosts are not deceived.
He knows all the right people, so he always wins.
He beats his rivals, though he can't conceal his sins.*   140
Yes, curse him, every time! It cuts me to the quick
To see him get away with every dirty trick.
Sometimes, it overwhelms me. I feel mortified
By all mankind, and long to run away and hide.

PHILINTE. For heaven's sake, don't try to be responsible
For all society. It's quite impossible
To be so critical of humans as a whole—
You'd better tone it down, and show some self-control.
You must live in the world, you can't stay on the side,
And people wouldn't think you wiser if you tried.   150
A reasonable man shouldn't go to extremes:
Be sensible, and don't indulge your crazy dreams.
The stuffy moral code our ancestors display
Is scarcely suitable for how we live today.
And nowadays, perfection's not what we expect—
We try to fit in, and be worthy of respect.
I'm telling you, my friend, it's madness to inform
Us all we're in the wrong, and tell us to reform.
I'm like you: I can see a hundred things each day
That could be better done, if done a different way;   160

But though I may be shocked, I don't, at any stage,
Make such a fuss as you, explode in fits of rage.
I take things easy, let men work their problems through;
I teach myself to put up with the things they do.
At court and in the town, I never intervene:
My phlegm's more philosophical than all your spleen.*

ALCESTE. I know—you're so phlegmatic, Monsieur Reasoner—
No feelings ever move that bland exterior.
What if it happens that a friend is treacherous,
And tries his tricks on you because you're prosperous,   170
Or does his best to spread false rumours, dare I bet
You won't stand calmly by, you'll find you're quite upset?

PHILINTE. Look, I agree, our fellow men have their defects,
But I see them as natural, normal effects.
It doesn't seem the thing to do to take offence
At people's dirty tricks, just as it makes no sense
To criticize a flock of vultures, beaks agape,
A pack of angry wolves, or an aggressive ape.*

ALCESTE. So I'm to watch the fellow fleece me, bleed me white,
And let him get away with it?... I find that quite   180
Outrageous. What an attitude! You're so absurd!

PHILINTE. Look here, take my advice: don't say another word.
And don't keep ranting that the fellow's a disgrace,
But pay attention to preparing your court case.

ALCESTE. Prepare my case? Certainly not—don't make me laugh.

PHILINTE. Which lawyer have you briefed to plead on your behalf?

ALCESTE. Why, justice, fairness, human rights. And I won't budge.

PHILINTE. What? Don't you plan to go and call upon the judge?*

ALCESTE. Why should I? Is my cause in any way unjust?

PHILINTE. No, but the other party's doing it, you must   190
Keep up...

ALCESTE.   My mind's made up. I'm not a hypocrite.
I'm wrong or else I'm right.

PHILINTE.   I wouldn't bank on it.

ALCESTE. I will not budge.

PHILINTE.   But you've a powerful enemy:
  He'll use his influence to win...

ALCESTE.   What's that to me?

PHILINTE. You're making a mistake...

ALCESTE.   That's for me to decide

PHILINTE. But...

ALCESTE.   If I lose my case, I'll be most gratified.

PHILINTE. Look here...

ALCESTE.   When I hear what the verdict is, I'll know:
  I'll have the confirmation men can sink so low;
  I'll know that they can be so wicked and perverse,
  That they deny my rights, before the universe.   200

PHILINTE. Oh, what a man!

ALCESTE.   I say, forget about the cost.
  I want the truth. No matter, if my case is lost.

PHILINTE. Well, everyone would laugh, they'd say you were far
    gone,
  If they could only hear the way you carry on.

ALCESTE. Too bad.

PHILINTE.   You're quite a paragon of rectitude,
  And you expect us all to share your attitude.
  But if you're looking for behaviour to approve,
  Then do you find it in the woman that you love?
  It seems that you're at odds with all the human race.
  Yet I'm surprised to find, with that being the case,   210
  That though you find the rest of us quite odious,
  You're charmed by a mere human being—one of us,
  And, more amazing still, it seems you want to take
  A wife, and then we see the choice you plan to make.
  You could have Eliante, who thinks the world of you;

The prude Arsinoë's a liking for you, too.
But you're not in the least attracted, and, instead,
Apparently, young Celimene has turned your head.
Yet she's a little flirt, and has a spiteful tongue:
In that, she's typical of all our modern young.   220
You hate the current trends, so how is it you let
This pretty girl enchant you? Don't you feel regret?
And does the fact she's charming mean you won't condemn
Her faults? Do you forgive them? Don't you notice them?

ALCESTE. No. This young widow charms me, makes me lose my
      mind,
   But I can see she has defects, for I'm not blind.
   Although I love her madly, yet I'm still the first
   To point them out, and try correcting what is worst.
   It's true I see that she's got faults; but, I confess,
   Although I criticize, they couldn't matter less.   230
   I'm weak as water with her. All that I can do,
   Is go on loving her. I'm sorry, but it's true.
   She charms me so, I can't resist—it's very strange—
   Let's hope my love can educate her, make her change.

PHILINTE. If you can work that miracle, hats off to you!
   But do you think she loves you?

ALCESTE.   Yes, indeed I do.
   Unless I thought she loved me back, I wouldn't care.

PHILINTE. But if she loves you, as you say, then why despair,
   If other young men come to call, and flirt with her?

ALCESTE. You know that when a man's in love, he'll much   240
      prefer
   To keep his mistress to himself. Right now, I plan*
   To tell her what I think, persuade her, if I can.

PHILINTE. Hmmm. For my part, if I could ever have the choice,
   Her cousin Eliante would always have my voice;
   But she admires *you*, and her feelings are sincere.
   She'd make a far, far better wife for you, I fear.

ALCESTE. That's true. My reason tells me, every day, it's so.
 But love is never ruled by reason, as you know.

PHILINTE. The whole thing makes me apprehensive. You're about
 To suffer...   250

SCENE 2

ORONTE, ALCESTE, PHILINTE

ORONTE.   Eliante and Celimene are out:
 The two of them are on a shopping trip, I hear.
 But when the servants told me you were waiting here,
 I came upstairs, to say—I mean it, now, it's true—
 That I respect you, most tremendously—I do.
 What's more, I've felt this way for ages. I intend
 To ask you: will you honour me, and be my friend?
 I know you're worthy of my friendship, I can tell.
 I long to for us to know each other really well.

        [ALCESTE *appears distracted, and seems not to hear*

 This isn't something to be sniffed at, I believe—
 The friendship of a well-bred man. Sir, by your leave,   260
 It's you that I've been talking to, if you don't mind.

ALCESTE. What, me, Monsieur?

ORONTE.   Yes, you, Monsieur. Is that a bind?

ALCESTE. No, Monsieur, but this comes as a complete surprise.
 I never asked for this. I didn't realize—

ORONTE. You shouldn't be surprised if I respect you so,
 For everyone admires your qualities, you know.

ALCESTE. Monsieur...

ORONTE.   I've yet to find your equal on this earth,
 A man who comes within a mile of what you're worth.

ALCESTE. Monsieur...

ORONTE.   Yes, I admit, I like you better than
 The most distinguished chaps I know, and you're my man.   270

ALCESTE. Monsieur...

ORONTE.   I mean it. Cross my heart, and hope to die!
Look here, to show you that I'm really serious, I
Would like to put my arms around you, if I may.
Well, do you think we can be friends, starting today?
Your hand, Sir, if you please. Now, do you promise me
Your friendship?

ALCESTE.   Monsieur...

ORONTE.   Oh, what's this? You don't agree?

ALCESTE. Monsieur, you honour me far more than I deserve;
But friendship really needs a little more reserve.
If we call everyone our friend, then we profane
The concept, and we take the name of 'friend' in vain.   280
A friendship can't be rushed or forced: it has to grow
At its own pace, and it won't prosper till we know
Each other. Things might not work out—it all depends.
If we don't suit, we might regret becoming friends.

ORONTE. By Jove! You don't find wisdom like that every day,
And I respect you even more for what you say.
So let's, by all means, take our time, if you prefer—
But, in the meantime, I am at your service, Sir,
And if, when you're at court, you need an opening,
Just come to me. I'm quite in favour with the King: 290
He always listens to the tales I have to tell,
And, damn it, Sir, he always treats me very well.
In short, Sir, I'm your man, and you can count on me;
And since I know you're wise and very scholarly,
I'd like to start the friendship we two have proposed
By reading you a sonnet that I've just composed.
I'd like your views—is it worth publishing, or not?

ALCESTE. Monsieur, don't ask me that—you may find that you've
    got
The wrong man.

ORONTE.   Why?

ALCESTE.   Because I tend to be uncouth—
I have an awful way of blurting out the truth.   300

ORONTE. But that's just what I want. I'm hoping you won't shrink
From making sure you say exactly what you think.
If you deceived me, I would feel I'd been betrayed.

ALCESTE. Oh, very well, if you're quite sure you're not afraid.

ORONTE. Hem! *Sonnet*—it's a sonnet. *Hope*—it was inspired
By someone who encouraged me, whom I admired.
Hope... Don't expect my verse to be great poetry:
It's intimate and tender, verbal coquetry.

> [*At every interruption, he looks at* ALCESTE

ALCESTE. Well, Sir, we'll soon see.

ORONTE.   *Hope*—I don't know if the style
Will strike you as convincing, clear, and versatile,   310
And if you think the language has a pleasing flow.

ALCESTE. Monsieur, I said we'll see.

ORONTE.   I think you ought to know
I dashed the whole thing off in less than half an hour.

ALCESTE. A piece that's dashed off rapidly can still have power.

ORONTE [*reads*].
> *Hope, it is true, alleviates our woe,*
> *And helps us for a moment to endure.*
> *But, Phyllis, this advantage brings us low,*
> *If nothing further comes to bring a cure.*

PHILINTE. I'm charmed already—that was such a brilliant start!

ALCESTE [*aside, to* PHILINTE]. Oh, what? You find that rubbish   320
good? You call that art?

ORONTE. *You showed me understanding, were so kind;*
> *But you allowed your goodness too much scope.*
> *To kindness you should have been less inclined,*
> *Since all you had to offer me was hope.*

PHILINTE. That's good! Your ideas are so eloquently framed!

ALCESTE [*aside, to* PHILINTE]. God damn it! What a hypocrite!
    Aren't you ashamed?

ORONTE.   *If I must wait for you eternally,*
            I won't hold out against my misery:
            By dying I will show you how I care.
            You won't keep me from death by being kind: 330
            Oh, Phyllis, we grow hopeless when we find
            That hope prolonged just turns into despair.*

PHILINTE. That ending! Brilliant! Romantic, yet so clear!

ALCESTE [*aside, to* PHILINTE]. I'll put an end to you, you devil, do
    you hear?*
    I wish you'd ended on your face, or even worse.

PHILINTE. I've never come across such well-constructed verse.

ALCESTE [*aside, to* PHILINTE]. Blast you!

ORONTE [*to* PHILINTE].   You're much too
    flattering, and my poor pen...

PHILINTE. No, I'm not flattering.

ALCESTE [*aside, to* PHILINTE].   What are you doing, then?

ORONTE [*to* ALCESTE]. But you, Monsieur, you know the bargain
    that we've made,
    So tell me what you think, straight out, don't be afraid.   340

ALCESTE. Monsieur, it's tricky criticizing, I admit—
    We like to be admired for our amazing wit.
    But someone I once knew, and I'll not tell you who,
    Was showing me his verse, and asking me my view.
    I said, a decent man should struggle to control
    The urge to write in verse, and bare his inner soul.
    I said that poems of this sort are frivolous,
    Their authors shouldn't try to show them off to us—
    The people who're most desperate to do just that
    Will end up looking pretty stupid, and that's flat.   350

ORONTE. In your opinion, then, my poetry's perverse?
    That's that?

ALCESTE.   That isn't what I said; it was his verse,
    Not yours. I told the fellow, poetry's a bore,
    It makes a man look stupid, when he holds the floor.
    However well you write the stuff, men are unkind:
    Most people judge you by your follies, as you'll find.

ORONTE. Make yourself clear. You say, you think my sonnet's trite?

ALCESTE. That isn't what I said. I told him not to write,
    I tried to make him see that, in this day and age,
    You shouldn't do things, just because they're all the rage.   360

ORONTE. You think I can't write? Am I like those other men?

ALCESTE. That isn't what I said. But what I told him, then,
    Was this: 'Why do you feel the need to write in rhyme?
    And why insist on publication, all the time?
    There's one excuse for writing rubbish. I'll forgive
    A man who needs the money, publishes to live.
    Believe me, do resist temptation, and don't try
    To show off your creation in the public eye.
    You've got a decent reputation at the court.
    Don't seek a reputation of another sort,   370
    And let your greedy publisher persuade you to
    Expose yourself to mockery with your debut.'*
    That's what I tried to make this other fellow see.

ORONTE. You don't need to explain how that applies to me.
    But what's the difficulty with my sonnet, pray?

ALCESTE. Quite frankly, you'd much better throw the thing away.*
    You took your inspiration from a doubtful source;
    The whole effect is artificial, and lacks force.
    What do you mean by *Hope alleviates our woe*?
    Or by the line *allowed your goodness too much scope*?   380
    Or by *I won't hold out against my misery*?
    Or by *You won't keep me from death, by being kind*?
    Or by *Oh, Phyllis, we grow hopeless, when we find
        That hope prolonged just turns into despair*?
    The precious way you write is popular, it's true,
    But, frankly, it's contrived, and unconvincing too.
    It's full of clever puns, elaborate word-play,

It's much too far removed from what real people say.*
Our literary scene is thoroughly debased.
Although our ancestors were crude, they had good taste,   390
And I would give up all your modern artifice
For one old-fashioned song, which goes something like this:

> *If the King had sold me cheap*
> *His great town of Paree,*
> *But I was not allowed to keep*
> *My darling there with me,*
> *I'd say to King Henri:*
> *'Take back your great Paree.*
> *For I would rather sleep,*
> *And my own dear with me.'*   400

The rhymes are rather brash, the style is out of date,
But, can't you see, that simple love song is first-rate,
Compared with all those trivial poems that make no sense?
In my example, the emotions are intense:

> *If the King had sold me cheap*
> *His great town of Paree,*
> *But I was not allowed to keep*
> *My darling there with me,*
> *I'd say to King Henri:*
> *'Take back your great Paree.*   410
> *For I would rather sleep,*
> *And my own dear with me.'*

Those really are a lover's words, they show he cares.

[*To* PHILINTE

Yes, you may laugh, and writers give themselves false airs,
But I've got more respect for honest, plain desire,
Than polished platitudes, for people to admire.

ORONTE. I'll have you know, I think my sonnet's very good.

ALCESTE. I'm sure you think so—it's quite normal that you
    should—
But I can have my own opinions, if I choose,
I don't feel I'm obliged to fit in with your views.   420

ORONTE. Well, many other people liked it quite a lot.

ALCESTE. Yes, that's because they're hypocrites, which I am not.

ORONTE. You think you're clever, yet you criticize my style.

ALCESTE. Not bright enough to find your poetry worthwhile.

ORONTE. Leave your opinions out—they couldn't matter less.

ALCESTE. That's just as well, I've no opinions to express.

ORONTE. You ought to try your hand at poetry, so why
Not have a go yourself? I'd like to see you try.

ALCESTE. My verses might be bad, like yours, that could well be:
But I'd be careful other people didn't see.   430

ORONTE. This is outrageous. I resent that nasty taunt.

ALCESTE. Don't come to me, then, if it's compliments you want.

ORONTE. Hey, there, my little man, don't take that tone with me.

ALCESTE. I'll take the tone I like, you don't have to agree.

PHILINTE [*placing himself between them*]. Messieurs, that's quite
enough—it's time for a reprieve.

ORONTE. You're right, and I was wrong; I think I'd better leave.
With all my heart, your most obedient servant, Sir.

ALCESTE. And I, too, am your humble servitor, Monsieur.

SCENE 3

ALCESTE, PHILINTE

PHILINTE. Look, can't you see you've been a good deal too sincere?
You've made things very awkward for yourself, I fear.   440
Oronte just wanted flattering, you should have known.

ALCESTE. Oh, go away!

PHILINTE.   But why?...

ALCESTE.   I want to be alone.

PHILINTE. It's too much!...

ALCESTE.   Oh, shut up!

PHILINTE.   I...

ALCESTE.   I don't want to hear!

PHILINTE. But what...?

ALCESTE.   Be quiet!

PHILINTE.   But...

ALCESTE.   Still going on?

PHILINTE.   Look here...

ALCESTE. Good grief! I'm off. Don't follow me. I've had enough.

PHILINTE. I'm coming too. You can't just go off in a huff.

ACT II

SCENE 1

ALCESTE. Madame, if you don't mind, I'd like to make things plain:
It's your behaviour—this time, I must complain.
I'm miserable—oh, it makes me sick at heart
To realize the two of us will have to part.   450
I can't pretend to you, it's time that I spoke out:
Yes, soon we'll have to break it off, I'm in no doubt.
Though I might swear to you I'd do the opposite,
I still would have to leave: I just can't cope with it.

CELIMENE. Aha! So you've come here to make a scene? I see.
Is that why you decided you'd come home with me?

ALCESTE. I'm not making a scene; but I detest the way
You open up your heart to every protégé.
The truth is, you've attracted far too many men,
I can't cope with this happening, time and again.   460

CELIMENE. Is it my fault if people fall in love with me?
Am I responsible? It's not that I agree
To welcome them: they come, and then try every trick.
Must I jump up and chase them, brandishing a stick?

ALCESTE. I'm not expecting you to grab a stick, and fling
Them out, but must you be quite so long-suffering?
I know you're most attractive, but it's more than that:
Young men are always free to come in for a chat,
Then you encourage them to fall in love with you,
And make sure they are well entangled, when they do.   470
You make them live in hope, and you've acquired the knack
Of getting them involved, so they keep coming back.
If you insisted liberties were not allowed,
Your suitors wouldn't gather round in such a crowd.
But, at the very least, I wish you'd let me know

How young Clitandre ever gets to please you so?
Is it his qualities that make him reign supreme?
Is that why you have honoured him with your esteem?
Is it the fact that he's got one long fingernail*
That makes him such a catch, his charms can never fail?   480
Are you impressed by his prestige, that idle sprig,
And totally won over by his fine blonde wig?
Or do you love him for his legs, all frilled with lace?*
Or is it all those ribbons he shows off with grace?
Is it the ample breeches that he wears, that gave
You cause to love a man who claimed to be your slave?
Or can it be his laugh, and high falsetto voice,
That won your heart, made him the lover of your choice?

CELIMENE. You shouldn't take offence at him—it's most unfair.
You know perfectly well why I must take such care   490
To humour him. My case comes up soon; he intends
To help me out, and plead my cause with all his friends.

ALCESTE. Well, lose your court case, then, and show you can be
       strong.
I find the man offensive—don't string him along.

CELIMENE. You're growing jealous of the entire universe.

ALCESTE. The universe pays court to you, it's too perverse.

CELIMENE. You should try to relax: I'm never going to fall
For any of them—I'm obliging to them all.
It would look bad, and you'd be quite right to condemn
Me, if I set my heart on any one of them.   500

ALCESTE. You say that I'm a lot too jealous. Tell me, what
Advantages do I have, that the rest have not?

CELIMENE. The joy of being sure that I'm in love with you.

ALCESTE. I feel so anxious—how can I believe it's true?

CELIMENE. Well since I've told you so, and I'm not one to bluff,
I think that my confession should be quite enough.

ALCESTE. But how am I to know? The truth may be that, when
You say you love me, you're two-timing other men...

CELIMENE. Oh, charming! You're some lover. What a compliment!
    You trust me absolutely. That's quite excellent!   510
    Well, then, to calm you down, and spare you all your dread,
    I take back everything I ever might have said,
    And you'll be free to make your own mind up—I trust
    That suits you better.

ALCESTE.   Damn it, this is hell. Why must
    I go on loving you? If I could only cease,
    I'd thank the Lord: at least I would have found some peace.
    I can't deny the facts: I've done my level best
    To break this strong attachment, rooted in my breast.
    I've had no luck with it, however hard I try:
    I'm being punished through my love for you, that's why.   520

CELIMENE. Your love for me is very powerful, it's true.

ALCESTE. Yes, I defy the world to match my love for you.
    My passion's carried me away—I can't define
    My feelings—no, I've never known a love like mine.

CELIMENE. The way you choose to show your love is very new:
    You make a point of arguing with what I do.
    The feelings you express are more like enmity,
    I think *I've* never known a love so crotchety.

ALCESTE. Well, you can easily win my approval back.
    Let's stop our arguments, we don't need to attack   530
    Each other, but let's talk instead, and try to win...

SCENE 2

ALCESTE, CELIMENE, BASQUE

CELIMENE. Well, what is it?

BASQUE.   Acaste's downstairs.

CELIMENE.   Then show him in.

ALCESTE. What? Can't we ever have a private tête-à-tête?
    Eh? Have you ever shown the door to someone yet?

Is it impossible to get you to announce
You're not at home to any callers, just this once?

CELIMENE. You want me to offend Acaste? He might complain.

ALCESTE. Oh, spare his feelings, then—it's driving me insane!

CELIMENE. I tell you, he's the type who might make open war
If he believed I found his visits here a bore.   540

ALCESTE. So what? Let him be vexed with you, what do you care?

CELIMENE. I've told you that I need him, that remark's not fair.
I don't know how they do it, but it's true, his sort
Are able to control what happens at the court.
When there's a royal audience, they hang about.
They can spoil things for you, if they won't help you out.
They can destroy your reputation on a whim:
Don't get on the wrong side of chatterers like him!

ALCESTE. Though your excuses may perhaps be genuine,
The fact is, you're prepared to let the whole world in.   550
I tell you that the way you're going, you'll soon be...

SCENE 3

ALCESTE, CELIMENE, BASQUE

BASQUE. Clitandre's here as well, Madame.

ALCESTE [*preparing to exit*].   There, now! You see?

CELIMENE. What? Are you rushing off?

ALCESTE.   I'm leaving.

CELIMENE.   Stay!

ALCESTE.   What for?

CELIMENE. Just stay.

ALCESTE.   I can't.

CELIMENE.   I want you to.

ALCESTE.   No. I'll withdraw.
Their conversation always seems so tedious—
So I'll not stick around and be obsequious.

CELIMENE. I want you to, I want you to.

ALCESTE.   Impossible.

CELIMENE. All right, then, go, don't think you're indispensable.

SCENE 4

ALCESTE, CELIMENE, ELIANTE, PHILINTE, ACASTE, CLITANDRE, BASQUE

ELIANTE [*to* CELIMENE]. The two marquis are here—in fact,
    they're on the stairs.*
Were they announced?   560

CELIMENE.   Oh, yes.

                                        [*To* BASQUE

        Run off and fetch some chairs.

                            [BASQUE *provides chairs, and exits*
                                        [*To* ALCESTE

    Oh, so you've not gone yet?

ALCESTE.   No, Madame, as you see.
    I want you to decide now: is it them, or me?

CELIMENE. Oh, do be quiet!

ALCESTE.   Today, I want you to confide...

CELIMENE. Have you gone mad?

ALCESTE.   No, but I want you to decide.

CELIMENE. Huh!

ALCESTE.   Quick, make up your mind.

CELIMENE.   Not me, I'll call your bluff!

ALCESTE. I really mean it. I've been waiting long enough.

CLITANDRE. I say! I've just come from attending the levée—
Cleonte was being too ridiculous today.
His manners are appalling. Should a caring friend
Try telling him that his behaviour's the end?   570

CELIMENE. In company, he swaggers, and he plays a part.
He's desperate to seem impressive, from the start.
If you don't see him for a while, then meet him, you'll
Agree he strikes you as a show-off, and a fool.

ACASTE. Gad! Talking of eccentrics, Ma'am, I've only just
Escaped from someone who is, frankly, dry as dust.
Damon, that prosy bore, who firmly buttonholed
Me by my sedan chair, and wouldn't leave his hold.

CELIMENE. It's odd how he's become a master of the art
Of droning on, when he's got nothing to impart.   580
The things he says are utter rubbish, as I've found,
And if you're there as well, *you'll* find they're empty sound.

ELIANTE [*to* PHILINTE]. Malicious gossip is to be today's concern:
The conversation's taking quite a lively turn.

CLITANDRE. Timante, Madame, seems like a decent chap to me.

CELIMENE. From head to toe, the man's a walking mystery.
He rushes past, and nods distractedly at you:
He's always busy, though there's nothing much to do.
He pulls the oddest faces that you ever saw;
He always makes a fuss—he's the most frightful bore.   590
He interrupts you, tries to whisper in your ear,
But all his secrets are a waste of time to hear.
A triviality will set him all aglow—
He even makes a point of whispering 'hello'.*

ACASTE. And what about Geralde?

CELIMENE.   Oh, isn't he a bore!
His grand connections—everyone from the top drawer!
He can't say anything without dropping great names:
Those dukes, princes, princesses—friends, or so he claims.

He's a colossal snob—the way he always hogs
The conversation with his horses, hunting, dogs.   600
The man's on first-name terms with every *grand seigneur*—
He knows them far too well to call them mere 'Monsieur'.

CLITANDRE. He knows Belise—I gather they're good friends all
    right.

CELIMENE. That dreary woman never fails to cast a blight.
    Whenever she turns up, I suffer agonies,
    And talking to her always brings me to my knees.
    Those dull remarks, that she occasionally drops
    Into the conversation, which abruptly stops:
    You try to break the silence, wildly introduce
    The most banal clichés, but no, it's all no use—   610
    You try the weather, but you find there's nothing new
    To say, and other topics—soon exhausted too.
    It's ghastly from the start, you wish that she'd be gone,
    Instead, she makes things worse by staying, on and on.
    You yawn, and ask what time it is, but it's no good:
    She goes on sitting there, like a dead log of wood.

ACASTE. What's your opinion of Adraste?

CELIMENE.   What arrogance!
    The gentleman's obsessed with his own brilliance.
    He doesn't feel appreciated by the court,
    And endlessly complains he lacks its full support.   620
    Another man's appointment fills him with despair—
    He should have had the job, it simply isn't fair.

CLITANDRE. I've noticed young Cleon is always in the swim,
    With heaps of visitors: what do you think of him?

CELIMENE. That people visit him because they like his cook,
    And it's his dining-room attracts them, in my book.

ELIANTE. It's true he serves up many a delicious dish.

CELIMENE. He shouldn't serve himself up then, that's what I wish.
    The man's a stodgy dish, he's indigestible—
    It makes his dinner parties quite detestable.   630

PHILINTE. Most people seem to like his uncle, old Damis.
   What do you say, Madame?

CELIMENE.   That he's good friends with me.

PHILINTE. He seems a decent sort—that's how he comes across.

CELIMENE. Yes, but he's clever-clever: that's what makes me cross.
   With every word he speaks, he's striving for effect;
   He works away at polishing his intellect.
   He wants his powers of thought to seem formidable;
   His standards are so high it's quite unbearable.
   He's the new arbiter of literary taste
   (Or so he thinks), and all our writers are debased.   640
   He won't admire them, for they make him want to choke:
   Only an idiot appreciates a joke.
   In fact, he thinks he's showing he's superior
   By claiming all our writers are inferior,
   And starting to attack what other people say:
   Their conversation is too vulgar, too risqué.
   He folds his arms in pity at our hopeless plight,
   And looks down on us all, from his exalted height.

ACASTE [to CELIMENE]. I say, God damn it, what a portrait! It's all
   true.

CLITANDRE. You paint them all from life, and no one matches   650
   you.

ALCESTE. Oh, very good, my friends, great work, please carry on,
   Give everyone his due, and don't spare anyone—
   Until one of your victims chances to appear.
   Then you come forward with an artificial leer,
   And shake his hand, and even kiss him on the cheek,
   Say you're his humble servant—I know your technique!

CLITANDRE. Well, what of it? If you believe we're doing harm,
   You shouldn't pick on us: your culprit is Madame.

ALCESTE. Damn it, you egg her on, and so it's all your fault.
   Why must you laugh each time she launches an assault?   660
   You flatter her until her mind is so inflamed
   She gets carried away. You ought to be ashamed.

She'd find her spiteful gossip wasn't quite such fun
If she wasn't admired, and praised by everyone.
I tell you, human vice is reprehensible,
And it's the flatterers that are responsible.

PHILINTE. Why are you on the side of all these people, since
You've said yourself that their behaviour makes you wince?

CELIMENE. The point is, Monsieur simply has to contradict.
Now, would we want to see him be a bit less strict?   670
If he tried to behave, things wouldn't be the same.
That's why he carries on, and plays the same old game.
What others think can never weigh with him one bit,
His attitude is always quite the opposite.
He'd see himself as dull and commonplace indeed
If he found that his fellow men and he agreed.
He so loves arguing, his feelings are so strong,
He even claims his own opinions are all wrong;
And he'll reject whatever other people say,
Although he's said the same himself, that very day.   680

ALCESTE. That's right, have a good laugh. Don't come to my
    defence:
You're free to go on making jokes at my expense.

PHILINTE. Yes, but you ask for it—and that's the price you pay
For taking such offence at everything we say.
You're so contrary, you admit it without shame:
You can't bear us to give you either praise or blame.

ALCESTE. Yes, blast you, that's because the lot of you are wrong:
That's why I take offence, and pitch the thing so strong.
At every turn, I find my fellow men perverse:
They heap up praise and blame—I don't know which is   690
    worse.

CELIMENE. But listen...

ALCESTE.   No, I won't. I know I've earned my fate,
But I won't let you talk this way, I tell you straight.
I'm horrified at how this company exalts
Your tendency to make a joke of people's faults.

CLITANDRE. Oh, gosh, Monsieur! I say! I know I'm not too bright,
     But till today, I thought Madame was always right.

ACASTE. Her looks and character are worthy of applause—
     She's not remarkable for her atrocious flaws.

ALCESTE. Oh, she has many faults. I know them all. No doubt,
     She understands it's right for me to point them out.   700
     The more you are in love, the less you are prepared
     To spare your lover—*you*'d confront her if you cared.
     It's time she learnt to banish men who humour her,
     And give in to her weakly, seeming to prefer
     Her when she's at her worst. They let her get away
     With wild extravagance, and have it all her way.

CELIMENE. Is this what you advise? I think I've got it right:
     If we're in love, we needn't try to be polite;
     We can adopt a less respectful attitude,
     And show how much we care by being very rude.   710

ELIANTE. But if you listen to the average lover's voice,
     You'll find that he'll be keen to boast about his choice.
     The woman that he loves is irreproachable,
     And everything about her's truly lovable.
     Defects become perfections, so he feels no shame
     At weaknesses, but gives them quite another name.
     A pasty girl's as like white jasmine as you'll get;
     A swarthy one is an adorable brunette.
     A skinny girl has verve and spontaneity;
     A plump one is majestic, moves with dignity;   720
     A scruffy one neglects herself, and lacks appeal—
     He thinks her beauty's natural, and much more real.
     A giantess is like a goddess, that's his claim;
     A dwarf embodies Heaven's delights in her small frame.
     A girl who's arrogant deserves a crown, he'll find.
     A sly one's brilliant, a fool is sweet and kind;
     A chatterer is always in a merry mood;
     A tongue-tied girl has such a tactful attitude.
     A man who truly falls in love, always adores
     His girl, both her good points, and her most blatant flaws.*   730

ALCESTE. Well, let me tell you, I insist...

CELIMENE.   Oh, don't let's talk.
Let's go into the gallery, and have a walk.
Oh, are you leaving?

ACASTE and CLITANDRE.   No, we've nothing else to do.

ALCESTE. The thought that they might soon be going bothers you.
You may go if you want, but me, I'm staying on,
And I won't budge from here till after you've both gone.

ACASTE. Unless Madame would rather that I went away,
I don't have to rush off—I've nothing on today.

CLITANDRE. I've got an evening duty to perform at court,*
But up till then Madame can count on my support.   740

CELIMENE. You're joking, I assume.

ALCESTE.   No, no, I quite agree:
Let's see, whom will you send off first—those two, or me?

SCENE 5

ALCESTE, CELIMENE, BASQUE, ELIANTE, ACASTE, PHILINTE, CLITANDRE

BASQUE [to ALCESTE]. Monsieur, a man's downstairs, waiting
impatiently:
He says he needs to see you, very urgently.

ALCESTE. What? This is news to me—is this some knavery?

BASQUE. He's wearing a smart coat—some kind of livery—*
It's covered in gold braid.

CELIMENE.   Just go and find out what
He wants, or show him in.

ALCESTE.   Come in. What have you got
To say, Monsieur?

SCENE 6

ALCESTE, CELIMENE, ELIANTE, ACASTE, PHILINTE, CLITANDRE,
THE CAPTAIN OF THE GUARD

THE CAPTAIN OF THE GUARD.   I'd like a brief word in your ear.

ALCESTE. You can say it out loud—I've got no secrets here.   750

THE CAPTAIN OF THE GUARD. I serve the Marshals as their captain
of the guard.*
Monsieur, come with me now, you may not disregard
This summons.

ALCESTE.   Me, Monsieur?

THE CAPTAIN OF THE GUARD.   That's right.

ALCESTE.   What do they want?

PHILINTE. It must be all that silly business with Oronte.

CELIMENE [to PHILINTE]. What's this?

PHILINTE.   Well, yes, the two of them have fallen out
About some verses on whose merit he cast doubt.
They want to patch things up, before they go too far.

ALCESTE. I'm not going to admit that I've made a *faux pas*.

PHILINTE. You must obey the summons, and it's best if you...

ALCESTE. How can they think it right to reconcile us two?   760
What will their judgement be? D'you think they can coerce
Me to say I approve of his atrocious verse?
I won't back down, and my opinion's still the same:
I say his poem's bad.

PHILINTE.   You'd better not inflame...

ALCESTE. His verse is execrable: I won't change my mind.

PHILINTE. You'll have to be accommodating, as you'll find.
Come on, let's go.

ALCESTE.   All right, I'll come. No need to shout.
  I won't give in, though.

PHILINTE.   We must try to sort this out.

ALCESTE. Unless His Majesty insists that I be found,
  And orders me to make a total turn-around,   770
  I'll still insist the fellow writes appalling verse,
  And he deserves to hang: his poem couldn't be worse.*

          [*To* ACASTE *and* CLITANDRE, *who are laughing*

  Oh, damn you, Sirs! I didn't know that I was such
  A laughing-stock.*

CELIMENE.   This situation is too much!
  Go quickly, sort it out.

ALCESTE.   It's most inopportune,
  Madame, but it won't take me long: I'll be back soon.

ACT III

SCENE 1

CLITANDRE. My dear Marquis, you're looking positively smug:
　　You laugh at life, dismiss your troubles with a shrug.
　　Be honest with me: do you think you've got it right?
　　Are you contented, is the future looking bright?　　　780

ACASTE. Oh, Lord! You want an honest answer? If I'm pressed,
　　I must admit that I've no cause to feel depressed.
　　I'm rich, I'm handsome, I'm a chip off the old block
　　(I can't deny the facts: I come from first-class stock).
　　In high society, I'm known as a good sort:
　　I do the right thing, I'm a good chap, and a sport.
　　To be a coward isn't done, and I admit
　　I'm foolhardy as anything, and proud of it.
　　I've fought a duel publicly; the whole world knows
　　How valiantly I brought the matter to a close.　　　790
　　I'm brainy too, you know, and ready to enthuse:
　　I never *read* new plays, but have decided views
　　On theatre. My passion is for novelty.
　　I sit in the best seats, and show my loyalty*
　　By leading the applause, and clapping the good bits,
　　And my support has carried all the latest hits.
　　I'm quite athletic; I've good manners, I look sleek,
　　My teeth are splendid, I've a jolly slim physique.*
　　In one thing I'm supreme, as all the chaps confess:
　　I beat the competition when it comes to dress.　　　800
　　I'm liked by all my friends, they find me quite the thing;
　　I'm popular with girls, a favourite with the King.
　　With all these fine advantages, my dear Marquis,
　　I'm right to feel content: I'm sure that you'll agree.

CLITANDRE. If you're so sociable, and anxious to impress,
　　Why waste your time round here, with no hope of success?

ACASTE. What, me? Deuce take it! Me? I'm not some kind of clown!
  Me, waste my time upon a girl who turns me down?
  I leave that to those fellows, with their dumb despair,
  Who dance attendance on a girl who doesn't care,   810
  And put up with her rudeness, hang about for years,
  And try to win her heart, with endless sighs and tears.
  They think that if they're always there, and keen to serve,
  They'll win the prize: the love they frankly don't deserve.
  That sort of thing's not done by gentlemen like me:
  I won't make all the running, in humility.
  A pretty girl's got qualities, I hear you say;
  But, damn it, I'm as good as she is, any day.
  She wants a man to keep her fully satisfied:
  It's not right if the effort's all on the one side.   820
  The point is not to show off your one-upmanship:
  It takes two to build up a good relationship.

CLITANDRE. I see. So your affair's progressing very well?

ACASTE. That's how it seems to me, as far as I can tell.

CLITANDRE. I'm sorry, but you've got it wrong, let me tell you:
  You're flattering yourself, and blinding yourself too.

ACASTE. I see. So I'm deluded. Blind as well, I hear.

CLITANDRE. But why do you believe you're making headway here?

ACASTE. Oh, I'm deluded.

CLITANDRE.   What makes you feel so secure?

ACASTE. I'm blind.   830

CLITANDRE.   D'you have real proof, old man? D'you know
  for sure?

ACASTE. I'm flattering myself.

CLITANDRE.   Has Celimene confessed,
  In secret, that she cares for you, more than the rest?

ACASTE. No, she's rejected me.

CLITANDRE.   Now, don't leave me in doubt.

ACASTE. I say she's turned me down.

CLITANDRE.   Do stop fooling about.
Tell me what tokens of her love you think you've won.

ACASTE. No, I'm not in the running, you're the lucky one:
The lady finds me horrible in every way.
I ought to go and hang myself, this very day.

CLITANDRE. We'd better sort this out, Marquis, and that's a fact.
Now, why don't we agree to make a mutual pact?   840
The moment one of us can get cast-iron proof
That Celimene prefers him, and she's not aloof,
The other one'll take the hint that's been implied,
Not stay to cramp his rival's style, but stand aside?

ACASTE. God damn it, what a good idea! Excellent plan!
Yes, I'm all for it. Count on me, for I'm your man.
But, hush!

SCENE 2

CELIMENE, ACASTE, CLITANDRE

CELIMENE.   Still here?

CLITANDRE.   We're waiting here, hoping for more.

CELIMENE. I say, I heard a carriage stop outside the door.
Do you know who it is?

CLITANDRE.   No.

SCENE 3

CELIMENE, ACASTE, CLITANDRE, BASQUE

BASQUE.   It's Arsinoë,
Madame. She's coming up.   850

CELIMENE.   What does she want to say?

BASQUE. She's in the hall, Madame, talking to Eliante.

CELIMENE. Oh, why's she turned up here? Whatever does she
  want?

ACASTE. Well, everybody says that she's a prude, you know,
  As holy as can be...

CELIMENE.   Yes, but it's all for show.
  She's worldly underneath, she uses all her skill
  To find herself a man—but never makes a kill.
  She's green with envy, and she casts a jealous eye
  On pretty girls, the ones who hardly need to try.
  She's stiff and arrogant, and always short of friends.
  She's very critical of all the latest trends.   860
  She lives an empty life, in dreary solitude,
  And tries to hide the truth, by acting like a prude.
  She's keen to save her honour, now her charms have paled,
  Insisting it's not right to triumph where she's failed.
  To get herself a man—that's what she'd like the best;
  In fact, the lady has a weakness for Alceste.
  She thinks his love for me is like some kind of slur,
  And she insists that I have stolen him from her.
  She finds it difficult to hide her jealousy—
  She can't control her angry outbursts properly.   870
  She's such an ass. I hope she gets what she deserves.
  The way she lectures, on and on, gets on my nerves,
  And...

SCENE 4

CELIMENE, ARSINOË

CELIMENE.   Marvellous to see you! What a nice surprise!
  Why haven't you been round? I can't believe my eyes!

ARSINOË. I've come because I want to give you some advice.

CELIMENE. Oh, goodness! I'm so happy! This is awfully nice!

            [*Exeunt* ACASTE *and* CLITANDRE, *laughing*

ARSINOË. Yes. Just as well they went away, it is indeed.

CELIMENE. Why don't you sit down, dear Madame?

ARSINOË.   No, there's no need,
Madame. When it comes to the things that matter, we
Can show each other what a true friend ought to be.   880
Since nothing can be more important in my view
Than decency and honour, I've come here to you
To tell you, as a friend, I'm worried for your sake,
And warn you that it seems your honour is at stake.
Some people I met yesterday, all most upright,
Began to talk of you, and were less than polite.
You make an exhibition of yourself, they say,
And, I'm afraid, they disapprove of your display.
The men that flock around your door in endless queues,
Your constant flirting, and the gossip that ensues,   890
Were criticized so strongly, it seemed quite unfair,
And judged so harshly, that I found it hard to bear.
You can imagine how I tried to do you good:
I took your part, defended you as best I could.
I said you meant no harm, they had to understand;
I tried to vouch for your good name, and make a stand.
But, you know how it is, sometimes it's all no use—
There are some things in life one simply can't excuse—
And in the end, I had no choice but to agree
With them that how you live's a little bit too free.   900
They say your reputation's suffering a knock,
They add that people talk about you, round the clock.
It's up to you to be a bit more moderate—
You'd give them less to talk about, at any rate.
Of course, I can't believe you don't do what you ought:
Ah! Heaven preserve me, dear, from having such a thought!
But folk are all too keen to swallow all that stuff,
And knowing that you're blameless isn't quite enough.
Madame, you're very reasonable, you'll receive
My warning in good part, and heed it, I believe.   910
I know you understand my motives, and I feel
A keen desire to serve you, with devoted zeal.

CELIMENE. Well, thanks, Madame, for warning me what people say.
It was too kind, and I won't take it the wrong way.

Instead, I'll do you the same for you, dear, in return:
Yes, I'll defend your honour, I'll be very stern.
You've been a good friend to me, I can clearly see—
You hear the gossip, and report it back to me.
You set a good example, but it's my turn now
To tell you how you strike your friends, if you'll allow.   920
The other day, as I was visiting somewhere,
I met some very worthy people gathered there.
They talked about the things that decent people do,
And then, Madame, the conversation turned to you.
They said you're so uptight, so prudish, and repressed,
You set a poor example: no one was impressed.
You always look so grim, respond so charmlessly,
You try to seem so wise, and drone on endlessly,
You shriek with horror at what's only harmless fun,
You sniff out innuendo, find it where there's none.   930
You think you're marvellous; you're full of arrogance,
You treat us all like dirt, and flaunt your insolence.
The way you snipe at us, your constant lectures, your
Attacks on things which should be innocent and pure,
In short, your whole behaviour, to tell the truth,
Was thoroughly condemned. They said that you're uncouth.
'So what's the point of being so superior
If she goes wild beneath that prim exterior?'
They said. 'She prays a lot, and at the right times, true,
But never pays her servants' wages, beats them too.   940
She goes to church all right, to show she's dutiful,
But paints her face, and struggles to look beautiful.
She claims that nudes in paintings are embarrassing,
And has them covered up, yet lusts for the real thing.'
I rushed to your defence, defying everyone,
And I maintained that their attack was overdone—
I couldn't get them to give in, couldn't compel
Them to agree. They said that it would be as well
For you to take less notice of what others do,
And concentrate a bit more carefully on you.   950
'Why don't you try some introspection, now and then,
Before you launch attacks upon your fellow men?
For criticizing people's actions always should

Be set against your own, or else they'll do no good',
They said. 'You'd do much better leaving all of that
To God's own ministers, and not give tit for tat.'
Madame, I know for sure you're much too sensible
To take offence—your faults are rectifiable.
You know that there's a secret movement of my heart
That spurs me on to help you out, and take your part.   960

ARSINOË. A person trying to do good must risk attack;
But even so, I never thought you'd answer back.
Your angry outburst's quite revealing. I observe
That my sincere advice has touched on a raw nerve.

CELIMENE. Oh, not at all, Madame. Why don't we both unite,
And make it the done thing to put each other right?
You know how people are: they never see their own
Shortcomings; these things can't be remedied, alone.
In good faith, we'd point out each fault, however small:
Our own faults couldn't blind us, no—we'd know them all.   970
We'd make a point of passing on the gossip, too—
You, everything you hear of me, and I, of you.

ARSINOË. No, no, Madame. Not you, you've got no cause for shame;
But in my heart of hearts, I know *I'm* much to blame.

CELIMENE. Things can look good or bad, Madame, it all depends.
An action sometimes seems quite right, sometimes offends.
It's fine to flirt a bit, as long as you're still young;
But when you're older, you'd much better hold your tongue.
A woman, when she's lost her youth and prettiness,
Can make her mind up to resort to priggishness—   980
If not, she may discover there's a price to pay.
I may decide to do the same as you one day;
But now, while I respect your prudent attitude,
At twenty, I've no need, Madame, to be a prude.

ARSINOË. You think you've got the upper hand? You go too far.
You make a song and dance about how young you are.
You've got a slight advantage as to age, I know,
But that's no reason to go on about it so.
I wonder why you're showing such aggressiveness,
And why on earth you need to sneer at me like this?   990

CELIMENE. You're not the only one: I'm quite taken aback
       At how you always get at me behind my back;
       But why blame me for all your problems, may I ask?
       If men neglect you now, must you take me to task?
       I may be lucky: I attract a lot of men,
       Who dance attendance on me daily: well, what then?
       You think they care for me, when they should care for you:
       You know it's not my fault, there's nothing I can do.
       The field's wide open, let's give every man his head.
       If you've got what it takes, make them love you instead.   1000

ARSINOË. Well, really! Do you think I care about that host
       Of lovers—hundreds of them, is it? You can boast,
       But, let me tell you, lots of people realize
       Precisely why young men come buzzing round, like flies.
       You think we all believe there's any likelihood
       The men all cluster round, because you're sweet and good?
       So they admire you, do they, place you on a throne,
       And worship you, because of your high moral tone?
       Some men may fancy you instead of me. So what?
       We all know what that means. A girl who hasn't got   1010
       Your reputation can be sweet as anything,
       And not have endless lovers dangling on a string.
       The explanation's clear—deny it if you can—
       If you don't make advances, you won't get a man.
       Men won't worship the ground you walk on from afar.
       They all want something back, that's just the way they are.
       So don't show off, and think it's satisfactory
       To boast of your pathetic little victory.
       Your beauty isn't really so superior;
       You've no call to look down—I'm not inferior.   1020
       If I were jealous of the hearts you say you've won,
       I'd play the game like you, and join in all the fun.
       A woman can make conquests, if she chooses to:
       If I let myself go, I could have lovers too.

CELIMENE. Well, have them then, Madame, and take their hearts by
           storm.
       You've got the secret: let's all see how you perform.
       Don't wait...

ARSINOË.   Oh, this is not a fight, so don't let's spar.
    Let's break off right away, before we go too far.
    I should have gone by now, it's getting very late:
    My carriage hasn't come, that's why I've got to wait.   1030

CELIMENE. Well, make yourself at home, Madame, please, stay on
        here.
    I won't show you the door, so you need have no fear.
    But I won't stand on ceremony, as you see:
    I'm going to leave you in much better company,
    For here's Monsieur now. Isn't that a lucky chance?
    He'll entertain you well—I say that in advance.
    Alceste, I'm sorry, there's a letter I must write.
    If I don't do it now, I'll seem most impolite.
    Will you stay with Madame? That would be very kind.
    I'm sorry if I'm rude—I do hope she won't mind.   1040

SCENE 5

ARSINOË, ALCESTE

ARSINOË. You see, she wants you to stay talking to me here,
    Until my carriage comes—so, will you volunteer?
    I must say that there's nothing she and I could do
    That I'd enjoy as much as talking here with you—
    For you're the kind of man whose merit is supreme,
    You're well respected, and you're held in high esteem;
    Then, in addition, you've your own *je ne sais quoi*,
    Which makes me want to share your thoughts, be where you are.
    I wish that you were better valued at the court.
    They should appreciate you better, yes, they ought!   1050
    I think you should complain—it makes me want to groan
    To see the way you're left to cope, all on your own.

ALCESTE. But why should I complain, Madame? I tell you straight
    I've never been of any service to the state.

Why should I have the right, I ask with all respect,
To make a fuss at court, accuse them of neglect?

ARSINOË. Because the court will often favour people who
    Deserve it, if at all, then much, much less than you.
    It's opportunity and power that counts, you know,
    And all the splendid qualities of mind you show   1060
    Should surely...

ALCESTE.   Don't go on about my virtues, please!
    Why should the court take note of people's qualities?
    They'd have so much to do, with spending all their time
    Discovering our merits—what a pantomime!

ARSINOË. But merit shines through from the start, can't be
      concealed.
    And everybody knows your worth—it stands revealed.
    I heard you praised, yes, twice, in an admiring way,
    By most important people, only yesterday.

ALCESTE. Yes, that's just it. These days, the whole world earns our
      praise:
    We're all in this together. It's a recent phase: 1070
    We all insist that everybody's virtuous.
    There's so much flattery, it's scarcely glorious—
    We're glutted with the compliments we give and get,
    And even my valet appears in the Gazette.*

ARSINOË. But you're much better than the others. Have you
      thought
    Of taking on a more official role at court?
    Bear it in mind. If you decide to go ahead,
    I'll do my best to help, you can take that as read.
    I've plenty contacts, and I'll use my influence:
    They'll help you out, I know that from experience.   1080

ALCESTE. Me, play a role at court? Why? What would be the point?
    I'd rather go away, I'd feel so out of joint.
    I've never been that sort of man, since I was small—
    I haven't got a courtier's character at all.
    I don't possess the qualities a fellow needs
    To get on well at court, and make sure he succeeds.

My greatest asset seems to be that I'm sincere,
And when I talk, I make my feelings very clear.
But blurting out your secret thoughts without disguise
Is scarcely admirable to a courtier's eyes.   1090
Away from court, I won't have any influence,
I'll have no title, no admiring audience.
But though I'll lose advantages, I must admit,
At least I won't be forced to play the hypocrite.
I'll not be made to suffer cruel snubs, or, worse,
To swoon with admiration at some idiot's verse,
Or compliment some fancy lady prettily,
Or roar with laughter, with those brainless young marquis.

ARSINOË. Let's drop the court, if you don't want to play a part,
And talk about your love affair. It wrings my heart   1100
To see you throw yourself away. I feel such pain—
I hope you don't mind, if I make myself quite plain.
You owe it to yourself to find a love that's true:
The girl you care for's not at all worthy of you.

ALCESTE. But when you say so, are you sure you comprehend,
Madame, that you're discussing your devoted friend?

ARSINOË. I know, but I've been most unhappy all along.
I can't stand back and watch the way she does you wrong.
I'm most upset at all the evil tricks she's played.
You've got to know the truth: your love has been betrayed.   1110

ALCESTE. Oh, very kind, Madame. You're so affectionate.
Just what a lover needs! Oh, how considerate!

ARSINOË. I know she's my close friend, but she doesn't deserve
Your love. She wants to keep you dangling, in reserve,
And when she says she cares, her words are just for show.

ALCESTE. You may be right, Madame, in love it's hard to know.
But I must say, it seems a little bit unkind
To put all these destructive thoughts into my mind.

ARSINOË. So you don't want to know, and wish you hadn't heard?
Fine. Let's forget it—I won't say another word.   1120

ALCESTE. I don't want to prevent the truth from coming out,

But there is nothing worse than being full of doubt.
It's rumours and half-truths I simply can't endure:
I only want to know what I can know for sure.

ARSINOË. Oh, yes, I take your point, it seems quite fair, and so
I'll tell you everything you really need to know.
I'll give you the whole truth about your future spouse,
But first, give me your arm, escort me to my house.
At home, I've got a most revealing document.
You'll see. It casts a light on your predicament.   1130
The best thing you can do is to forget her charms,
And seek your consolation in another's arms.

ACT IV

SCENE 1

PHILINTE, ELIANTE

PHILINTE. I've never known a man be quite so hard to shake,
　　A reconciliation, quite so hard to make.
　　The Marshals did their best, and tried in vain to find
　　A way to coax Alceste to stop, and change his mind.
　　The whole affair was running at a breakneck pace—
　　The Marshals said they'd never seen a stranger case.
　　'No, gentlemen, I won't take back my words,' said he.
　　'I'll do whatever else you may require of me.　　　　　　　　1140
　　What does Oronte want? Why's he so dissatisfied?
　　Does writing rubbish seem to him a source of pride?
　　He got me wrong, I know, which made things even worse:
　　I meant, a gentleman can still write awful verse.
　　His honour isn't touched—it's quite irrelevant:
　　The fact that he's a decent sort is evident.
　　He's well born, he's deserving, thoughtful, kind, polite,
　　He's everything I say, but still the man can't write.
　　I'll say he's very rich, that I admire his skill
　　At riding, fencing, dancing, anything you will,　　　　　　1150
　　But when it comes to praising what he writes, no way.
　　He's got no talent, he can't write, so I won't play.
　　He ought to give up all this rubbish, save his breath;
　　That kind of man should only write on pain of death.'
　　They worked on him for ages, tried to put him wise,
　　And finally persuaded him to compromise.
　　He found a form of words to say, with this result:
　　'Monsieur, I'm sorry if I'm being difficult,
　　I wish with all my heart you didn't feel so sore:
　　And if I could, I would have liked your sonnet more.'　　1160
　　That seemed to be the best the judges could impose,
　　And so a brief embrace brought matters to a close.

ELIANTE. He really does behave in an eccentric way,

But I think that he's special too, I have to say.
The way he won't agree to play the hypocrite
Does have a noble and heroic side to it.
It's not his fault, you know—our modern life's to blame—
If only other people tried to do the same!

PHILINTE. I find it more and more surprising, for my part,
That he's let passion conquer him, and win his heart.   1170
He's not the same as other people. Heavens above!
I can't see how he's had the face to fall in love.
And why on earth pick on young Celimene, what's more?
Is she the sort a man like him ought to adore?

ELIANTE. It only goes to show love's unpredictable,
And people rarely fall for someone suitable;
I know there can be sympathies on which to base
A love affair, but you won't find them in this case.

PHILINTE. And do you think he's courting her with much success?

ELIANTE. That is the question, and it's very hard to guess.   1180
I don't know how you'd tell, the whole thing's so obscure.
In fact, I don't think she herself is really sure.
You may wake up one day, and be in love, or find
That what you thought was love, is nothing of the kind.

PHILINTE. Our friend's obsessed with her, I told you so before;
But things may turn out worse than he has bargained for.
If I were in his shoes right now, I have to say,
My preference would guide me quite another way.
I'd make a better choice, Madame, and you'd soon see
The way I'd take advantage of your love for me.   1190

ELIANTE. Well, I believe in being honest, and you'll find
In matters of the heart, I'll always speak my mind.
I don't mind that he loves my cousin, not one bit.
In fact, I hope that he can make a go of it,
And if the outcome of his love rested with me,
I'd make sure they were married, quickly as can be;
But if—and these things happen—something should go wrong,
And if their love affair should meet some contretemps,
And then, one day, she falls in love with someone new,

I hope he'll turn to me, and tell me that I'll do.   1200
Another woman might have turned him down—so what?
I'd like him just as much—I wouldn't care a jot.

PHILINTE. And, for my part, Madame, I tell you I don't mind
That you think he's attractive, and, in fact, you'll find
That I've said much the same to him myself. It's true,
You only have to ask him, we've talked about you.
But if his love for her should one day pass the test,
And Celimene should bring herself to take Alceste,
Then I'd set out to win the favour you show him:
For it's my dearest wish, it's not an idle whim.   1210
If you'll uproot your love from where it was before,
And give your heart to me, I'll ask for nothing more.

ELIANTE. Philinte, you must be joking.

PHILINTE.   No. I've never been
More serious, Madame. I'm saying what I mean:
That it's my dearest wish to bring this to a close.
One day, I hope, it will be my turn to propose.

SCENE 2

ALCESTE, ELIANTE, PHILINTE

ALCESTE. I've got to talk to you—I'm in a dreadful state—
I've always been so faithful, too!... Now it's too late.

ELIANTE. Why? What's the matter? What's brought all this to a
head?

ALCESTE. It's terrible—I can't... I wish that I were dead—   1220
If all the world were ripped to shreds, I wouldn't care,
For nothing matters now, and I'm in such despair:
It's over, and... My love... I can't find words to say...

ELIANTE. Just keep your self-control, and try not to give way.

ALCESTE. Oh, Heavens! Though the girl has such a lovely face,
She's vicious underneath. How can she be so base?

ELIANTE. What's happened? Tell us quickly.

ALCESTE.   How could she degrade
  Herself like that? I'm done for! I've... I've been betrayed!
  Yes, Celimene—oh, who'd believe it, is it true?
  Oh, Celimene's unfaithful, and a traitor too!   1230

ELIANTE. Oh, come! Have you got proof? How can you be so sure?

PHILINTE. Is there a chance your misery is premature?
  You know you tend to be too ready to infer...

ALCESTE. Good grief! Confound it all! Mind your own business,
    Sir.
  Do you think I'm so stupid I can't understand?
  The proof's here, in my pocket, written in her hand.
  Oh, yes, Madame, in here, a letter to Oronte,
  That makes her shame as plain to see as you could want—
  Oronte! Whom she avoided, whom she called a beast—
  Of all my rivals, he's the one I feared the least.   1240

PHILINTE. A letter isn't always quite what it appears,
  It may mean nothing much, so calm your jealous fears.

ALCESTE. Must I repeat myself, Monsieur? Leave me alone!
  Don't sort out my affairs, just look after your own.

ELIANTE. You must try to control yourself. If this is true...

ALCESTE. Madame, you've got to help me, I rely on you.
  I've come to you today because I'm sore at heart.
  You can help calm me down, but you must play your part:
  I want to get my own back on your cousin for
  Her wicked treachery. Oh, help me fight this war.   1250
  I must have my revenge—she owed me more respect.

ELIANTE. What, me avenge you? How?

ALCESTE.   That's easy. Just accept
  My hand in marriage now, instead of her, Madame.
  That way, I'll be avenged. There's no cause for alarm—
  To punish her I'll dedicate myself to you.
  I'll make you happy, more than other lovers do;

I'll worship you. You'll see, it'll be paradise—
I'll give you all my heart, an ardent sacrifice.

ELIANTE. You're suffering agonies—I truly sympathize;
You offer me a love that's worthy in my eyes.   1260
But things may not be quite as awful as they seem,
And later you may find you'd rather drop this scheme.
You're eager for revenge right now, but you may find,
Since you love your tormentor, you may change your mind.
You may hate her for now, your feelings may be strong,
But you may soon forget the way she's done you wrong.
The anger that you feel can melt away, and fast:
We all know that a lover's fury doesn't last.

ALCESTE. No, no, Madame: the injury goes much too deep.
There's no way back. I say I'm leaving her, I'll keep   1270
My word. Nothing on earth can make me change my mind:
I'd hate myself if my resolve was undermined.
She's coming now. Oh, God! she makes me furious!
I'm going to tell her that, this time, it's serious;
My heart is free again. I'll tell her that we're through;
I'll put her in her place, and then come back to you.

SCENE 3*

ALCESTE, CELIMENE

ALCESTE. Oh, God! I can't control myself—I'm in a state!

CELIMENE. Oh, what's the matter now? Why are you so irate?
Why are you heaving all these big, dramatic sighs,
And gazing at me with such sombre, tragic eyes?   1280

ALCESTE. For horror at its worst, and vicious cruelty,
There's nothing to compare with your disloyalty.
And Heaven, and hell, and cruel fate, and devil's brew,
Have never made a monster quite as vile as you.

CELIMENE. Well, now, for sheer politeness, that's a masterstroke.

ALCESTE. Oh, don't start laughing, please. This is no time to joke.
Why aren't you blushing? Tell me that. You've got good cause.

I've proof that you've deceived me: that should give you pause.
I was uneasy, and I knew that things weren't right—
I felt this coming, that's why I was in a fright.   1290
You didn't like the fact that I was full of doubt;
I thought there would be trouble: now the truth's come out.
Although you played things very cool indeed, my dear,
A secret instinct warned me what I had to fear.
But don't think I'm prepared to go along with this:
I'm going to be revenged for all your wickedness.
I know these things can happen, and can't be controlled,
That sometimes unexpected love can gain a hold—
And I accept that one can't win a girl by force,
She must be free to love as she sees fit, of course.   1300
I would have felt that I'd no reason for complaint,
If you had spoken honestly, without constraint,
And if you had rejected me right from the start,
I would have taken my misfortune in good part.
But you pretended that you cared, encouraged me,
Told me you loved me. Oh, what cruel mockery!
I'm going to punish you, for that's what you deserve.
I'm going to hunt you down, keep nothing in reserve.
You can expect the worst, after this last outrage:
Now nothing matters, I'm out of my mind with rage.   1310
You've struck the final blow, you cruel murderess,
And I've lost all the self-control I could possess;
I've given in to my just anger against you,
And I can't answer now for anything I do.

CELIMENE. Excuse me—do you think it's perfectly all right
To shout at me like this? You're spoiling for a fight!

ALCESTE. That's right—I lost control the day that I set eyes
On you: you'll be the death of me, I realize.
I trusted you, believed you'd never do me harm,
And let myself be taken in by your false charm.   1320

CELIMENE. What is this harm I've done, and how am I to blame?

ALCESTE. Ah! See how cleverly you play a double game!
But, this time, I've the trump card, I can call your bluff.
Just take a look at this—don't you think it's enough?

This letter demonstrates the kind of game you play:
Now you've seen this, I'm sure you've nothing more to say.

CELIMENE. I see. So this is what the fuss is all about?

ALCESTE. Look, here's the letter. Go on, blush: you've been found
out.

CELIMENE. Why should I blush? I don't see why—I feel no shame.

ALCESTE. You're devious, and bold as well. Next thing, you'll   1330
claim
The thing's not in your writing, as the note's not signed.

CELIMENE. Of course I wrote it—so? Are you out of your mind?

ALCESTE. But how can you be so unmoved, and can't you see
This letter makes it clear you've been deceiving me?

CELIMENE. Well, I must say that you're a perfect idiot.

ALCESTE. The proof's right here. Are you admitting it, or not?
Look, here you write you love Oronte, and I'm supposed
To think that's quite all right, best say the matter's closed?

CELIMENE. Oronte? Who said I wrote it to him, anyway?

ALCESTE. The people who gave it to me, only today.   1340
Perhaps you wrote it to another man. So what?
D'you think I'm happy that you write such things, or not?
You're every bit as guilty, I'm no less upset.

CELIMENE. If it was written to a girl, would you still fret?
It would mean nothing then, you surely must agree.

ALCESTE. Oh, brilliant! That changes everything for me.
I'm so astonished. Who would have expected it?
Oh, yes, I'm utterly convinced, I must admit.
How dare you lie to me so crudely? What contempt!
You think you can deceive me with this botched attempt?   1350
Come on, then, do your worst, just show me how and why
You aim to make me swallow this outrageous lie.
Let's see you take this letter, tender to the end,
And show me that it's written to a female friend.

I'll read it to you. Listen, let's see if you can't
Invent some good excuses. Come on...

CELIMENE.   No, I shan't.
 You have a nerve to tell me that I'm in disgrace,
 And make these devastating comments to my face!

ALCESTE. Keep calm, now. Don't start off on an aggressive note.
 Give me an explanation of the things you wrote.   1360

CELIMENE. I don't see why I should, I'm not under duress.
 You can think what you like, it couldn't matter less.

ALCESTE. Let's see. A woman reader—how is that implied?
 Explain, please. Then I promise I'll be satisfied.

CELIMENE. No. It was written for Oronte, as you can see.
 I revel in the way he pays his court to me,
 I do admire him, yes, and I respect him too,
 And I agree with what you say: it's all quite true.
 Go on, jump to conclusions, won't you? Why refrain?
 But stop abusing me, it's driving me insane.   1370

ALCESTE [aside]. Oh, heavens, what a twisted, cruel thing to say!
 How can she torture me in such a heartless way?
 I'm duped, I'm angry, but I'm told to be correct,
 She takes it out on me when I try to object!
 She plays on my suspicions, drives me to extremes,
 Tells me it's all quite true, rejoices in her schemes—
 And even so, I'm still so weak that I can't break
 The chains that bind me, and I stay here for her sake!
 I can't see how to arm myself with proud disdain
 For such a worthless girl, who causes me such pain!   1380

[To CELIMENE

You treat my weakness for you as a weapon to
Destroy me, for I'm helpless when it comes to you:
You know I love you to distraction, and you use
My fatal love, because you know I can't refuse.
At least defend yourself against this hateful crime,
And don't keep telling me you're guilty all the time;
Try to persuade me that your letter's innocent.
I'll try to help you out, for that's my firm intent:

Tell me you're not unfaithful, please, I beg you to,
And I'll try to believe this latest story's true.   1390

CELIMENE. Come on! You're raving mad, you and your jealous
    scenes.
It seems that you can't grasp what my love for you means.
Do you really believe that anyone could force
A girl like me to tell such lies without remorse?
If I preferred another man, would I deny
The truth, not say so openly? And if so, why?
It's just too bad: when I've paid you the compliment
Of telling you how much I care, you're not content.
I've told you how I feel, and that should be enough:
It hurts me when you blurt out all this jealous stuff.   1400
It isn't easy for a woman to come clean;
It's difficult to make a man know that she's keen
On him, because it's not considered quite the thing
To make such declarations—it's embarrassing—
So if a girl speaks up, it's scarcely courtesy
To doubt her word and give in to this jealousy.
The fact is that my declaration's cost me dear:
You ought to be ashamed of doubting I'm sincere.
All your suspicions do is make me very cross:
If I had any sense, I wouldn't give a toss   1410
For you. I can't believe that I'm so crazy that
I care for you, when I should really drop you flat.
I should find someone else, I feel I've every right.
I know I ought to break with you; in fact, I might.

ALCESTE. I've such a passion for you that it's quite absurd,
For I'm convinced you're duping me, with every word.
Alas, there's nothing for it but to meet my fate—
My soul is in your hands, you minx: I abdicate.
I want to test you out, and see how far you'll go.
Will you betray me heartlessly? I've got to know.   1420

CELIMENE. Don't count on me: you don't care for me as you
    should.

ALCESTE. Oh, no one loves as you as I do, and no one could.
What's more, I want the world to know about it too—

I even wish that things would go all wrong for you.
I wish people would tell you you were hideous,
I wish that you'd become degraded, piteous;
I wish that you'd been born a beggar girl, or worse,
No pedigree, no home, no money in your purse:
I'd sacrifice my heart to you, and I'd make sure
That I repaired the dreadful wrongs you might endure.   1430
And on that glorious day, why, I'd rejoice to see
You owing all your wealth and happiness to me.

CELIMENE. I must say, that's the oddest way to wish me well!
I do hope things don't turn out quite as you foretell.
Here comes your man Dubois—I think he looks distressed.

SCENE 4

ALCESTE, CELIMENE, DUBOIS

ALCESTE. Why're you in such a state? And why so oddly dressed?
What's wrong?

DUBOIS.   Monsieur...

ALCESTE.   Well, what?

DUBOIS.   A private matter, Sir.

ALCESTE. What is it?

DUBOIS.   We've got problems, Monsieur, as it were.

ALCESTE. Eh?

DUBOIS.   Do I tell you now?

ALCESTE.   Yes, now, and make it quick.

DUBOIS. Should I speak out?   1440

ALCESTE.   Get on with it! My God, he's thick!
Will you explain?

DUBOIS.   Monsieur, I think we'd best get out.

ALCESTE. What's that?

DUBOIS.   It's as I say, we'd best go walkabout.

ALCESTE. But why?

DUBOIS.   I'm telling you, Monsieur, we must depart.

ALCESTE. What for?

DUBOIS.   Come on, Monsieur, be quick, it's time to start.

ALCESTE. Why are you going on like this? And what's the snag?

DUBOIS. I'm going on because it's time to pack your bag.

ALCESTE. I'll wallop you if you don't stop being maddening.
Now, try to say exactly what is happening.

DUBOIS. As I sat by the kitchen fire, who should appear
But this here man in black—his face was all severe.   1450
He had a paper, there were scribbles over it:
The devil himself could scarcely read the writing bit.
It's all about that wretched case, without a doubt,
But it would take a demon brain to make it out.

ALCESTE. But how this means I'm in a mess, I can't conceive—
And why do you keep telling me I have to leave?

DUBOIS. Now, try to keep your hair on, Sir, and I'll begin.
A man who often comes to visit you dropped in
Soon afterwards—or, rather, rushed straight in to find
You, but you weren't at home, so he says, nice and kind,   1460
Because he knows I care for you, he says: 'Tell him I came
To find him urgently... ' But what the hell's his name?

ALCESTE. Oh, never mind his name! What did he say, blockhead?

DUBOIS. Well, anyway, the man's a friend of yours, 'nuff said.
He told me you're in danger here, you'd best get out,
For you might get arrested if you hang about.

ALCESTE. But didn't he explain? I don't know what to think.

DUBOIS. No. He told me to give him paper, pen, and ink,
And wrote a note for me to give you, to explain
The mystery to you, and make the matter plain.   1470

ALCESTE. Well, hand it over.

CELIMENE.   Don't you find this rather queer?

ALCESTE. Yes, very odd—I hope the note will make things clear.
  Well, come on, hurry up, you devilish young cur!

DUBOIS [*after a lengthy search*]. Oh, drat, I must have left it on the
  table, Sir.

ALCESTE. That's it. You're for it now!...

CELIMENE.   Oh, there's no need to shout.
  You'd better hurry off and try to sort things out.

ALCESTE. For all my trying, I can see that fate is set
  Against us ever managing a tête-à-tête.
  But lovers won't give up until the battle's won—
  So let me come back here before the day is done.   1480

ACT V

SCENE 1

ALCESTE, PHILINTE

ALCESTE. You heard. I'm telling you that I've made up my mind.

PHILINTE. It's a hard blow, but are you sure that you're inclined...?

ALCESTE. It's no use reasoning, and talking on and on:
You can't stop me, I'm leaving—high time I was gone.
There's far too much corruption in the world today;
I want to leave my fellow men, get right away.
Can you believe it? Everything was on my side—
My honour, honesty, the law were satisfied,
And everybody was agreed my cause was just.
The fact that I was in the right led me to trust   1490
That I would win—but no, the judgement's a disgrace!
With justice on my side, I've gone and lost my case!
We're all aware that monster's life's an evil one—
He told a pack of lies—and now the wretch has won!
The man's betrayed me—never mind that I was right!
He proved me wrong, he cut my throat, out of sheer spite!
His phoney smirk, which he parades all over town,
Perverts the truth, turns common justice upside down;
Then he compounds his wrongs by prosecuting me.
I think that things have got as bad as they can be,   1500
But now, they're passing round a most appalling book—
You can be prosecuted if you take a look—
It should be banned, or worse: it's truly sickening—
And now he's telling everyone I wrote the thing.*
And then, guess what? Oronte decides to add his bit,
Pretending that he knew full well I'd written it.
When you remember he's respected by the court,
A man I treated honestly, said what I thought,
When he approached me, and would not let me refuse,
Read me his sonnet, asked to hear my honest views.   1510

And then, because my answer *was* an honest one,
And when I wouldn't hide the truth, once I'd begun,
The man's become my most determined enemy,
He won't forgive me, and he's out to torture me.
He tries to charge me with imaginary crimes—
And all because I didn't like his little rhymes!
Our fellow men behave like that, I think it's great!
They like to see the right thing done, I tell you straight.
They're always out to tell the world how good they are,
Show off the dazzling virtues in their repertoire!   1520
I've had enough of all this abject misery—
I want to leave this cut-throat world of roguery:
I want to turn my back on them, yes, that's my plan,
Since man is nothing but an arrant wolf to man.*

PHILINTE. You're mad, so don't pretend you know what you're
     about.
Things aren't nearly as desperate as you make out.
Your rival's accusations haven't stood the test:
He hasn't managed to arrange for your arrest.
Our reputation suffers from the lies we tell:
His bad behaviour may discredit him as well.   1530

ALCESTE. What, him? Those minor setbacks matter not a whit.
Just call him scoundrel—it won't bother him one bit.
His reputation will be none the worse; you'll see
That in a day he'll be triumphant as can be.

PHILINTE. Meanwhile, the fact is, almost nobody has paid
Attention to his gossip; don't you be afraid:
All his insinuations scarcely count, I feel.
You may have lost your case, but you can still appeal.
That's not a legal problem, it's expected, and
The verdict's doubtful...   1540

ALCESTE.   No, the verdict has to stand.
Although it's quite unjust, I know when I've been spurned,
I'm still determined not to have it overturned.
It shows up justice in its fallibility,
It's got to be preserved for all posterity,
A fine example, to enable men to gauge

The vile corruption of this modern day and age.
So—I'll lose twenty thousand francs out of my purse:
Money well spent in giving me the right to curse
Against the wickedness of the whole human race,
And prove that all humanity is a disgrace.   1550

PHILINTE. Look here...

ALCESTE.   No, you look here, don't try, you'll never sway
My judgement. It's the truth—what can you find to say?
And would you have the cheek to tell me to my face
That you can sympathize with what's done in this place?

PHILINTE. Oh, no. You're right to feel a sense of injury.
The world's run by a selfish, greedy coterie.
Low cunning is the greatest new accomplishment,
That's how to win—I wish things could be different.
But, granted that injustice and foul play are rife,
Is that a reason to abandon public life?   1560
Humanity's a mess, but let's be practical,
And make sure our approach is philosophical.
That's the best way to demonstrate we're really good;
For if we tried to be as honest as we could,
And everyone was decent, fair, and virtuous,
Most of *our* virtues would become superfluous,
Since what we use them for is helping us to bear
Our grievances, when other people are unfair.
A truly decent fellow can assimilate...

ALCESTE. Monsieur, I know that you are most articulate;   1570
You've all the answers, and your reasoning's sublime,
But still your speechifying's just a waste of time.
It stands to reason that I can't live here, among
My fellows, since it's clear I can't control my tongue,
And I can't answer for the things that I might say.
I'd find myself in constant trouble, every day.
Don't argue, leave me here to wait for Celimene.
Will she approve my plan to leave the world of men?
Will she commit herself, or else remain aloof?
It's time now, time for her to give me proper proof.   1580

PHILINTE. Well, while we wait, let's go upstairs to Eliante.

ALCESTE. No, thanks. I'm too upset to meet her now—I can't.
　　You go on up, I'll stay, and try to find relief,
　　In this dark corner, here, alone, me and my grief.

PHILINTE. If you ask me, you're piling on the agony:
　　I'll go find Eliante to keep you company.

SCENE 2

ORONTE, CELIMENE, ALCESTE

ORONTE. I want you to decide: accept me, or refuse.
　　It's up to you, Madame. I leave you free to choose,
　　But you must make your mind up. I'm here, in your hands:
　　A lover likes to know exactly where he stands.   1590
　　If, as I hope, my love for you has touched your heart,
　　I want you to declare it now, not play a part.
　　But one thing you must do, to pass the lover's test,
　　And that is to turn down your other man, Alceste.
　　Yes, sacrifice him to my love, send him away,
　　And tell him never to come back, after today.

CELIMENE. But why? What is this clash of personalities?
　　You say yourself he's got outstanding qualities.

ORONTE. Madame, that sort of talk is quite irrelevant:
　　Tell me your feelings, don't let's have an argument.   1600
　　You've got two lovers, you can keep one of the two,
　　So which one will you choose? You know it's up to you.

ALCESTE [coming out of his corner]. Yes, Monsieur's right,
　　　　Madame—I see I share his views,
　　And I agree the time has come for you to choose.
　　I'm here, like him, to learn the truth: I want to know.
　　I need the final proof: do you love me, or no?
　　This has been going on too long—it's quite a strain.
　　We can't go on like this—so make your feelings plain.

ORONTE. If you're the lucky one, I want to know, today.
Monsieur, I wouldn't dream of standing in your way.   1610

ALCESTE. Monsieur, although my jealousy may drive me spare,
I will have all her love or none, and I won't share.

ORONTE. If she finds your love more acceptable than mine...

ALCESTE. If she says what she feels, or gives the smallest sign...

ORONTE. I swear I'll go away from here: I know what's right.

ALCESTE. I swear I'll leave at once: I won't put up a fight.

ORONTE. Madame, it's your turn now. Don't be afraid to speak.

ALCESTE. Madame, explain yourself—and no more hide-and-seek.

ORONTE. All you need do is give your answer—that's the deal.

ALCESTE. All you need do is say exactly how you feel.   1620

ORONTE. What's this? You find it hard, do you? So we're unkind?

ALCESTE. What? Are you at a loss? Can't you make up your mind?

CELIMENE. My goodness, why insist? It's quite intolerable!
I must say, you are both a bit unreasonable.
Not that you've put me on the spot: I've got my views.
My heart's not undecided, I know which to choose.
No, I'll not hesitate, you'll see, and you'll both find
A girl is quick to act, once she knows her own mind.
The thing that holds me back is that I'm rather proud:
It's so embarrassing to say one loves, out loud.   1630
A nice girl doesn't wear her heart upon her sleeve:
These things should be discussed in private, I believe.
If you're the favoured one, I'm not obliged to dwell
On it, for you can guess, so don't force me to tell.
And as for turning down a man, it isn't done:
Far better break it gently that he's not the one.

ORONTE. This is an opportunity not to be missed:
You must speak out, I say.

ALCESTE.   For my part, I insist.
We need to know: come on, don't spare your audience.
You must give us the truth, speak out, no reticence.   1640

I know that keeping people happy is your aim,
We're both unhappy, but you think it's all a game;
So now you must be frank, we want you to come clean—
And if you won't, I'll know precisely what you mean:
Your silence will be my rejection—I'm well versed
In what to think—I'll know I can expect the worst.

ORONTE. Yes, Monsieur, that's well said. In fact, I quite agree,
And she will hear the very selfsame words from me.

CELIMENE. I must say, you're a bossy and demanding pair,
And what you're making me go through is most unfair.   1650
I've told you I won't put my feelings on display—
Here's Eliante. Let's hear what she has got to say.

SCENE 3

ELIANTE, PHILINTE, CELIMENE, ORONTE, ALCESTE

CELIMENE. Oh, cousin, these two gentlemen are hounding me.
They've got together to upset me cruelly.
They're terribly insistent they must have their way:
They're forcing me to choose between them, right away.
I've got to turn one of them down, now, to his face,
Reject his love, and send him straight off in disgrace!
Now, tell me, did you ever hear of such a thing?

ELIANTE. Oh, don't expect me to relieve your suffering.   1660
You'll see you've not picked the right person, for I find
That I prefer it when a woman speaks her mind.

ORONTE. You'll have to tell the truth, we won't take an excuse.

ALCESTE. Don't try to wriggle out of this, for it's no use.

ORONTE. Speak up—you can't string us along, it's not polite.

ALCESTE. Or else say nothing, and we'll guess, that's quite all right.

ORONTE. Just say one word, I'll understand perfectly well.

ALCESTE. I'll understand your silence, there's no need to tell.

SCENE 4

ACASTE, CLITANDRE, ARSINOË, PHILINTE, ELIANTE, ORONTE,
CELIMENE, ALCESTE

ACASTE [*to* CELIMENE]. Madame, we've come to talk to you, if you
  don't mind.
  There's something bothering the two of us, we find.   1670

CLITANDRE [*to* ORONTE *and* ALCESTE]. Ah, gentlemen, we're very
  pleased to find you here:
  For you're both implicated too, as you'll soon hear.

ARSINOË [*to* CELIMENE]. Madame, you must be quite surprised at
  seeing me:
  These gentlemen insisted I must come, you see.
  They came to see me, in a fine state, to complain
  At something that you'd done, and that I can't explain.
  I've got a very high opinion of you, I'm
  Convinced you'd be incapable of such a crime,
  So I've denied the evidence of my own eyes—
  Though we may disagree, our friendship's one I prize—   1680
  I told them that I'd come, and keep them company,
  To see you clear yourself of vicious calumny.

ACASTE. That's what we want to see. We think it'll be fun
  To watch you try and justify the things you've done.
  This letter to Clitandre—was it written by you?

CLITANDRE. And did you send Acaste this tender billet-doux?

ACASTE. Now, gentlemen, her writing's quite familiar.
  I'm sure you've both had lots of friendly notes from her:
  You know the sort of thing the lady tends to write—
  But this one's well worth reading—it's a sheer delight: 1690

  *You are an odd creature to blame me for being too merry; how can you
  reproach me for seeming most cheerful when I'm not with you? It's so
  unfair. Unless you come soon to beg my pardon for the wrong
  you've done, I'll never forgive you as long as I live. As for that great
  galumphing Vicomte...*

  He should be here too...

... As for that great galumphing Vicomte, who heads your list of complaints, I can't stand the man. Ever since I saw him spend three-quarters of an hour spitting in a well to make ripples,* I've never had a high opinion of him. And as for the little Marquis—

She's speaking of your humble servant, gentlemen—

... As for the little Marquis, who insisted on keeping me company yesterday, he's the puniest fellow imaginable. He's one of those deserving people who have nothing but a cloak and sword to their name. As for the man with the green ribbons...

[*To* ALCESTE

Your turn now, Monsieur...

... As for the man with the green ribbons,* he can be quite amusing, with his rudeness and his sulks; but time and time again, I find him a crashing bore. And as for the man with the coat-tails...*

[*To* ORONTE

You next...

... As for the man with the coat-tails, who has worked himself into a creative lather, and wants to be a writer, whatever people think, I can't be bothered to listen to what he says. He's equally tedious in prose and verse. Believe me, I don't always enjoy myself as much as you think. When they drag me off to parties, I miss you more than I care to admit. Happy moments seem twice as delightful in the company of people you love.

CLITANDRE. My turn now.

You go on about Clitandre, who simpers so sweetly; but he's the last man I could care for. He's mad to believe I love him—and you're mad to think I don't love you. Show some sense, and try to copy him; come and see me as often as you can, to help me bear it when he insists on hanging around.

These letters show you up in quite a novel light,
Madame. You know what name we use when people write
Such things? But now we'll spread the word, both near and far,
And tell the world just what a charming flirt you are.

ACASTE. I'm sure that you'll agree there's plenty I could say,
But you're not worth my getting angry, anyway,
And you'll soon find that even little, thin marquis
Can find love in superior places—wait and see!

ORONTE. I'm horrified, I'm speechless, words stick in my throat.
What! After all those flattering letters that you wrote,   1700
And all your vows of love, it seems you've got the face
To offer yourself up to all the human race?
This time, I've had enough. I won't remain your dupe—
I'm grateful I found out how low a girl can stoop.
My heart's my own again, the future's looking bright—
You've lost me now, my dear, and, frankly, serves you right.

[*To* ALCESTE

I won't stand in your way, Monsieur. Bask in her charm—
You're welcome to commit your future to Madame.

ARSINOË [*to* CELIMENE]. Oh, this is the most shocking thing I've
    ever heard!
I'm so upset, I can't walk off without a word.   1710
Ugh! What a carry-on these billets-doux disclose!
Of all the men that you've been leading by the nose,
It's Monsieur here, who loved you so devotedly,
An honourable man, full of integrity,
A man who idolized you, worshipped on his knees—
How could you have...?

ALCESTE.   Madame, just drop it, if you please.
I know how to stand up for my own interest,
And I don't need your help, so let the matter rest.
Although I'm well aware you always take my part,
Your zeal has made no strong impression on my heart.   1720
I wouldn't turn to you, despite your many charms,
If I looked for revenge in someone else's arms.

ARSINOË. Well, really! What makes you think you can take that
    tone?
You think I'm desperate to have you for my own?
I don't know where you get your monstrous vanity,
To assume I'm capable of such insanity.

Used goods are not for me, I find they're lacking charm,
And I won't feast upon the leavings of Madame.
Try not to aim so high in finding your new bride,
For you won't get yourself a girl with any pride.   1730
My best advice to you is: carry on with her.
I long to see the wedding—should make quite a stir.

[*Exit* ARSINOË

ALCESTE. I stood there quietly through everything I heard.
The others ranted on, I didn't say a word.
So have I held back long enough now? Does it strike
You I've a right to speak?

CELIMENE.   You can say what you like.
You've every right to make the bitterest complaint.
Reproach me all you want: no need for self-restraint.
I'm in the wrong, I know. I've earned all your abuse.
I won't defend myself, for I've got no excuse.   1740
I didn't care when they were furious, it's true,
But I agree that I've been horrible to you.
It's understandable I've lost your high esteem:
I fully realize how guilty I must seem.
There's no two ways about it, you must feel betrayed.
Of course you hate me, seeing how you've been repaid.
So hate me, if you want.

ALCESTE.   How can I, traitress?
D'you think I can dislodge my former tenderness?
I long to hate you, and I wish we two could part;
But still I can't control my ever-loving heart.   1750

[*To* PHILINTE *and* ELIANTE

You see, I'm showing you a most ignoble streak.
You're witnesses to how my love has made me weak.
But that's not all, there's something else you both must know,
If you're to see how far my helplessness will go.
Believe me, don't trust human nature if you can:
At heart, the wisest sage is nothing but a man.

[*To* CELIMENE

You little minx, I'm ready to forget the whole,
To pardon all your crimes, forgive them in my soul.
I'll say it's only weakness, swear that it's the truth,
Say it's the fault of modern life, and blame your youth.   1760
But, in return, my dear, I want you to agree
To follow me. I'm leaving high society.
I've sworn to live alone in some deserted spot:
You've got to come with me, at once, no matter what,
For that's the only way to find an antidote
To make up for those dreadful letters that you wrote.
What you've done's unacceptable, you know it's true:
This is the only way I'll keep on loving you.

CELIMENE. What, me? At my age? Do you think I could survive
Away from town, in some dull hole, buried alive?   1770

ALCESTE. But if we love each other truly, don't you see,
You won't need any others, seeing you've got me:
If we're together, surely you'll be satisfied?

CELIMENE. At twenty, girls like me can't stand the countryside.
I don't feel I'm mature or serious enough
To cope with moving out—it'd be much too tough.
If it would make you happy, I can demonstrate
How much I care about you now: no need to wait,
Let's just get married...

ALCESTE.   No. That's it now. I detest
You—now you've turned me down, you can forget the rest.   1780
Since you're not ready to give up the things you do,
And come away with me, as I would do for you,
You'd better go. I feel disgusted, and I find
This latest insult's wiped all feeling from my mind.

                    [*Exit* CELIMENE. *To* ELIANTE

Madame, I like your looks. I know you're virtuous;
And, better still, it's plain you're never devious.
For some time now, I've watched, admired you from afar—
But now, I'm sorry, things must stay the way they are.
I'm troubled, disappointed, miserable, and
I simply can't request the honour of your hand.   1790

I don't deserve you, I've begun to realize
That I'm not meant to marry: dreadfully unwise.
I mean, how could I ask someone superior
To love the cast-off of a mere inferior?
I don't think it would be a good idea...

ELIANTE.   Oh, quite.
Don't try to change your mind—it's perfectly all right.
I've got no need to hunt for husbands: in the end
I might just find myself deciding on your friend.

PHILINTE.   Madame, there's nothing I want more, I've told you so,
And I'd do anything to win you, as you know.   1800

ALCESTE.   Ah! May you both be happy as the day is long;
I hope your feelings for each other stay so strong!
But me, I've been betrayed, I've got to pay the price:
I plan to leave this world, this filthy den of vice,
And find a place where I don't need to socialize,
Where I can be myself, don't have to compromise.

PHILINTE.   Let's follow him, Madame, and let's do all we can
To try to change his mind, and make him drop this plan.

THE END

THE CLEVER WOMEN

1672

CHARACTERS

CHRYSALE,* a worthy bourgeois
PHILAMINTE,* wife to Chrysale
ARMANDE,* daughter to Chrysale and Philaminte
HENRIETTE,* daughter to Chrysale and Philaminte
ARISTE,* brother to Chrysale
BELISE,* sister to Chrysale
CLITANDRE,* lover to Henriette
TRISSOTIN,* man of wit
VADIUS,* man of letters
MARTINE,* scullery-maid
L'EPINE, footman
JULIEN, valet to Vadius
A LAWYER

*The scene is set in Paris**

ACT I

SCENE 1

ARMANDE, HENRIETTE

ARMANDE. What? Are you getting married? Is it really true,
When living as a single girl's the thing to do?
I hear you're looking forward to your wedding day?
How can you? It's so vulgar! You, a fiancée?

HENRIETTE. Yes, sister.

ARMANDE.   How can you say 'yes'? Eh? Tell me, quick!
To hear you say it—ugh!—it makes me feel quite sick.

HENRIETTE. What view of marriage have you got into your head?

ARMANDE. Ugh! God, it's so revolting!

HENRIETTE.   What's that?

ARMANDE.   Ugh, I said!
That word—it's utterly disgusting, and I find
Just hearing it's enough to discompose my mind.*   10
The pictures that it conjures up inside my brain—
It makes me think strange thoughts, too shaming to explain!
So aren't you quaking, sister? How can you decide
To be a wife?... That word... we both know what's implied.

HENRIETTE. No. What's implied for me, when I think of that word,
Is husband, children, family: I'm not deterred.
And, thinking that, I know I'm making no mistake
That's liable to give offence, or make me quake.

ARMANDE. Good God! Is an engagement really to your taste?

HENRIETTE. At my age, I believe I've got no time to waste.   20
The best thing I can do is marry the right man,
A man who loves me, and whom I love. That's my plan.
I'll stay with him, and live a happy married life.

I'm looking forward to becoming that man's wife;
I think it all sounds wonderful, and I can't wait.

ARMANDE. Good grief! How common! Let me tell you, any rate,
You'll seem a nobody in decent people's eyes,
Stuck in the house, weighed down with dreary household ties.
Never a glimpse of pleasure, not a joy for you,
Only your lord and master, and a brat or two!   30
You shouldn't want those things. I'm telling you to leave
All that alone. Some people like it, I believe,
But you should live your whole life on a higher plane,
And opt for nobler joys. Look here, let me explain:
You should give up the senses, scorn base things like that,
And use your brain, don't waste your time in idle chat.
Your mother sets a wonderful example here;
Her reputation's known to scholars far and near.
So try to copy her; try to be more like me:
You've excellent examples in the family.   40
Oh, let yourself enjoy the exquisite delight
Of loving scholarship. You'll see that I was right.
Don't be a husband's slave—reject the marriage vow—
Instead take up philosophy, and do it now.
You'll see, you'll rise above the common human race.
Philosophers alone put reason in its place;
They teach us to control our brutish appetite,
That makes us seem like beasts (I'm trying to be polite).
You should respect your brain, not live as someone's wife,
You'd love your learning every moment of your life.   50
When I see women waste time on futility,
Their life shows up in all its imbecility.

HENRIETTE. We all know God controls the Heavens and the earth,
We know he's destined us for different roles from birth.
And some of us, if you'll excuse the metaphor,
Are not cut from the cloth of the philosopher.
You think great thoughts, you've got a lofty turn of mind,
And scholarly debate's the way that you're inclined.
My mind's of a more humble, ordinary sort,
So leave me to indulge in undemanding thought.   60
I'm sure God's got it right. Indeed, I see no case

For changing things: let's each take our allotted place:
You've got your intellect which men can't overwhelm,
You can have high philosophy's exalted realm,
While I, with my low mind fixed on material things,
Enjoy the earthly happiness that marriage brings.
Although there's a great difference between us two,
I'll imitate my mother just as well as you:
You'll represent the aspirations of the soul,
And I'll adopt a baser, much more earthy role;   70
While your approach is noble and ethereal,
The angle that I'll choose is more material.

ARMANDE. When you set out to imitate a person's ways,
You ought to concentrate on earning people's praise;
And you can never say your imitation fits
If all you do is ape the way she coughs and spits.*

HENRIETTE. Yes, but where would you be, for all your scornful
      pride,
If Mother only had her pure, high-minded side?
It's just as well for you our mother's noble mind
Was crude from time to time, not totally refined.   80
It's lucky she was gross, or you wouldn't be here.
I'll do as she did, I don't plan to be austere.
Don't set a harsh example; don't repress with scorn
A future little scholar waiting to be born.

ARMANDE. Oh, how pathetic! Isn't she stuck in her ways?
You're set on marrying, no matter what one says.
But tell me, who's the lucky man? Your sights are set
On someone—not Clitandre? That isn't etiquette.

HENRIETTE. Why? is there any reason not to choose Clitandre?
He's very eligible, worthy of a *tendre*.   90

ARMANDE. Oh, don't be so unfair! I can't allow this match:
You know that you'd be poaching someone else's catch.
Hands off! Let me tell you, the gentleman's not free:
In fact, he's made no secret of his love for me.

HENRIETTE. I know, but being in love with you gave him such pain,
For you view earthly passion with such deep disdain.

You won't get married, and you think yourself above
That bestial way of life: philosophy's your love.
You don't want him yourself, since marriage is taboo:
If someone else takes him instead, what's that to you?   100

ARMANDE. Though I admit my reason dominates my mind,
    I've not become unfeeling, and I always find
    I like it when men worship me. He can't aspire
    To marry me, but still he's welcome to admire.

HENRIETTE. I never made him stop, he could have carried on
    Insisting you were such a perfect paragon;
    But then, after you'd dropped him, I felt I was free
    To take the gift of love he came to offer me.

ARMANDE. But if I drop him, and he turns to you instead,
    How can you trust him? Are you sure you're not misled?   110
    Can you believe he's really offered you his heart,
    And that his love for me has died, now we're apart?

HENRIETTE. That's what he tells me, sister. I believe him, too.

ARMANDE. Don't be so trusting, sister. What if it's not true?
    When he says he's left me to worship at your feet,
    Could it be wishful thinking, simple self-deceit?

HENRIETTE. I couldn't say. But if you want to clear the air,
    I'll tell you what to do next, sister, if you care
    To know the truth: just ask him. Here he comes—don't go,
    He'll tell us both exactly what we want to know.   120

SCENE 2

ARMANDE, HENRIETTE, CLITANDRE

HENRIETTE. My sister's got some doubts that you're one to clear.
    Can you decide between us two? We'd like to hear
    The truth. Be honest, tell us, is it me or her?
    Out of the two of us, which one do you prefer?

ARMANDE. No, really, I don't mind. There's no need to explain.
    I know that speaking out would only cause you pain.

I'd rather spare your blushes, knowing what distress
A modest person feels, when bullied to confess.

CLITANDRE. I'm not a hypocrite. In fact, I'm quite content
To tell you both the truth, so you've my full consent.   130
Let's go ahead. It doesn't bother me a bit.
I tell you straight, I make no mystery of it.
I do love one of you, and one of you alone.

                              [*Indicates* HENRIETTE

My heart belongs to Henriette, I'm proud to own.
But let's have no hard feelings at my change of heart:
You wanted it this way, you drove us two apart.
I was besotted, but I sighed for you in vain—
You knew I cared for you, you made that very plain.
I loved you, and my feelings seemed unshakeable,
But you said that my love was unacceptable.   140
I suffered so much degradation at your side:
You ruled over my heart, and tortured me with pride.
I'd had enough. Exhausted by the whole affair,
I found a kinder love, and chains less hard to bear.

                              [*Indicates* HENRIETTE

I gazed into her eyes, found what I hoped to see—
The way she looks seems quite adorable to me.
She made me dry my tears, took pity on my pain,
She loved me. She was not like you, full of disdain.
She was so kind to me, she touched me to the heart,
And nothing you can do will ever make us part.   150
There's one thing you must know, Madame, I'm warning you:
Don't try to split us up, whatever else you do.
It won't be any use, however hard you try—
I'll be in love with her until the day I die.

ARMANDE. Why should I split you up, Monsieur? Can you believe
I care for you? I never said so, by your leave.
Well, really! The idea! You must be off your head.
And what a cheek! I can't believe the things you've said.

HENRIETTE. Now, take it easy, sister. You've a noble mind,

You can control the animal side of mankind,   160
Remember? So, stay cool. Why all this angry speech?

ARMANDE. Control? It's up to you to practise what you preach.
So you're in love with him, you say? You're too naive:
You haven't tried to ask your parents for their leave.
A daughter's duty's to obey when they command—
They'll tell you what to do: you can make no demand.
They can control your heart, that's unconditional;
Don't take control of what you feel, it's criminal.*

HENRIETTE. Oh, goodness, you're quite right. You know, I needed
    you
To tell me what to do. I value duty too: 170
I'll model my behaviour on what you say.
So let me show how I obey you right away
By asking you, Clitandre, to find my parents, and
Get their approval for the marriage that we've planned.
You've got to ask for their consent, and in good time,
Not leave it till my love for you seems like a crime.

CLITANDRE. I'll go off now and do my best—it's time I went.
I only wanted you to give me your consent.

ARMANDE [to HENRIETTE]. You're gloating, and it shows—that
    smug look on your face!
Don't flatter yourself—you're not causing my disgrace.   180

HENRIETTE. Me? Not at all. I know you're very self-controlled,
You listen to your reason, so I'm always told.
Your wisdom governs you, you're logic's protégée,
And you've no weakness, for you're under reason's sway.
I know that you don't mind at all, and I believe
That you'll be good enough to help us both achieve
Our aim. You'll back us up and lend us your support—
Help us get married. We're both eager, time is short,
So I appeal to you. Give us your help, and we...

ARMANDE. You think you're being clever, making fun of me.   190
His heart was tossed to you—you picked it up with pride.

HENRIETTE. And now you want the very heart you tossed aside.

The fact that he's rejected you has made you mad—
If you could win his heart again, you'd be too glad.

ARMANDE. I won't just stand here listening, that's not my way.
I've no call to dispute the silly things you say.

HENRIETTE. Oh, what a good example! We're outclassed by far.
It's unbelievable how moderate you are.

SCENE 3

HENRIETTE, CLITANDRE

HENRIETTE. I think your frank confession took her by surprise.

CLITANDRE. Well, she deserved plain speaking, cutting down to   200
size.
Her arrogance is ludicrous, but you'll agree
She had a perfect right to learn the truth from me.
I'll go and find your father, since you've said I may,
Madame...

HENRIETTE. My mother's more important, I should say.
My father's easygoing, always keen to please,
He never seems to stand by what he first agrees.
He's born with a compliant attitude to life
Which means that he submits in all things to his wife.
She rules the roost; she's bossy, and she's much inclined
To laying down the law once she makes up her mind.   210
Humour my mother and my aunt, you know you should—
The ladies, both of them—and do our cause some good.
If you could just pretend you like their make-believe,
At least you'd earn respect—that much you could achieve.

CLITANDRE. I couldn't flatter them—that way just isn't mine.
Why, even in your sister's case I drew the line.
Pedantic women never have been to my taste.
Some schooling in a woman may not be misplaced,
But being passionate about it's a mistake—
She mustn't cultivate learning for learning's sake.   220

And if she doesn't want to end up on the shelf,
She'll have the sense to keep her knowledge to herself.
If she intends to study, she should hide the fact,
Conceal her learning with discretion and with tact,
Refrain from quoting authors and from wise critiques,
And try not to seem clever with each word she speaks.*
I do believe your mother's worthy of respect,
But self-deception's quite a character defect.
I find I can't agree with most of what she says,
For instance in the compliments she always pays   230
To Monsieur Trissotin. I loathe that charlatan—
It drives me mad to see her worship of the man.
She places him among the great minds of the age,
And yet his writing's second rate on every page.
He's so prolific—just with what he throws away,
You'd wrap up all the groceries on market day.*

HENRIETTE. I feel the same as you. The man's a frightful bore—
His books, his conversation when he takes the floor—
But as he has great influence here in the house,
You've got to be polite. It means you'll have the nous   240
To play a part. You lovers have to do your bit,
Gain favour in the household, try to score a hit,
Check everyone's included in your dialogue—
And even make advances to the family dog.*

CLITANDRE. You're right; but Trissotin, and all his rigmarole,
Repels me from the very bottom of my soul.
I need his good opinion, but I can't agree
To lie about his work and its effect on me.
I'd read some of his books before he showed his face;
I knew of him before he turned up in this place.   250
The endless stream of rubbish he kept pouring forth
Revealed what this pedantic person thinks he's worth:
He's so complacent that he's very hard to beat,
And nothing shakes his arrogance and self-conceit.
He constantly declares his superiority
And seems quite unaware of his infirmity.
He likes himself so much he laughs at his own jokes,
And thinks the words he writes are little masterstrokes.

He wouldn't change his role as intellectual
For all the medals of an army general.*   260

HENRIETTE. How perspicacious to see all that in his books!

CLITANDRE. It even went so far I felt I knew his looks.
We'd been bombarded by so many poems, I guessed
What he must look like by the way they were expressed.
I knew what to expect when first I saw his face—
So one day, when I saw him in a public place,*
'That must be Trissotin!' I said. I laid a bet,
And found I'd wagered right before we'd even met.

HENRIETTE. You're joking.

CLITANDRE.   No I'm not. That's how it really was.
Here comes your aunt. Leave me alone with her, because   270
If I tell her our secret hopes, and make her see
Our side, she might persuade your mother to agree.

SCENE 4

CLITANDRE, BELISE

CLITANDRE. Madame, will you excuse my importunity?
I want to use this lucky opportunity
To have a heart to heart. Look, I'm a man in love...

BELISE. Hold on! Don't tell me what you feel! For I'm above
All that. I know that you're my suitor, like the rest—*
Keep silent!—Your two eyes alone may try their best
To plead your cause, for I forbid you to use speech
To express desires which shock me. You may dwell on each   280
Of my perfections, love me, burn with ardour, if
You make quite sure that you don't speak. No, not a whiff
Of passion! I'm prepared to overlook your zeal,
As long as you dissemble what you really feel.
But if you should attempt a speech, however light,
Then that's the end, and you'll be banished from my sight.*

CLITANDRE. True, I'm in love, but there's no need to feel alarm.
It's Henriette, Madame, who's won me with her charm.
And I've come here to ask you if you'd be so kind
As give us your support—that is, if you don't mind.   290

BELISE. How cleverly you turn the thing! I must admit
That naughty trick's quite brilliant. Who'd have thought of it?
I've read a hundred novels with these very eyes,
And never found a more ingenious device.

CLITANDRE. It's no device, Madame. I'm trying to explain
The way I really feel. Let me make myself plain.
My love is Henriette—*her* beauty's won my heart.
It's *Henriette* who rules my life; I wouldn't part
From *Henriette* for anything. If we can wed,
We'll ask for nothing more. Oh, please, don't be misled,   300
But help us. You've great influence. Can we depend
On your support? We need your help—please condescend.

BELISE. He's very circumspect, but I can guess the truth.
I know what I'm supposed to think—I'm not uncouth.
He talks in metaphors, but I can play that game:
I'll take your part and I'll promote your secret aim,
By telling everyone that Henriette rejects
Your love: I'll say that you've proposed, but she objects.

CLITANDRE. But why must you twist everything into a knot,
And why, Madame, insist on thinking what is not?   310

BELISE. Oh, come, come, don't be coy. And don't try to deny
What I see in your eyes. There's no need to reply,
Just let me tell you that one's pleased that you're discreet,
And your respectful subterfuge is rather sweet.
One won't object—one's satisfied you will be good;
You may pay homage from a distance, but you should
Take care. Don't go too far. Let honour be your guide.
Enough to say you worshipped me, so lived and died.

CLITANDRE. But...

BELISE.   I've encouraged you enough for just one day,
And also said a lot more than I meant to say.   320

CLITANDRE. But you're mistaken...

BELISE.   Stop! You're putting me to
      shame...
   My modesty... my blushes... Oh, I'm all aflame.

CLITANDRE. I'm hanged if I love you. This really is absurd!

BELISE. Be quiet! I won't listen to another word.

                                        [*Exit* BELISE

CLITANDRE. The woman's mad. To hell with her illusions!
   And have there ever been such mad delusions?
   But we still need support—that's indispensable.
   I'll go and ask for help from someone sensible.*

ACT II

SCENE 1

ARISTE, CLITANDRE

ARISTE [*speaking to* CLITANDRE *as he exits*]. All right, I'll let you
    have the answer when I can.
    I'll plead your cause, I promise... Yes, I'll be your man.   330
    Will you young lovers never stop your chattering?
    You're so impatient! The effect is shattering.
    I never...

SCENE 2

ARISTE, CHRYSALE

ARISTE.   Oh, hallo there, brother!

CHRYSALE.   Ah! good-day
    To you.

ARISTE.   Can you guess why I'm here? What do you say?
    Eh?

CHRYSALE.   No, but tell me why, you know I'll be all ears.

ARISTE. I understand you've known Clitandre for many years?

CHRYSALE. That's right. He spends a lot of time with us, you know.

ARISTE. And is he in the way? Do you find him *de trop*?

CHRYSALE. Of course not! He's a splendid fellow! I respect
    The boy. You won't find many like him, I suspect.   340

ARISTE. I think so too. In fact, I've come at his request,
    And I'm delighted if you think that he's the best.

CHRYSALE. I met his father when I made that Roman trip—

ARISTE. Indeed!

CHRYSALE.   Great chap! We made a lively partnership.

ARISTE. They say he's nice.

CHRYSALE.   We weren't much more than twenty-eight,
   Both ladies' men, and always ready for a date.

ARISTE. I'm sure you were.

CHRYSALE.   We'd hunt the Roman ladies down.
   What sport! We soon became the talk of that great town.
   The men of Rome were jealous.

ARISTE.   Happy souvenir!
   But can we talk about the reason why I'm here?   350

SCENE 3

CHRYSALE, ARISTE, BELISE [*enters silently and listens*]

ARISTE. I'm here to speak for young Clitandre, for he's set
   On marrying—he loves your daughter Henriette.

CHRYSALE. What's that, my daughter?

ARISTE.   Yes; that's what the boy's confessed.
   I've never seen a man so utterly obsessed.

BELISE [*stepping forward*]. No, no, that isn't true. You just don't
      know the half,
   You've got it wrong. I'll speak on Clitandre's behalf!

ARISTE. What, sister?

BELISE.   Yes, he's pulled the wool over your eyes,
   Another woman is the object of his sighs.

ARISTE. You're joking. He's in love, but not with Henriette?

BELISE. I'm certain of it.   360

ARISTE.   But he says his heart is set...

BELISE. Well, yes...

ARISTE.   I'm only here because he wanted me
   To break it to her father, get him to agree.

BELISE. Quite so.

ARISTE.   And when formalities have been exchanged,
   To name the day, as soon as it can be arranged.

BELISE. Ha, ha! That's better still! What a romantic ruse!
   Between ourselves, poor Henriette is an excuse.
   She's camouflage, dear brother, useful to conceal
   A more mysterious love, which I can now reveal.
   My duty is to see you don't make a mistake.

ARISTE. Well, sister, if you've solved the problem, could you   370
   make
   It clear just who this secret love of his can be?

BELISE. You want to know?

ARISTE.   Yes, who?

BELISE.   *Moi.*

ARISTE.   What?

BELISE.   Yes, little me.

ARISTE. Pshaw, sister!

BELISE.   What on earth do you mean by that 'Pshaw'?
   What's so surprising? Never heard of love before?
   I happen to believe my beauty says it all,
   And I have more than one adoring heart in thrall.
   Dorante, Damis, Cleonte, and Lycidas all came*
   To worship at my altars, with their hearts aflame.

ARISTE. You say they love you?

BELISE.   Passionately! They're consumed.

ARISTE. And have they told you so?   380

BELISE.   No, for they've not presumed.
   They show so much respect that to this very day
   They haven't said a word. Of course they won't betray
   Their passion. Though their feelings almost overflow,
   They pay me homage, but it's always in dumb show.

ARISTE. Where visits are concerned, Damis is circumspect.

BELISE. Yes, that's to demonstrate the depth of his respect.

ARISTE. Dorante makes mock of you—it's almost an outrage.

BELISE. Those are the transports of a lover's jealous rage.

ARISTE. Cleonte and Lycidas have taken wives elsewhere.

BELISE. Yes, that's because their love's reduced them to despair. 390

ARISTE. You've made it all up, sister. Stop, admit defeat.

CHRYSALE. You'd really better rid yourself of this conceit.

BELISE. *Conceit* indeed! I see. It's a *conceit*, you say!
        Conceit, that's me. That word *conceit*'s just made my day.
        Well, brothers, I'm delighted with *conceit*; thank you.
        So I'm full of *conceit*, you say. At least that's new.

SCENE 4

CHRYSALE, ARISTE

CHRYSALE. Our sister's raving mad.

ARISTE.   She gets worse every day.
        But can I go on with what I was trying to say?
        Clitandre hopes that Henriette can be his wife.
        So what d'you say? I know he'll love her all his life.   400

CHRYSALE. You needn't even ask. I'm happy to agree.
        The marriage is an honour to the family.

ARISTE. He's not very well off, you may not realize.
        And he...

CHRYSALE. Oh, that's of no importance in my eyes.
        I know that he's hard up, he never did pretend.
        So what? I like the lad. His father was my friend.

ARISTE. Shall we speak to your wife, get her consent before
        Going on with this?...

CHRYSALE.   I've said he'll be my son-in-law.

ARISTE. That's fine; but it would help to back up your consent
If we could get hers too: your time would be well spent.   410
Let's go now...

CHRYSALE.   There's no need, when I've said I agree.
I'll answer for my wife: the matter's up to me.

ARISTE. But what...

CHRYSALE.   Let me decide, I say, and have no fear.
I'll go and sort things out. The situation's clear.

ARISTE. I'll sound out Henriette, check her agreement's won,
Then I'll be back to hear...

CHRYSALE.   The thing's as good as done.
I'll speak to my dear wife, myself, and make things plain

SCENE 5

MARTINE, CHRYSALE

MARTINE. Just my bloomin' bad luck! Now what's that thing again
'Bout giving dogs bad names to hang 'em?—so they say,
And being in service never gets you far, no way.   420

CHRYSALE. Martine, so what's the matter now?

MARTINE.   Well, sad to say...

CHRYSALE. Yes?

MARTINE.   I've been given notice, Sir, as of today.

CHRYSALE. Given your notice?

MARTINE.   Yes, Madame has thrown me out.

CHRYSALE. I don't agree with this. How come?

MARTINE.   And with a clout

Around the ear'ole too, so I best get out quick.*

CHRYSALE. No, you're a good girl. Here you are and here you'll
　　stick.
On a bad day my wife's hot-headed, I admit,
But me, I don't intend...

SCENE 6

PHILAMINTE, CHRYSALE, BELISE, MARTINE

PHILAMINTE [*catching sight of* MARTINE]. What, hussy, not gone
　　yet?
Get out, you wretch! Look sharp now. Go on. Disappear,
And don't you dare come back! You're not wanted round here. 430

CHRYSALE. Hold on...

PHILAMINTE.　　　　　My mind's made up.

CHRYSALE.　　　　　　　　　　Eh?

PHILAMINTE.　　　　　　　　　　　　She must go, right now.

CHRYSALE. All right, so she's to blame, but could you tell me how?

PHILAMINTE. What! So you're sticking up for her?

CHRYSALE.　　　　　　　　　　　　　　Me? Not at all.

PHILAMINTE. And taking sides with her against me?

CHRYSALE.　　　　　　　　　　　　　Don't let's brawl—
I just wanted to know what she was doing wrong.

PHILAMINTE. Would I dismiss her for a minor contretemps?

CHRYSALE. That isn't what I said; but don't you think our staff...?

PHILAMINTE. No. She must go. Don't try to plead on her behalf.

CHRYSALE. I quite agree, my dear. I only thought I'd ask...

PHILAMINTE. I'm mistress here. Don't think you can take *me*　　440
　　to task.

CHRYSALE. Of course not.

PHILAMINTE.   Husbands ought to let their wives decide.
    What you must do is back me up, and take my side.

CHRYSALE. Of course, my dear.

                                        [*Turns to* MARTINE

                    My wife's quite right to throw you out,
    You baggage; you've been very bad, without a doubt.

MARTINE. But, Sir, what have I done?

CHRYSALE [*quietly*].   Oh, gosh, I've no idea.

PHILAMINTE. She's playing down her wickedness, that much is
    clear.

CHRYSALE. What's she done wrong, my dear? Can she have
    overspent,
    Or smashed a precious vase, or dropped an ornament?

PHILAMINTE. Would I dismiss her for a silly thing like that?
    That wouldn't make me cross—I'm not an autocrat.   450

CHRYSALE. I see—then has she done something considerable?

PHILAMINTE. Indeed she has. You know I'm not unreasonable.

CHRYSALE. Oh, so it's something much, much worse? Well, at that
    rate...
    Can she have let a thief get at the silver plate?

PHILAMINTE. That would be nothing.

CHRYSALE.   Ho! Upon my word, my girl!
    What, did you catch her out, giving romance a whirl?

PHILAMINTE. It's far, far worse than that.

CHRYSALE.   Far worse than that?

PHILAMINTE.   Yes, worse.

CHRYSALE. The little minx! You mean you find she's not
    averse...

PHILAMINTE. She made a coarse remark I chanced to overhear—
    We gave her lessons too!—It grated on my ear.   460
    She used a certain vulgar word, made a *faux pas*,
    Which was condemned decisively by Vaugelas.*

CHRYSALE. So...

PHILAMINTE.   After all we've said, the hussy has the gall
    To disregard the noblest science of them all?
    It's grammar that I mean: it governs even kings.
    They're regulated by it, like their underlings.

CHRYSALE. And I thought what she did was something chargeable.

PHILAMINTE. What? So you don't agree it's unforgivable?

CHRYSALE. I do.

PHILAMINTE.   You can't excuse her. Don't make the attempt.

CHRYSALE. No, no.   470

BELISE.   You'll find her use of words beneath contempt:
    Forget the syntax, all the girl can do is stammer,
    Although we've tried to teach her all the rules of grammar.

MARTINE. Correct me if you like; I don't mind; I agree,
    But talking posh like you two ladies's not for me.

PHILAMINTE. Impertinence! What she calls 'posh' is proper
    speech.
    It's based on usage and the rules grammarians teach.

MARTINE. If people understand me, why all this abuse?
    And all your fancy talk, let's face it, ain't no use.

PHILAMINTE. You hear the things she says? Her language is a joke:
    'Let's face it, ain't no use'!   480

BELISE.   Her brain's gone up in smoke.
    We've tried so hard to teach the girl, for all our sakes,
    But can't make her see sense, and speak without mistakes.
    That 'ain't' followed by 'no' is so rebarbative—
    We've told you not to use a double negative.

MARTINE. Well I ain't got book-learning same as what you got,

And we all talks the same back home with all our lot.

PHILAMINTE. This is beyond belief!

BELISE.   Yes, what a solecism!

PHILAMINTE. She'll be the death of me. The girl's a barbarism!

BELISE. You needn't make mistakes with your vernacular—
   The pronoun 'We''s a plural, 'talks' is singular.   490
   You should show more respect for simple rules of grammar.

MARTINE. Who says I don't respect my grandpa or my grandma?*

PHILAMINTE. Oh, Lord!

BELISE.   'Grammar' is what I said. You've got it wrong,
   I've told you where the word comes from.

MARTINE.   Oh, get along!
   Who cares if it's from Finland or from Timbuctoo?
   It's all the same to me.

BELISE.   You country bumpkin, you!
   The adjective, the verb, the noun, the parts of speech,
   It's grammar teaches us to show respect for each,
   And makes us learn their rules.

MARTINE.   Madame, I've got to say
   I never met them people.   500

PHILAMINTE.   God, what a display!

BELISE. Those are the names of words; and we're supposed to see
   The best way we can find of making them agree.

MARTINE. Let them agree or have a row: what do I care?

PHILAMINTE. Stop reasoning with her: it drives me to despair.

                                        [*To her husband*

And as for you, do as I say and show her out.

CHRYSALE. Of course.

                                        [*To* MARTINE

> She's in a mood. I don't quite like to flout
Her wishes. Don't annoy her. Yes, you'd better go.

PHILAMINTE. What's that? You don't want to offend that so-and-
so?
Your tone was too obliging. Must you mollify
The girl?   510

CHRYSALE.   No. Go away, now. Scram!

> [*Quietly*
Poor child, goodbye.

SCENE 7

PHILAMINTE, CHRYSALE, BELISE

CHRYSALE. We've thrown her out. I hope that you're both satisfied;
As for my part in this, I don't feel edified.
She did her job quite well, and took good care of us.
Your reasons for dismissing her were frivolous.

PHILAMINTE. I see; you'd rather I kept her in service here,
Although she tortures me, and irritates my ear.
Her speech is an uncouth collection of mistakes:
With every syllable, she slaughters speech, and breaks
The rules of common usage; then she'll intersperse
Her speech with homespun proverbs—those are even worse.   520

BELISE. It's true that hearing her's enough to make one sweat—
With every word she says, poor Vaugelas's under threat,
And at her vulgar best the chit accompanies
Her speech with pleonasms and cacophonies.

CHRYSALE. Who cares if she has never studied Vaugelas?
Her cooking's where she needs a varied repertoire.
She needn't have a clue which nouns go with which verbs;
I'd rather that she knew a thing or two on herbs.
She's welcome to display her failure to construe,
If she won't burn the meat or over-salt the stew.   530

I live off tasty soup, not off a learned book
And Vaugelas's grammar book can't teach a girl to cook.
Malherbe and Balzac knew the literary rules*
But in the kitchen they'd have looked a pair of fools.

PHILAMINTE. Oh! What a speech! It ended worse than it began—
And how degrading that you call yourself a man!
You know, you're so material it's quite insane,
You ought to change, and strive to reach a higher plane.
This body now, this husk, is trivial, and you ought
To do the right thing by it: don't give it a thought.   540
You ought to leave this grossness far behind, you know.

CHRYSALE. My body's what I am. I care for it, and though
It seems a husk to you, that husk is dear to me.

BELISE. But minds and bodies go together, don't you see,
And if we take the men of learning at their word,
The mind ought to take precedence, or so I've heard.
Now, cherishing the mind should be our prime intent:
Essential knowledge ought to form its nourishment.

CHRYSALE. Good grief! If your chief aim is nourishing the mind,
You're feeding it starvation rations, shells, and rind.   550
You couldn't care less. No, you've no solicitude
For...

PHILAMINTE.   Ah! that word 'solicitude' is very crude.
It's out of date: it has an odour of decay.

BELISE. It has a rather starchy sound to it, today.

CHRYSALE. Look here, I've had enough, I'm going to make a scene.
I've lost control, I see I've got to vent my spleen.
Our friends think you've gone mad, it's making me feel blue...

PHILAMINTE. What's this I hear?

CHRYSALE.   Sister, it's you I'm talking to.
You talk of 'solecisms', which bother you in speech;
But in behaviour you don't practise what you preach.   560
Your everlasting books don't fit with my beliefs.
A tome of Plutarch to press down my neckerchiefs*

Is all we need. Just burn the rest or let them drown,
And leave book-learning to the scholars of the town.
Then climb up to the loft—I'm sure you can both cope—
And make sure you remove that monstrous telescope,
And all those other bits and pieces. Do it soon.
Stop looking into what you've seen up on the moon,
And look into what's going on under your nose,
Where everything is topsy-turvy, goodness knows.   570
The honest truth is, sister, it's not quite the thing
To be a clever woman, and a bluestocking.
The subject of your study, your philosophy,
Should be to keep the house, practise economy,
Bring up the children to know how things should be done,
See that the staff behave, and that the home's well run.
Our elders knew a thing or two in this respect,
They claimed that with a woman all you could expect
Was that, with training, she might manage to expose
What makes a doublet different from a pair of hose.   580
Their women never read, but they knew how to live,
And housekeeping for them was something positive.
Their books were needle and thread, their daily task to sew;
Their work was for their daughters, and the girls' trousseaux.
You modern women won't consent to stay at home.
You long to be the authors of a learned tome.
You want to shine, to be the ones with all the nous;
The worst offenders live right here, here, in my house.
The secrets of the universe are here for free,
And you know everything except what pleases me.   590
The pathways of the pole-star, Venus, Mars, the moon,
Are plotted in this house, here, in this very room.
You study futile subjects, ranging far and wide,
But overcook my food, leave me dissatisfied.
To please you, all the servants, bogged down in their books,
Neglect their household tasks—I don't need clerks but cooks.
The staff's commitment to their learning's quite immense,
But so much reasoning has banished common sense.
One, reading, burns the roast: the story made him think;
Another dreams up verses when I ask for drink.*   600
They follow your example, as I have observed,

And I have servants, but I never can get served.
One single girl was left to keep me from despair:
She hadn't been infected by the noxious air.
And now you throw her out with maximum fracas,
Because her speech would not appeal to Vaugelas.
I can't bear it much longer, sister, nor condone
Your lifestyle (what I say is meant for you alone).
And I could do without your Latin-speaking gang,
And in particular that Monsieur Trissotin.   610
He's made a fool of you in public with his verse,
And everything he says is nonsense, if not worse.
Deciphering his poetry's quite an affair,
And if you ask me he's as mad as a March hare.

PHILAMINTE. Oh, Lord! He plumbs the depths, in mind and
    language too!

BELISE. I never saw a baser clump of cells, did you?
    His brain's made up of atoms, all too too bourgeois.*
    How can he be the brother of a girl like *moi*?
    It makes me sick at heart to be of the same race.
    I'm in too much confusion—better leave this place.   620

SCENE 8

PHILAMINTE, CHRYSALE

PHILAMINTE. Do you have any further crude attacks to make?

CHRYSALE. Me? No. Let's drop all this. That's it—had my
    outbreak.
    To change tack now, your older daughter can't adjust
    To marrying—she views the whole thing with disgust.
    She's a philosopher—enough said, call a halt.
    She gets advice from you, that's true, I can't find fault.
    Our younger daughter's in a different frame of mind;
    Yes, Henriette would benefit if we could find
    A husband...

PHILAMINTE.   Yes, I've thought of that. I have a plan—

It's time to tell you who's to be the lucky man.   630
That Monsieur Trissotin, whose presence is taboo,
Who hasn't had the luck to be admired by you,
I've chosen him for this eventuality—
I'm better placed than you to judge his quality.
Don't try to answer back—it's useless to protest,
My mind's made up, I know my choice is for the best.
Don't say a word to her about this marriage; I
Will tell the girl myself, so don't you even try.
I'll handle this one. Till I tell you you may speak,
Keep quiet. I'll know at once if you have dared to squeak.   640

SCENE 9

ARISTE, CHRYSALE

ARISTE. Well? Off sweeps Philaminte. It's very plain to see,
    You've had it out between you. What did she decree?

CHRYSALE. Well...

ARISTE.   Do we get our wedding, did you win the day?
    Did she agree to everything? What did she say?

CHRYSALE. No, not exactly.

ARISTE.   She refused?

CHRYSALE.   Oh, no, not so.

ARISTE. So is it that she can't make her mind up, then?

CHRYSALE.   No.

ARISTE. What then?

CHRYSALE.   I find she's chosen quite another man.

ARISTE. Another man?

CHRYSALE.   That's right.

ARISTE.   And it's none other than?...

CHRYSALE. It's Monsieur Trissotin.

ARISTE.   That boring waste of time?

CHRYSALE. That's him—the one who talks in Latin and in   650
rhyme.

ARISTE. Did you accept him?

CHRYSALE.   Me? Of course not, God forbid!

ARISTE. You answered?

CHRYSALE.   Nothing, and I'm very glad I did.
I didn't say a word, I needed no defence.

ARISTE. How sensible, how wise to sit upon the fence!
Did you mention Clitandre, as we agreed before?

CHRYSALE. No; when she offered me a different son-in-law,
I thought it better not to try to press my point.

ARISTE. How thoughtful! Keep it up, you'll never disappoint.
But aren't you ashamed to be so very wet?
You really are the weakest man I've ever met.   660
Your wife rules over you, you're horribly henpecked;
When she makes up her mind, you never dare object.

CHRYSALE. Look, brother, it's all very well for you to talk.
You can't imagine how I squirm when women squawk.
I like a quiet life, restraint and self-control,
And my wife's moods strike abject terror to my soul.
She makes a thing of being a philosopher,
But nothing stops her temper overwhelming her.
Material things to her are far beneath contempt,
But she can't curb her rages, won't make the attempt.   670
If you dare to object to what she has in mind,
You're buffeted all week by tempest, storm, and wind.
I start to quake as soon as she begins to shout.
I just can't cope—she's like a dragon; she wipes out
My peace of mind with her brutality. And yet,
I have to tell her she's 'my darling' and 'my pet'.

ARISTE. Now, brother, don't pretend. Your meekness helps to give
Your wife the upper hand: you're much too sensitive.
Her strength depends upon your weakness, and that's that:

It's you who've turned her into such an autocrat.   680
When you give in to what she thinks she can impose,
You let her lead you, like a donkey, by the nose.
Yes, you've become a laughing stock. Can't you decide
To stand up like a man, not run away and hide?
To make that woman realize she must obey,
And have the guts to say: 'I'll run the place my way'?
This madness draws your women like a kind of spell.
Don't let them sacrifice poor Henriette as well!
What? Give away your worldly goods to this dumb fool,
Who knows six words of Latin, learnt by heart at school?   690
At least with him your wife is deferential:
He's a philosopher, an intellectual;
She thinks his poems are incredible, first class,
But you and I both know he's just a silly ass.
Stop fooling, that's enough. It's high time that you woke—
Your cowardly behaviour's nothing but a joke.

CHRYSALE. Yes, I can see it now. You're right, I know I'm wrong.
I'm going to have to show the woman that I'm strong,
Dear brother.

ARISTE.   Yes, well said!

CHRYSALE.   The time has really come.
I'm not prepared to live under a woman's thumb.   700

ARISTE. Yes.

CHRYSALE.   I've been much too soft, she took me for a ride.

ARISTE. That's true.

CHRYSALE.   When I was kind, she pushed me to one side.

ARISTE. Oh, yes.

CHRYSALE.   All that must stop, today. I'll have her know
My daughter's mine to give, and what I say must go.
The husband that she gets must be the man I choose.

ARISTE. At last you're talking sense, I see you share my views.

CHRYSALE. You're on Clitandre's side, you know where he must be:
Quick, brother, seek him out, and bring him here to me.

ARISTE. I'll go at once.

CHRYSALE.   Her reign is over. Change of plan.
No matter how she rails, I'll show her I'm a man.   710

ACT III

SCENE 1

PHILAMINTE, ARMANDE, BELISE, TRISSOTIN, L'EPINE

PHILAMINTE. Come on, let's settle down to listen at our ease:
We'll need to concentrate on clever lines like these.

ARMANDE. I'm frantic with impatience!

BELISE.   Oh, I'm burning, *moi*!

PHILAMINTE. I'm charmed by all the poems in your repertoire.

ARMANDE. I know this will be ecstasy—I'm quite sincere.

BELISE. Like a delicious meal: you'll pour it down my ear.

PHILAMINTE. Don't keep us in suspense! We must have our desire.

ARMANDE. Be quick!

BELISE.   We're longing for it, and we're all on fire.

PHILAMINTE. We've such an appetite! Let's hear your epigram.

TRISSOTIN. Alas! It's just a newborn infant, dear Madame,   720
But I know you'll appreciate my little man:
For it was in your court my labour-pains began!

PHILAMINTE. Of course he'll touch my heart, since you're his fond
papa.

TRISSOTIN. You favour him, so you can be his proud mamma.

BELISE. Oh, that's so witty!

SCENE 2

PHILAMINTE, HENRIETTE, ARMANDE, BELISE, TRISSOTIN,
L'EPINE

PHILAMINTE.   Hey there! Don't you sneak away!

HENRIETTE. I don't want to disturb the charming things you say.

PHILAMINTE. I want you here with us. You'd better be all ears:
This conversation's like the music of the spheres.

HENRIETTE. I can't appreciate such erudite delights:
The treasures of the mind are way beyond my sights.   730

PHILAMINTE. It doesn't matter; and, when this is over, you
Must learn a secret which it's more than time you knew.

TRISSOTIN. Now, why should you be clever? Why take up your pen?
Your energies go into captivating men.

HENRIETTE. I don't care to do either, Sir. You've got me wrong.

BELISE. Oh, please let's hear the new-born baby's cradle-song!

PHILAMINTE. Come on, young man, be quick, and bring us chairs
all round.

> [*The footman falls with the chair*

Oh, what an idiot! You land flat on the ground,
When you've been taught the laws of equilibrium.

BELISE. You clumsy ignoramus, must you be so dumb?   740
You moved your fulcrum—goodness, what depravity!—
And disregarded all the laws of gravity.

L'EPINE. Madame, I knew that when I landed on my arse.

PHILAMINTE. You lout!

TRISSOTIN.   It's just as well he isn't made of glass!

ARMANDE. Ah! Brilliance everywhere!

BELISE.   An ever-flowing source!

PHILAMINTE. Oh, hurry! Do serve up your exquisite first course!

TRISSOTIN. Oh, now I realize your hunger's so extreme,
I fear one little dish of eight lines is too lean.
I've had a good idea. I'll be more prodigal,
And I'll top up my epigram and madrigal*   750
With this, a sonnet titbit, which a princess thought

Quite delicate in flavour, and with Attic salt
Well seasoned (so she said), and redolent of Greece.
I think you'll all consider it a tasty piece.*

ARMANDE. We know it!

PHILAMINTE. Hurry, please, I'm greedy for a bite!

BELISE [*every time he tries to read, she interrupts*]. I can already feel
  my heart beat with delight.
I so love poetry! There's nothing more worthwhile,
Particularly when I can admire the style.

PHILAMINTE. If we talk on and on he'll never get to start.

TRISSOTIN. *SO...* 760

BELISE. Silence, niece, I tell you!

ARMANDE. Let him show his art!

TRISSOTIN.

SONNET TO PRINCESS URANIE ON HER FEVER*

> *Your prudence must be sound asleep!*
> *By grandly entertaining—*
> *This hostile guest retaining—*
> *Your own worst enemy you keep.*

BELISE. Ah! That begins so well!

ARMANDE. How gracefully it's turned!

PHILAMINTE. Such easy, flowing verse! What treasures I discerned!

ARMANDE. At *Prudence sound asleep* we three lay down our arms.

BELISE. *This hostile guest retaining*'s packed chock-full of charms.

PHILAMINTE. That *grandly entertaining* goes together well—
  Adverb and gerund juxtaposed—it casts a spell. 770

BELISE. Oh, do let's hear the rest!

TRISSOTIN. *Your prudence must be sound asleep!*
> *By grandly entertaining—*
> *This hostile guest retaining—*
> *Your own worst enemy you keep.*

ARMANDE. *Prudence sound asleep!*

BELISE. *Hostile guest retaining!*

PHILAMINTE. *Grandly entertaining!*

TRISSOTIN.   *Make her leave, though tongues can cluck,*
       Your sumptuous apartment:
       Her insolent comportment
   At your life's precious heart has struck.

BELISE. Oh, wait! I need to think! I'm burning! I'm on fire!

ARMANDE. Oh, please, let's have a moment's leisure to admire!

PHILAMINTE. I can't explain what's flowing through me. Look, I melt,
I'm quivering with joy—those lines—so deeply felt!

ARMANDE. *Make her leave, though tongues can cluck,*
       Your sumptuous apartment.

Sumptuous apartment! Could one ask for more?   780
How cleverly you put that witty metaphor!

PHILAMINTE.   *Make her leave, though tongues can cluck.*

Ah! *Tongues can cluck!* That's in the very best of taste!
In my view it's sublime, and admirably placed.

ARMANDE. That *Tongues can cluck*—it makes my heart beat fast.
What bliss!

BELISE. Oh, you're so right, that *Tongues can cluck*'s a masterpiece.

ARMANDE. I wish I'd thought of it.

BELISE.   It's poetry in itself!

PHILAMINTE. But do you understand its craft? I do, myself.

ARMANDE and BELISE. Oh, oh!

PHILAMINTE.   *Make her leave, though tongues can cluck.*
So what, if the observers take the fever's side?
Relax, try not to mind, though people may deride.

       Make her leave, though tongues can cluck,
       Tongues can cluck, tongues can cluck.

There's more to *tongues can cluck* than would at first appear: 790
I don't know if you two can grasp my meaning here;
But I can see it speaks a volume with each word.

BELISE. In one suggestive phrase whole epics can be heard.

PHILAMINTE. But at the time you wrote that gorgeous *tongues can cluck*,
Did you, the author, feel its force and see your luck?
Did you appreciate its concentrated wit,
And did you realize what charms you'd put in it?

TRISSOTIN. Hey, hey!

ARMANDE.   And as for *hostile guest*, I'm quite obsessed:
That fever, what a poisonous, ungrateful pest,
Ungrateful to the host who kindly took her in!   800

PHILAMINTE. Your quatrains seem to me superbly genuine.
And now, let's have the tercets, quickly, if you please!

ARMANDE. Just one more *tongues can cluck*, I beg, a short reprise!

TRISSOTIN.   *Make her leave, though tongues can cluck,*

PHILAMINTE, ARMANDE, and BELISE. *Tongues can cluck!*

TRISSOTIN.   *Your sumptuous apartment*

PHILAMINTE, ARMANDE, and BELISE. *Sumptuous apartment!*

TRISSOTIN.   *Her insolent comportment*

PHILAMINTE, ARMANDE, and BELISE. That *insolent* fever!

TRISSOTIN.   *At your life's precious heart has struck.*

PHILAMINTE, ARMANDE, and BELISE. Ah!

TRISSOTIN.   *What! No respect for your high rank!*
                Attack your blood? She never shrank!

PHILAMINTE, ARMANDE, and BELISE. Ah!

TRISSOTIN.   *She night and day your life doth blast!*
                To the bath-house! Understand
                The time for tender mercy's past:
                Drown her there with your own hand.

PHILAMINTE. I can't go on...   810

BELISE.   I'm fainting!

ARMANDE.   I'm half dead with bliss!

PHILAMINTE. I'm quivering all over! Oh, what happiness!

ARMANDE.   *To the bath-house! Understand*

BELISE.   *The time for tender mercy's past:*

PHILAMINTE.   *Drown her there with your own hand.*

There, drown her in the bath, yourself, you understand!

ARMANDE. Our path is strewn with loveliness—a charming touch!

BELISE. One moves in holy rapture—this is just too much!

PHILAMINTE. One walks on perfect beauty everywhere one goes.

ARMANDE. At every step one treads upon another rose.

TRISSOTIN. And so you find my sonnet...

PHILAMINTE.   Admirable, new,
And such high quality! You poets, happy few...

BELISE. What? Niece, he reads his sonnet out, it leaves you cold?
You are the strangest girl, if I may make so bold!   820

HENRIETTE. You know we simple girls can only do our best.
I wish you joy of it, but spare me all the rest.

TRISSOTIN. Perhaps my little poem irritates Madame?

HENRIETTE. I wasn't listening.

PHILAMINTE.   Let's have the epigram!

TRISSOTIN.

*ON A LAVENDER-COLOURED CARRIAGE GIVEN TO A LADY-FRIEND**

PHILAMINTE. Each title always has a brand-new twist to it.

ARMANDE. The prologue to a feast of scintillating wit.

TRISSOTIN.   *Love cost me dear when it took me in thrall:*

BELISE, ARMANDE, and PHILAMINTE. Ah!

TRISSOTIN. *By now my fast-dwindling fortune's grown small.*
      See this carriage so fair,
        With its opulent air,   830
    Its gold knobs are a wonder to all, far and wide—
    My Lais's a triumph when she rides inside!*

PHILAMINTE. Ah! My Lais! How classical! How erudite!

BELISE. I think I know who she must be, at least, I might!

TRISSOTIN. *See this carriage so fair,*
        With its opulent air,
    Its gold knobs are a wonder to all, far and wide—
    My Lais's a triumph when she rides inside!
    But sadly of all my shares I was a vendor,
    When I bought this carriage, colour of lavènder!

ARMANDE. Oh, oh! How unexpected! Doesn't it have bite!

PHILAMINTE. Oh, what good taste he has! This man knows how to
    write!

BELISE. *But sadly of all my shares I was a vendor,*
    When I bought this carriage, colour of lavènder!

Construe it: *a* vendor, *the* vendor, *la* vendor!

PHILAMINTE. I can't tell what it is: it's got to be some quirk,
    Perhaps I'm prejudiced in favour of your work,   840
    But I love everything you write, in verse and prose.

TRISSOTIN. Why don't you let us see the verses you compose?
    We'd be all admiration, listening to you.

PHILAMINTE. I never write in verse, but hope, and shortly too,
    To let you see eight chapters I've been working on.
    I'm planning our Academy. It's time we shone.
    Now, Plato thought of it, but didn't see it through
    When writing his *Republic*—it was all too new.*
    It's up to me to carry on what he began
    And my prose exposition demonstrates my plan.   850
    When I see men observing women with distrust,
    I'm overcome by potent feelings of disgust.

I want to take revenge for what they do to us—
The way they relegate us to a lower class,
Expecting us to waste our time on paltry things,
Excluding women from the rapture wisdom brings.

ARMANDE. It's awful. Do you wonder if we feel offence
When we're expected to use our intelligence
To help us analyse fine lace, or judge a dress,
And waste our time on things that couldn't matter less?   860

BELISE. It's shameful how they treat us. Time we made a stand.
The hour will strike! Our liberation is at hand!

TRISSOTIN. The fair sex is perfection. Who could criticize?
But though I am enchanted by your dazzling eyes,
I find your women's minds illuminating too.

PHILAMINTE. We know it, and that's why our sex thinks well of
     you.
But men who will insist they've left us far behind
Must think again. A woman can have a good mind.
We're founding our Academy like anyone,
We know how learned institutions should be run.   870
We'll make new rules to fit the structure we create,
And link together subjects men keep separate.
It's time for language and pure science to unite,*
We'll do research. Why shouldn't we be erudite?
You'll see, we'll always be impartial in debate,
And give each philosophical approach due weight.

TRISSOTIN. The finest logic is Peripateticism.*

PHILAMINTE. I value abstract thought, and favour Platonism.

ARMANDE. For powerful dogma, Epicurus pleases me.

BELISE. Atoms can really seem quite pleasing, I agree;   880
But I have problems coping with the vacuum,*
So subtle matter is my favourite medium.*

TRISSOTIN. Cartesian magnetism makes sound sense, in my eyes.*

ARMANDE. I love his vortices.*

PHILAMINTE.   His falling worlds are wise.*

ARMANDE. I long to see the birth of our society,
  And demonstrate our worth by some discovery.

TRISSOTIN. We all expect great things of each outstanding mind,
  And nature's mysteries will never leave you blind.

PHILAMINTE. My first discovery's been very opportune—
  I've actually observed some men upon the moon.*   890

BELISE. I haven't seen men yet, but by my reckoning,
  I've seen church steeples up there, clear as anything.

ARMANDE. We'll study science in depth, together with a mix
  Of grammar, history, morals, verse, and politics.

PHILAMINTE. I love moral philosophy, it thrills my heart.
  The finest minds in past times used to take its part.
  But Stoicism's the best of all. It's all the rage,
  And nothing can quite match the perfect Stoic sage.*

ARMANDE. We'll show you language study can be feminine:
  We plan to revolutionize the discipline.   900
  A natural reaction happily inspired
  In us a real disgust for some words we're required
  To use—some nouns and verbs are such a waste of breath,
  That we've decided we must put them all to death.
  We don't want them to live on under sufferance.
  That's the Agenda for our opening conference:
  We're going to do away with all these divers words
  And sterilize our spoken language, prose and verse.*

PHILAMINTE. We've got a master-plan for our Academy
  A noble enterprise, and very dear to me,   910
  A glorious plan and one which certainly will be
  Remembered by great thinkers of posterity.
  You'll see—we'll clean up every smutty syllable
  Whose shocking presence makes nice words despicable,
  Whose innuendo keeps poor stupid fools amused,
  Providing tasteless puns for wisecrackers to use,
  Provoking the eternal vulgar grubby joke,
  Offensive and insulting to us womenfolk.

TRISSOTIN. The projects that you plan are wonderful indeed!

BELISE. When we've set out our rules, we'll give you them to   920
read.

TRISSOTIN. They'll be worthwhile and sensible, and no mistake.

ARMANDE. We'll be the judges, make the laws, and plan to take
Control of prose and verse, and literary trends.
We'll say no one has brains except us and our friends.
We'll pick on everyone, we're spoiling for a fight,
And nobody but us will be allowed to write.

SCENE 3

L'EPINE, TRISSOTIN, PHILAMINTE, BELISE, ARMANDE,
HENRIETTE, VADIUS

L'EPINE [to TRISSOTIN]. Monsieur, a man's outside. He tells me
that he's known
To you. He's dressed in black, talks in an undertone.*

TRISSOTIN. Oh, yes—my friend who's longing to be introduced.
He's quite a scholar—and, I fear, can't be refused.   930

PHILAMINTE. Ah, show him in. A friend of yours is welcome here.
We'll introduce him to a learned atmosphere.

[To HENRIETTE

Hey, you! I thought I'd made it very clear before:
You've got to stay right here.

HENRIETTE.   You said so, but what for?

PHILAMINTE. Just stay by me. You'll hear about it, presently.

TRISSOTIN. Ah, here's the man. He wants to meet you urgently.
I told him he could come. You'll find I'm not to blame—
In fact, I know you'll be delighted that he came:
He holds his own among the finest minds in town.

PHILAMINTE. Well, he's a friend of yours; that speaks for his   940
renown.

TRISSOTIN. He knows the classics—has a perfect cognizance—
And speaks in Greek as well as anyone in France.*

PHILAMINTE. What, Greek? Oh, sister, Greek! The gentleman
speaks Greek!

BELISE. Oh, niece! He can speak Greek!

ARMANDE.   Oh, God! My knees—they're weak!

PHILAMINTE. What, Monsieur! You speak Greek? Oh, paradise!
Oh, bliss!
For love of Greek, will you give all of us a kiss?

                    [VADIUS *kisses them all except* HENRIETTE, *who turns away*

HENRIETTE. Not me, Monsieur, for it's a language I don't speak.

PHILAMINTE. I have a great respect for works composed in Greek.

VADIUS. I would have come to pay you homage long ago,
But reverence held me back. I trust I'm not *de trop*?   950
I fear I interrupt your learned gathering.

PHILAMINTE. No, Monsieur, you speak Greek. Your visit's
flattering.

TRISSOTIN. Besides, he's eloquent in verse, as well as prose.
Perhaps you'd like to hear how well he can compose?

VADIUS. Those writers who complete a composition
Tend to monopolize the conversation.
All over Paris, in the salons or in town,*
They read their works aloud, refuse to put them down.
I think you'll find an intellectual resents
Brash writers of that sort, fishing for compliments.   960
They bend the ear of everyone who comes their way,
And torture hapless victims, who can't get away.
I've never been like them, crude and belligerent;
I sympathize with that Greek writer's sentiment*
When he opines that every wise man should disdain
To read his verse out loud: it's wiser to refrain.
Here are some little verses all about young love.
I'd like to have your views, and see if you approve.

TRISSOTIN. Your verses are unique—I'm not being polite.

VADIUS. The three Graces and Venus reign in what you write.*   970

TRISSOTIN. Your syntax is so skilled, your turn of phrase so terse.

VADIUS. There's *ithos* and *pathos* pervading all your verse.*

TRISSOTIN. I love your eclogues. Who can match the things you
    do?*
Theocritus and Virgil could have learnt from you.*

VADIUS. Your odes are so light-hearted, yet so grave, I find.*
You know, you've left your master, Horace, far behind.

TRISSOTIN. Is anything so charming as your canzonets?*

VADIUS. Would it be possible to match you in sonnèts?

TRISSOTIN. What could be more delightful than your sweet
    roundels?*

VADIUS. What could be wittier than your dear madrigals?*   980

TRISSOTIN. Your *ballades* are innovative, and so *au fait*.*

VADIUS. I find you quite adorable in *bouts-rimés*.*

TRISSOTIN. If only France appreciated what you're worth...

VADIUS. If only intellect was valued on this earth...

TRISSOTIN. You'd ride a golden coach if they gave you your due.

VADIUS. They'd put up statues everywhere to honour you.
Ahem! It's a *ballade*. Please listen to this page,
And judge it frankly.

TRISSOTIN.   There's a sonnet—all the rage—
It's on the fever of the Princess Uranie.

VADIUS. Yes, it was read aloud to me in company.   990

TRISSOTIN. You realize who wrote it?

VADIUS.   No, I wasn't told;
But to be frank, the composition leaves me cold.

TRISSOTIN. But people who have heard it say it's very fine.

VADIUS. That doesn't stop it being a total waste of time,
And if you'd read it you would think the same as me.

TRISSOTIN. You know, that isn't so. I beg to disagree.
Not many poets could demonstrate such expertise.

VADIUS. The gods protect me from composing lines like these!

TRISSOTIN. They're excellent, and I'm prepared to take a stand.
My reason is that they were written by my hand.   1000

VADIUS. You?

TRISSOTIN.   Me.

VADIUS.   I don't know how it can have happened, then.

TRISSOTIN. Monsieur fails to admire the children of my pen.*

VADIUS. Perhaps the reader didn't do it justice, or,
When he was reading, I should have attended more.
Let's drop the subject and move on to my *ballade*.

TRISSOTIN. The *ballade* in my view is scarcely avant-garde.
It's colourless and dull, and very out of date.

VADIUS. Yet it's a form of verse that some appreciate.

TRISSOTIN. The fact remains that I can't stand this type of verse.

VADIUS. Your disapproval doesn't make it any worse.   1010

TRISSOTIN. The pedants are the ones who think it's full of charms.

VADIUS. That can't be so. Why, look at you—you're full of qualms!

TRISSOTIN. If you think I'm like you, you must be ignorant.

VADIUS. And if you think the same, then you're impertinent.

TRISSOTIN. Be off, you pompous twit, you scribbling featherbrain!

VADIUS. Be off, you cheapskate poet, you put our craft to shame!

TRISSOTIN. Be off, you copycat, you pushy plagiarist!

VADIUS. Be off, you wretched hack...

PHILAMINTE.   Please, gentlemen, desist!

TRISSOTIN. Go and give back the shameful passages you stole
  From Greek and Latin, which you took, and swallowed   1020
  whole.

VADIUS. You go, and make amends to the poetic Muse
  For making Horace suffer hideous abuse!

TRISSOTIN. Think of your book: how many copies have been sold?

VADIUS. Think of your publisher—he's down and out, I'm told.

TRISSOTIN. My reputation's made—you'll never bring it low.

VADIUS. You took a drubbing in the *Satires* of Boileau.*

TRISSOTIN. He mocks at you as well.

VADIUS.   At least I can reflect
  That, criticizing me, he's very circumspect.
  He gets at me in passing, it's a mild attack,
  No worse than other writers making up the pack.   1030
  But you're eternally the butt of his caprice,
  He sneers at you, and never leaves you any peace.*

TRISSOTIN. That only goes to show that I'm superior.
  He leaves you in the crowd like an inferior.
  The smallest blow's enough to knock you to the ground,
  You don't deserve the honour of a second round.
  But me, I'm singled out, a worthy challenger;
  He uses all his art to score a leveller.
  The reason that he's constantly attacking me
  Is that he's nervous, and unsure of victory.   1040

VADIUS. My pen will show you whom you're fighting, never fear.

TRISSOTIN. And you will learn from mine just who's the master
  here.

VADIUS. I challenge you in verse, prose, Latin, and in Greek.

TRISSOTIN. And I choose Barbin's bookshop for the place to meet.*

SCENE 4

TRISSOTIN, PHILAMINTE, ARMANDE, BELISE, HENRIETTE

TRISSOTIN. I lost my temper, but don't blame me, dear Madame,
    I was defending you. He was intent on harm,
    Presuming to attack my sonnet, witless man.

PHILAMINTE. I'll reconcile you both, and do the best I can.
    But now let's change the subject. Henriette, come here.
    It's high time I took steps to sort you out, my dear.   1050
    You seem so very stupid—such a dreadful plight:
    I've hit upon a way of putting matters right.

HENRIETTE. Oh, you've no need to bother; why not leave me be?
    Your learned gatherings are not the thing for me.
    For me, an easy life is an undoubted perk,
    And making clever talk seems too much like hard work.
    It's quite beyond me to show much intelligence,
    Or suffer in the cause of verbal elegance.
    I don't want to be brainy, my ambition's gone:
    You know, I'm quite content to be a simpleton.   1060

PHILAMINTE. My honour is at stake, and I won't listen, Miss.
    Yes, you're my flesh and blood, you won't shame me like this.
    The beauty of the face can't be relied upon—
    A transitory flower, it blooms and then it's gone.
    It's skin-deep, nothing more. But beauty of the mind
    Reflects the inner soul, that flower of womankind.
    The time has come for us to help you to infuse
    Your soul with beauty of a kind you'll never lose.
    We must instil the love of learning into you,
    And waken up your mind. The world will seem quite new!   1070
    You see, I've hit upon a very clever plan.
    We'll marry you at once, and to a learned man;
    And that man is Monsieur. I tell you to rejoice.
    From now on, he's your husband, and I've made my choice.

HENRIETTE. What, mother? Me?

PHILAMINTE.   Yes, you. Don't play the innocent.

BELISE [*to* TRISSOTIN]. That look speaks volumes. Yes, you're still
   my supplicant.
Can you be marrying another, when you're mine?
Go on—I give you up most gladly. I resign.
If you marry my niece, your future is secure.

TRISSOTIN. I can't find words to speak... you are my cynosure, 1080
   Madame. I'm honoured that my ardent suit has met
With your approval...

HENRIETTE.   Wait. We're not quite married yet.
   Don't rush things...

PHILAMINTE.   What's this? Do you want to make a scene?
   Do as I say, or else... Yes, you know what I mean.
Oh, she'll see sense. Let's go and leave her here, in thought.

SCENE 5

ARMANDE, HENRIETTE

ARMANDE. You've got yourself a most illustrious consort.
   With mother's loving help, you'll soon find that you're wed.

HENRIETTE. If you like him that much, why not take him instead?

ARMANDE. Because he's pledged his word to you and not to me.

HENRIETTE. But you're the elder sister. Take him, I'll agree.   1090

ARMANDE. If I found marriage charming in the way you do,
   I'd take up your kind offer without more ado.

HENRIETTE. If I had pedants and their learning on the brain,
   As you do, then I'd take him on and not complain.

ARMANDE. Well, even if our views on marriage aren't the same,
   Obedience to our parents has to be our aim.
A mother's power over us is absolute,
So don't think you've a hope, if you stay resolute...

SCENE 6

CHRYSALE, ARISTE, CLITANDRE, HENRIETTE, ARMANDE

CHRYSALE. Come here. It's time to take the action that I've
planned.
Take off your glove, my daughter, give Monsieur your   1100
hand.*
You must accept his love, and this time it's for life—
This man will be your husband, and you'll be his wife.

ARMANDE. You're following your inclinations now, that's plain.

HENRIETTE. Obedience to our parents, sister, is our aim.
A father's power over us is absolute.

ARMANDE. A mother's influence should be beyond dispute.

CHRYSALE. What do you mean?

ARMANDE.   I mean that as it seems to me,
In this affair you and our mother don't agree:
She's picked another man...

CHRYSALE.   Don't be impertinent.
Go and philosophize to both your hearts' content,
And don't dare poke your prying nose in my affairs.
Go, tell her what I say, stop giving yourself airs,
And tell her not to come and make her mischief here.
Be off with you!

ARISTE.   That's excellent! Now persevere.

CHRYSALE. What ecstasy! What joy! Oh, happy, happy day!
Come on, Clitandre. Take her hand and lead the way.
Take her off to her room. Oh, what a sweet caress!
I say, my heart is moved by all this tenderness.
This brings back memories of all my youthful flings—
I feel a lad again, and ripe for naughty things.   1120

ACT IV

SCENE 1

ARMANDE, PHILAMINTE

ARMANDE. Yes, not for one split second did she hesitate.
  She said that she'd obey, was most articulate.
  She's not prepared to wait, but readily complies.
  She's given away her heart before my very eyes.
  But don't think that it's through obedience to papa—
  She's showing her bravado, flouting her mamma.

PHILAMINTE. Her father or her mother—who must take control?
  Is it form or matter, body or pure soul?*
  She can't make such a choice alone—she needs a guide.
  I'll show her which of us has reason on her side.   1130

ARMANDE. They could at least have asked you what your feelings
        were,
  And I am shocked at that impertinent Monsieur,
  Who plots behind your back to be your son-in-law.

PHILAMINTE. He still has far to go before he wins that war.
  I liked his looks and favoured his and your romance,
  But in our dealings he took up a hostile stance:
  Although he knew I wrote, his conduct was absurd—
  He never asked me to read out a single word.

SCENE 2

CLITANDRE [enters quietly, and listens without being seen], ARMANDE,
        PHILAMINTE

ARMANDE. If I were in your shoes, you know, I wouldn't let
  That man become the husband of our Henriette.   1140
  But don't misjudge me, for I mean it for the best:
  I'm not just saying it out of self-interest.

Although he left me, and played quite a shabby part,
I don't resent it, I've no anger in my heart,
For these things happen; and the soul finds its support
In wise philosophy and solid serious thought.
And that's the way I've placed myself above the fray.
But now he's gone too far, in treating *you* this way.
You must oppose the man—your honour is at stake.
You can't be seen to favour him, and you must make   1150
A stand. For when we met and talked, as lovers do,
He never showed the slightest reverence for you.

PHILAMINTE. How paltry!

ARMANDE.   When your reputation brought you fame,
He always seemed indifferent to your acclaim.

PHILAMINTE. The brute!

ARMANDE.   Not letting on who wrote it, for a ploy,
I read him verse by you which he did not enjoy.

PHILAMINTE. What nerve!

ARMANDE.   We quarrelled over his hostility,
And you would not believe that man's stupidity...

CLITANDRE [*stepping forward from his hiding-place*]. Hey, take it easy,
     now. Let's have less spitefulness,
Madame, or at the least, a bit more truthfulness.   1160
What harm have I done you? Tell me, what's my offence,
And why pile into me with all your eloquence?
You're hell-bent on destroying me, mean to succeed,
And make me look a cad to people whom I need.
Come, tell us what you think of me. Why so severe?
I'm willing for Madame to judge between us here.

ARMANDE. If what you said about my bitterness were true,
I'd surely have good reason to feel hurt by you.
Love has its obligations: lovers surely owe
A sacred duty to their first romance, and so   1170
You should be giving up your money and your life
Before you take another woman for your wife.
There's nothing quite so loathsome as a faithless heart,
And fickle lovers always play a shoddy part.

CLITANDRE. Can you complain that I was fickle then, Madame?
 You made a point of ditching me without a qualm.
 You laid down all the rules—all I did was obey;
 And you're the one to blame if I offend today.
 You fascinated me, I loved you from the start.
 For two whole years you had possession of my heart.   1180
 Whatever I held dear, I gladly sacrificed;
 I paid you constant court; but no, nothing sufficed—
 Despite my efforts, you remained indifferent,
 I lived in hope, but you were still recalcitrant.
 I chose another love—of course you knew the cause.
 Tell me, Madame: is this my fault, or is it yours?
 Was I the fickle one? And is there any doubt?
 Was I the one to leave, or did you throw me out?

ARMANDE. But, Monsieur, can you say I really had no heart?
 I tried to purge your love of all that vulgar part.   1190
 I wanted to distil it, keep that purity
 Which gives a perfect love its true nobility.
 For my sake, couldn't you refine your worldly mind,
 Forget about your senses, leave them far behind?
 You should have tried to keep your body in control,
 Cast off your earthly side, and loved me with your soul.
 Can't you imagine perfect love, or see beyond
 The vulgar, gross encumbrance of an earthly bond?
 How is it that your feelings ultimately fail
 Unless you take a wife, with all that may entail?   1200
 Oh, what a view of love! It shocks me, and I find
 Such coarse desires offensive to a noble mind.
 Love can be ardent, though the senses play no part:
 True lovers can unite—a marriage of the heart.
 They cast aside the rest, the side that gives us shame;
 Their passion is as pure as a celestial flame.
 They sigh, it's true, but not because of gross desire,
 They don't want filth but purity, and they aspire
 To love for love's sweet sake. Indecency's taboo:
 There's nothing smutty in the things they like to do.   1210
 They melt with passion, but it's an ethereal flood,
 And they don't deign to notice that they're flesh and blood.*

CLITANDRE. Unfortunately, though, I'm not the same as you:
  I don't just have a soul, I've got a body too.
  It means too much to me, I won't cast it aside:
  I don't possess the art of being rarefied.
  The good Lord has denied me your philosophy;
  My body and my soul keep perfect company.
  There's nothing more enchanting, I believe you find,
  Than love that's consummated only in the mind,   1220
  Two hearts that beat as one in tender purity,
  And utterly removed from sensuality.
  But I can't imitate your dainty attitude:
  And you're so right to say that I'm a trifle crude.
  I love with all of me, and not just with my soul;
  My love's directed at my mistress as a whole.
  I don't feel I deserve your condemnations,
  And notwithstanding all your reservations,
  Such purity might seem, to others, rather odd,
  And marriage in society is *à la mode*.   1230
  It's perfectly respectable and pleasant too;
  All right, I did decide I'd like to marry you,
  So what? It's normal practice in society.
  You didn't have the right to feel annoyed with me.

ARMANDE. Well, then, if you won't listen to the things I say,
  If your base sentiments must have their brutal way,
  If your fidelity can't otherwise be won,
  Except by fleshly bonds and chains, let it be done.
  If mother will agree, then I'll take on the task—
  And I'll resign myself to do the things you ask.   1240

CLITANDRE. It's much too late, Madame. Your sister's won my
    heart.
  To give her up would be to play a shabby part.
  She was a refuge for me, comforted my pain
  When you made me unhappy with your proud disdain.

PHILAMINTE. You think you can rely upon my full support
  In planning this new marriage—have you given it thought?
  And in your mad arrangements have you noticed yet
  I have another man in mind for Henriette?

CLITANDRE. Madame, your plans for her deserve fresh scrutiny.
    And spare me too, I beg, this crude ignominy: 1250
    The rival of your Monsieur Trissotin must be
    A role I wouldn't wish on my worst enemy.
    You favour intellectuals to my detriment,
    Set me against a fellow who's impertinent.
    The current lack of taste has given prominence
    To writers with pretensions to intelligence;
    But Monsieur Trissotin has taken no one in,
    And everyone can see his talent's very thin.
    He's valued much as he deserves, except for here,
    It's always taken me aback that you revere   1260
    The man, and praise the rubbish he sees fit to write.
    If you'd composed it, you would be far less polite.

PHILAMINTE. You have a right to your opinions. So do we.
    We view him in a different light, as you can see.

SCENE 3

TRISSOTIN, ARMANDE, PHILAMINTE, CLITANDRE

TRISSOTIN. Madame, I bring great news! The horror makes me
    gape!
    While we were sound asleep, we had a near escape:
    Another alien world passed close to earth last night.*
    It fell right through our vortex in its hurtling flight;
    It could have bumped right into us as it did pass—
    It would have smashed us into pieces just like glass!   1270

PHILAMINTE. Oh!... Look, let's talk about all that another time,
    For Monsieur here'd be bound to say that there's no rhyme
    Or reason in it. Yes, he values ignorance,
    And looks on wit and learning with indifference.

CLITANDRE. If I may put my case in rather fairer terms,
    I'll make myself quite plain. My whole approach confirms
    That I see wit and learning as worthwhile *per se*,

But when they ruin men, they fill me with dismay.
I'd rather be an ignoramus than aspire
To act the learned man, like someone you admire.   1280

TRISSOTIN. Whatever you may say, I don't believe it's true
That learning ever harms a man: it's good for you.

CLITANDRE. If learning's wrongly used, it makes you look a fool;
Pedantic speech can often lead to ridicule.

TRISSOTIN. A clever paradox!

CLITANDRE.   It isn't difficult
To make out a good case, and show you the result.
And if I couldn't prove it through plain argument,
I'd find examples illustrating what I meant.

TRISSOTIN. There'll be some false examples in your repertoire.

CLITANDRE. I'll find a real one. I don't need to look too far.   1290

TRISSOTIN. Oh? I can't see a specimen that proves your case.

CLITANDRE. And I see one right here—it stares me in the face.

TRISSOTIN. Until today I thought, in all my innocence,
That learning didn't make men fools, but ignorance.

CLITANDRE. Let me assure you that the case is the reverse:
An untaught fool is bad, a learned fool is worse.

TRISSOTIN. I think you'll find that you've misunderstood the rule.
Most people tend to link up 'ignorant' with 'fool'.

CLITANDRE. If synonyms and ways with words move you to think,
Then look up 'fool' and 'pedant', and you'll find a link.   1300

TRISSOTIN. Stupidity seems worse in an untutored state.

CLITANDRE. But nurture adds to nature in the pedant's pate.

TRISSOTIN. True learning has great merit, and it's not a crime.

CLITANDRE. But learning in a fool is just a waste of time.

TRISSOTIN. Sheer ignorance to you must have enormous charms:
You're fighting for it, and we see you take up arms.

CLITANDRE. I do find ignorance's charms congenial
Since I have witnessed pedants in tutorial.

TRISSOTIN. Those pedants, when you get to know them, are as good
As certain gentlemen who haunt the neighbourhood.   1310

CLITANDRE. Well, yes, if you're prepared to take the pedants' word;
But other people would maintain that they're absurd.

PHILAMINTE. It seems to me, Monsieur...

CLITANDRE.   There's no need to persuade.
Monsieur's quite strong enough—he doesn't need your aid.
He's such a mighty foe, I'm threatened with defeat;
Though I protect myself, I'm beating a retreat.

ARMANDE. Your repartee is most offensive, and your wit
Malicious...

CLITANDRE.   What, another ally? I submit.

PHILAMINTE. A true debater can feel free to make such cracks,
Provided he avoids the personal attacks.   1320

CLITANDRE. All this is nothing. There's no need to take offence.
He's constantly attacked—he's got his own defence.
The whole of France joins in, he knows how people scoff;
Yet out of pride he always tries to laugh it off.*

TRISSOTIN. That crude attack does not surprise me. By his speech,
Monsieur shows he believes you practise what you preach.
He's well up in court circles—I need say no more:
We all know that the court finds intellect a bore.
It's not for nothing that it values ignorance—
It's as a courtier that he takes up its defence.   1330

CLITANDRE. You seem to bear a grudge against the hapless court,
And not a day goes by without men of your sort,
The literati, launching a severe assault
And blaming the poor court for something not its fault.
The courtiers have no taste, at least that's what you claim,
And when your work is booed, you say that they're to blame.
You're famous, Trissotin, and worthy of respect,

But let me tell you this: I think you should correct
The things you say about the court, and watch your tone.
Your crude remarks are most unwise. You're not alone   1340
In this, but you should learn the court is less naive
Than you and all your colleagues want us to believe.
The courtiers have sophistication, common sense,
And their good taste and *savoir-vivre* are immense.*
Society's idea of wit means more to me
Than all your erudition and your pedantry.

TRISSOTIN. And yet their admiration's frequently misplaced.

CLITANDRE. Monsieur, where do you see this so-called lack of
    taste?

TRISSOTIN. In Rasius and Baldus, glories of the state,*
With their great learning, which one cannot overrate.   1350
Their wisdom is well known by general report,
And yet they fail to gain their just reward at court.*

CLITANDRE. I understand why you're indignant. Yes, you're shy
Of telling us that you're involved. I can see why.
But, putting to one side your role in this debate,
What do your learned men contribute to the state?
What service do their stuffy manuscripts provide
That justifies your feeling so dissatisfied,
And constantly complaining that the luckless court
Is too slow to reward the pedants as it ought?   1360
So scholarship's of vital consequence to France!
These books will all enrich our lives, given the chance!
Your three small-minded fools assume that they're renowned,*
Because their works are all in print and vellum-bound.
They call themselves important figures in the land
Who shape the destiny of monarchs, pen in hand.
If they find anyone to bother with their work,
They think they've earned a pension or some other perk,
And that the universe admires their fame. What pride!
To claim that they've a reputation, far and wide,   1370
And that they're such distinguished prodigies of wit
Because they've copied down what other men have writ,
Because for thirty years they've used their eyes and ears

In staying up, night after night, as volunteers,
And dabbling tirelessly in Latin and in Greek,
While cramming full their minds with stuff that's all antique,
The useless, outworn rubbish lurking in old books.
These men are drunk on their own wit, or so it looks.
They babble on and on, and that's their claim to fame.
They've got no common sense, no talents to their name;   1380
They claim they're learned; but I tell you, they debase
The whole idea. Those learned fools are a disgrace.

PHILAMINTE. You're very heated, Sir. You're showing so much zeal
Your secret's out, and we can all see how you feel.
Monsieur's your rival, and that's what's behind this row...

SCENE 4

JULIEN, PHILAMINTE, ARMANDE, TRISSOTIN, CLITANDRE

JULIEN. The gentleman who came to visit you just now,
And whom, I'm proud to say, I serve as his valet,
Madame, begs you to cast your eye o'er this billet.

PHILAMINTE. Oh, never mind the letter. What an attitude!
Young man, has no one told you that it's very rude   1390
To come and interrupt the conversation here?
It's proper to go through the servants. Is that clear?
A valet with good manners wouldn't just barge in.

JULIEN. I'm writing my first book—I'll note it down therein.

PHILAMINTE [reads]. *Madame, Trissotin has boasted that he is to marry your daughter. I must warn you that his philosophy is directed at your money; you would do well to put off the marriage until you have read the poem I am composing against him. Whilst you are awaiting this portrait, in which I flatter myself I will paint him in his true colours, I am sending you Horace, Virgil, Terence, and Catullus,* with all the passages he has plundered marked in the margins.*

PHILAMINTE. I owe myself this marriage. See how harsh it is
When merit is assailed by troops of enemies!

This corporate attack convinces me today
To take the final step. Let envy stand at bay,
Let our opponents see that I don't care a whit,
Since all their efforts will achieve the opposite.   1400

[*To* JULIEN

Take back these volumes to your master, straight away,
And make sure that he gets my message. You must say
That as I set great store by all his good advice,
And as I see I must obey, at any price,

[*Indicates* TRISSOTIN

Monsieur will marry Henriette, this very night.

[*To* CLITANDRE

You, Monsieur, as a family friend will have the right
To see their wedding contract signed at my behest.
I'm happy to invite you. Please come as my guest.
Armande, will you make sure you get the lawyer here,
And go and tell your sister quickly, do you hear?   1410

ARMANDE. I needn't go and tell my sister what you're at—
Monsieur who's standing here will take good care of that.
He's itching to run off, and give her all the news,
And work on her till she's determined to refuse.

PHILAMINTE. Well, we'll see which of us can have the stronger hold,
And I'll make sure the hussy does as she is told.

[*Exit* PHILAMINTE

ARMANDE. Monsieur, it seems a shame that though you took a
    stand,
The thing has not turned out exactly as you planned.

CLITANDRE. Madame, I'll do my best to put the matter right.
I wouldn't leave you with regrets, however slight.   1420

ARMANDE. I fear that all your efforts, though, won't help you much.

CLITANDRE. Perhaps your fears will not be realized, as such.

ARMANDE. I hope it will be so.

CLITANDRE.   Madame, I know you do—
  I also know my efforts will be backed by you.

ARMANDE. Indeed, I'll try to help in every way I can.

CLITANDRE. I'm sure you will—and I shall be a grateful man.

SCENE 5

CLITANDRE, CHRYSALE, ARISTE, HENRIETTE

CLITANDRE. I must have your support, or else we're both undone.
  Madame's just turned me down. She's deaf to everyone.
  She says that Trissotin must be her son-in-law.

CHRYSALE. Now, what's come over her? Why does she want   1430
  that bore?
  That Monsieur Trissotin! Why must she be his fan?

ARISTE. It's all because he spouts in Latin when he can.
  It makes her think that he's a cut above the rest.

CLITANDRE. The wedding is to be tonight, at her request.

CHRYSALE. Tonight?

CLITANDRE.   Tonight.

CHRYSALE.   Tonight, I know what I must do:
  I'll show her who's the boss, by marrying you two.

CLITANDRE. The lawyer's on his way, to draw the contract up.

CHRYSALE. I'll send for him as well. Tell him to hurry up!

CLITANDRE. Her sister's gone to Henriette, to tell the news,
  And get her ready now, so we've no time to lose.   1440

CHRYSALE. Well, I've some power round here, I'm going have my
  say.
  I'm marrying her to you, and giving her away.
  I tell you, I've the right to choose my daughter's spouse;
  It's time I showed them who's the master in this house.
  I'll sort this out. Be back directly. Then you'll see.
  Come, brother, come on, son-in-law, quick, follow me.

HENRIETTE. Oh, dear! Don't let him waver, back him if you can.

ARISTE. I'll do the best I can, to help you get your man.

CLITANDRE. I know our friends will do their best, and play their
    part,
But you're the one who has to keep a constant heart.   1450

HENRIETTE. My heart, you can be sure, will still belong to you.

CLITANDRE. In that case I'll be happy, knowing that it's true.

HENRIETTE. You realize they'll try their best to force my hand?

CLITANDRE. I'm not afraid. I know that you will make a stand.

HENRIETTE. Yes, I'll do all I can to fight for our romance;
But if I fail unhappily, through some mischance,
I'll go on a retreat. At least that can be done.
In there, they can't force me to marry anyone.*

CLITANDRE. Let's hope it doesn't come to that. Oh, heavens above,
May you not need to give me such a proof of love!   1460

ACT V

SCENE 1

HENRIETTE. Ah, there you are, Monsieur. I wanted to discuss
This hasty marriage mother's organized for us.
I hope to get you to see reason—that's my aim.
The family's upset, and I think that's a shame.
I know you realize that with my hand I bring
A dowry that is large by any reckoning;
But money's vulgar, isn't it, my dear Monsieur?
It's worthless to a genuine philosopher;
And all the high contempt for riches that you preach
Should be reflected in your actions, not your speech.   1470

TRISSOTIN. Indeed, it's not your money that I find most fair.
Your dazzling loveliness, your brilliant eyes, your air
Of elegance and grace, these riches, these alone
Have earn'd themselves my love and tenderness, I own:
These are the only treasures that I now adore.

HENRIETTE. Oh thank you! How polite. How could one wish for
    more?
It's most obliging. I confess, I'm overcome—
I'm truly sorry that your passion leaves me numb.
I think of you with feelings of profound respect,
But there's an obstacle, which means I must reject   1480
Your love. A heart may not belong to more than one:
Clitandre is the man for me, my heart's been won.
I'm well aware his merit's far, far less than yours.
It just shows my bad taste, that I can plead his cause,
Since you've a thousand talents that should weigh with me;
I know I'm in the wrong, but, no, it's not to be.
So if you try to pressurize me, then you'll find
You just make me ashamed, because I know I'm blind.

TRISSOTIN. Don't worry, that'll change the day I win your hand;
You'll soon forget you ever loved the fellow, and   1490

I'll do a thousand pretty things to you; you'll see:
I'll quickly find a way to make you care for me.

HENRIETTE. My heart's so set on my first love, I know you'll find
That all your efforts fail to make me change my mind.
Monsieur, since I've presumed to make my meaning plain,
My frank confession shouldn't give you any pain.
A love that steals up on us, sets our hearts aglow,
Is not provoked by worth, as I'm convinced you know.
It happens on a whim, and even as we sigh,
We find it difficult to say exactly why.   1500
If people fell in love because of common sense,
Your merit would have earned my love in recompense;
But love just doesn't work that way, as you can see.
Please don't attempt to cure my blindness: leave me be.
Don't take advantage of the cruel violence
That's being done to force me to obedience.
A gentleman should never force a girl to yield,
Exploiting the control her parents choose to wield;
He shouldn't feel the need to hold his bride in thrall.
She ought to marry willingly, or not at all.   1510
By urging mother on, you force me through her voice,
Impose yourself on me, because you are her choice.
Give up your love for me, let someone else delight
In capturing your heart, so fine and erudite!

TRISSOTIN. But how can my poor heart agree to your demand?
It hasn't got the power to do what you command.
Do you think I could ever stop adoring you?
You must become less lovable before I do,
And cease to thrill my gaze with your celestial charm...

HENRIETTE. For goodness's sake, Monsieur, why do you have   1520
to smarm?
It's Philis, Iris, Amarante in all your verse;*
Their charms are trumpeted throughout the universe.
Your poems are filled with protestations on your part...

TRISSOTIN. My intellect speaks in my poems, not my heart.
Expressing love for them is purely etiquette:*
My real affection's for my darling Henriette.

HENRIETTE. Oh, please, Monsieur, I'm begging you...

TRISSOTIN.   If I offend,
    Don't think that my wrongdoing's ever going to end.
    You know my ardour, and by now you recognize
    That I intend to dwell forever in your eyes.   1530
    Nothing can stop my ecstasies—I'm resolute.
    And even if, my fair one, you reject my suit,
    I won't refuse your mother's willing help, if she
    Promotes a marriage that's so very dear to me.
    I aim to win the happiness I long for, now:
    Provided I get you, it doesn't matter how.

HENRIETTE. But do you know the risks you're running, when you
    start
    Proposing to do violence to someone's heart?
    To put it plainly, Sir, you're lacking in finesse,
    In forcing me to marry you under duress.   1540
    A girl who hates her husband won't need asking twice:
    If I'm coerced, you'll find you have to pay the price.

TRISSOTIN. I don't mind. You won't put me out of countenance:
    A wise man is prepared for every mischance.
    His reason cures him of such vulgar weaknesses.
    He knows he is above such inconveniences.
    He won't allow himself to be discomfited
    By situations he has not elicited.

HENRIETTE. If that's the case, then I'm delighted at the news.
    I never knew philosophy could so infuse   1550
    Her followers with fortitude, to help them bear
    Behaviour which, in normal men, would cause despair.
    Your constancy of purpose is exceptional,
    All credit to you, for it's quite sensational.
    A man like you should marry nothing but the best—
    Your partner's aim should be to put you to the test.
    That partner won't be me. I'm too unworthy, and
    I wouldn't do you credit, if I gave my hand
    To you. Take this on board: I swear, upon my life,
    I'll never have the privilege of being your wife.   1560

TRISSOTIN. We're soon to see the outcome of this whole affair.
The lawyer has been sent for: he's already there.

SCENE 2

CHRYSALE, HENRIETTE, CLITANDRE, MARTINE

CHRYSALE. Ah! daughter. Good!... I'm awfully glad to find you
here.
Come on, it's time to do your duty, do you hear?
I want you to obey my wishes, make your vow:
It's time I showed your mother who's the master now.
Though she may show her teeth, to demonstrate who's boss
I've brought Martine back home. I want to make her cross.

HENRIETTE. What resolution! You deserve the highest praise.
But, father, please don't let this be a passing phase.   1570
Don't stop insisting. Make your point. Try to stay true,
And don't let your good nature get the better of you.
Remember what's at stake, and don't let matters rest,
Until you're sure that you, not mother, come off best.

CHRYSALE. What do you take me for? Am I a silly fool?

HENRIETTE. Far from it!

CHRYSALE.   What's the meaning of this ridicule?

HENRIETTE. I only meant to...

CHRYSALE.   Do I seem incapable?
Has anybody said I'm not dependable?

HENRIETTE. No, father.

CHRYSALE.   Are you saying I don't have the nous,
At my age, to be master here, in my own house?   1580

HENRIETTE. No, no!

CHRYSALE.   So do you think that I'm a fool, like those
Who let their bossy women lead them by the nose?

HENRIETTE. Of course not. I...

CHRYSALE.   You think I'm talking through my hat?
Impertinence! How dare you speak to me like that?

HENRIETTE. I didn't mean to make you cross in any way.

CHRYSALE. Look, I take the decisions, you do what I say.

HENRIETTE. Of course I will.

CHRYSALE.   I tell you, nobody but me
Is master in this house.

HENRIETTE.   I thoroughly agree.

CHRYSALE. I'm the head of the family, you understand.

HENRIETTE. I do.   1590

CHRYSALE.   It's up to me who gets my daughter's hand.

HENRIETTE. Oh, yes!

CHRYSALE.   And I'll dispose of you as I think best.

HENRIETTE. I'll do my bit.

CHRYSALE.   I'll choose your husband. That must rest
With me. Do as you're told. A girl has to obey
Her father, not her mother. I must have my way.

HENRIETTE. Oh, dear! Of course I will. There's nothing I'd like
more.
Just tell me what to do, that's all I'm hoping for.

CHRYSALE. And Heaven help her if she tries to overthrow...

CLITANDRE. She's coming, and she's got the lawyer there in tow.

CHRYSALE. Oh, goodness!... Back me up!

MARTINE.   Just leave it all to me.
I'll prop you up, Sir, and I'll speak up, if need be.   1600

SCENE 3

PHILAMINTE, BELISE, ARISTE, TRISSOTIN, LAWYER, CHRYSALE,
CLITANDRE, HENRIETTE, MARTINE

PHILAMINTE [*to* LAWYER]. You ought to modify your language,
    which is vile,
And formulate the contract in a pleasing style.

LAWYER. Our style is excellent, and it would be absurd,
    Madame, to try to modify a single word.

BELISE. I find it shocking that we don't have censorship
    Of legal jargon. In the name of scholarship,
    Instead of écus, livres, and francs, it would make sense*
    To calculate the sum in mines and in talents,
    And date the document in ides and in calends.*

LAWYER. What, me? I'd be a laughing stock to all my friends   1610
    If I agreed, Madame, to do as you request.

PHILAMINTE. They'll keep their barbarisms, so don't try to protest.
    Come, sit down at this table, then we can begin...

                                        [*Noticing* MARTINE

What's this? Who let that cheeky baggage sneak back in?
Now why was she brought back to my house, if you please?

CHRYSALE. I'll tell you later, dear. I can explain with ease,
    But not now—I can see you're fully occupied.

LAWYER. Let's move on to the contract. Which girl is the bride?

PHILAMINTE. I'm marrying my youngest—

LAWYER.   This one, *scilicet.*

CHRYSALE. Yes, here she is, Monsieur, her name is Henriette.   1620

LAWYER. That's fine. And who's the groom?

PHILAMINTE.   The husband I select
    Is Monsieur.

                                        [*Indicates* TRISSOTIN

CHRYSALE.   I'm afraid that isn't quite correct.
She's marrying Monsieur.

[*Indicates* CLITANDRE

LAWYER.   What, more husbands than one?
But that's against the law.

PHILAMINTE.   Oh, come on, get it done.
Just write down Monsieur Trissotin, for he's my choice.

CHRYSALE. Write down Monsieur Clitandre: he has a father's voice.

LAWYER. Agree between yourselves, I can't do any more.
You must decide which one's to be the son-in-law.

PHILAMINTE. Monsieur, do as I ask, I've said how it's to be.

CHRYSALE. Monsieur, do as I ask, you can depend on me.   1630

LAWYER. Just tell me whom I am expected to obey.

PHILAMINTE [*to* CHRYSALE]. What's this? You won't let me
arrange things my own way?

CHRYSALE. I find it most upsetting when I realize
He wants her for her money: she's a wealthy prize.

PHILAMINTE. As if your family money made a difference!
A wise man wouldn't stoop to such a lame pretence.

CHRYSALE. I've made my choice, and Henriette's to have Clitandre.

PHILAMINTE. And Trissotin's the man to whom I've pledged my
bond.
Don't bother to protest, I've said I'm resolute.

CHRYSALE. Indeed! Your tone, Madame, is very absolute.   1640

MARTINE. A wife didn't ought to wear the trousers. Looks bad
when
Us women won't give in, and listen to the men.

CHRYSALE. Well said!

MARTINE.   Give me my cards, don't pay me what I'm owed:
The hen shouldn't never cackle, till the cock has crowed.

CHRYSALE. That's right.

MARTINE.   We all know how it is, and people mock:
When woman wears the breeches, man's a laughing stock.

CHRYSALE. Too right.

MARTINE.   If I was to get married, then my spouse
Would always be the lord and master in our house.
I wouldn't love him if he was an idiot.
And if I argufied, and put him on the spot,   1650
Or yelled at him, I wouldn't turn a hair if he
Knocked me about a bit—that'd be fine by me.

CHRYSALE. That's what I like to hear.

MARTINE.   Monsieur was doing well:
He hit upon a man who's just right for his gell.

CHRYSALE. Yes, yes!

MARTINE.   Monsieur Clitandre's a right good-looking bloke.
So why not go for him? Is it some crazy joke
To give her to a crank who's always droning on?
She needs a proper husband, not some kind of don.
She just don't want to know that Latin and that Greek.
Your Monsieur Trissotin would drive her up the creek.   1660

CHRYSALE. Quite right.

PHILAMINTE.   We stand about here, while she holds the floor.

MARTINE. All he can do is spout, that's why he's such a bore.
I've said a thousand times, that, when I take my pick,
For husband I won't never choose a clever dick.
You don't need lots of brains for running happy homes,
And marriage is enough—forget the great big tomes.
If ever I get hitched to anyone, you'll see,
I'll pick a man who reads no other book but me,
Who don't know A from B, and leads a normal life,
And only acts the doc in private, with his wife.   1670

PHILAMINTE. Now have I listened long enough, and will that do?
You've found a worthy spokesman.

CHRYSALE.   What she says is true.

PHILAMINTE. I've had enough. Let's put a stop to all of this.
I've got to be obeyed, so no more stubbornness.
She'll marry him today, it's got to happen now,
And that's an order, so don't try to make a row.
You went and gave Clitandre your word, so I suggest
You offer him your elder girl, as second best.

CHRYSALE. That's certainly a way of sorting matters out.
A new approach! Do you accept this turnabout?   1680

HENRIETTE. Oh, father!

CLITANDRE.   Oh, Monsieur!

BELISE.   It's true that you could find
Solutions that she might prefer, but never mind,
For we are setting up an admirable love.
You'll see, it's pure and sacred as the moon above;
The soul will matter, in the marriage that we've planned,
But anything to do with bodies will be banned.

SCENE 4

ARISTE, CHRYSALE, PHILAMINTE, BELISE, HENRIETTE, ARMANDE,
TRISSOTIN, LAWYER, CLITANDRE, MARTINE

ARISTE. I'm sorry I must interrupt this gathering,
Particularly as my news is shattering.
I've got two letters here. It's bad news, I'm afraid,
Arising from some grave mistakes you both have made.   1690
The first one is for you, from your solicitor.
The other one for you, from Lyon.

PHILAMINTE.   So, Monsieur,
What is there in the letters that's so horrible?

ARISTE. Just read this and you'll see—it's quite deplorable.

PHILAMINTE [reads]. *Madame, I have begged Monsieur your brother**
to give you this letter, which will tell you what I could not face saying

to you in person. As a result of your great neglect of your affairs, the
clerk reporting on your trial failed to keep me informed, and you have
completely lost your case, which you should have won.

CHRYSALE. You've lost your court case!

PHILAMINTE.   Well, so what? Don't make a scene.
You won't see me break down: I stay calm and serene.
Try not to go to pieces when you're feeling low,
And be like me, stay cool, don't flinch beneath the blow.

Your carelessness will cost you 40,000 écus, and, by order of the court,
you are condemned to pay that sum with all costs.

Condemned! Oh, what a crude expression! It's reserved
For criminals.   1700

ARISTE.   Your criticism is well observed,
And you were right to draw the line at what he said.
He should have asked you, most respectfully, instead,
According to court orders, to be sure to pay
The forty thousand écus, with the costs, today.

PHILAMINTE. Let's see the other one.

CHRYSALE. *Monsieur, my friendship for Monsieur your brother means*
that I feel great concern for everything that involves you. I am aware
that you placed your wealth in the hands of Argante and Damon, and
I must inform you that they have both gone bankrupt on the same day.

Oh God! To lose my fortune all in one fell swoop!

PHILAMINTE. Your outburst's so embarrassing. Wise men don't
     stoop
So low when things don't go their way. What do you care?
We're ruined, but philosophers never despair.
Let's get on with the wedding, now. Stop looking grim—
His money is enough for us, as well as him.   1710

TRISSOTIN. No, no, Madame. Stop there. Don't force the marriage
     through.
I see that everyone's against it, except you,
And I don't want a match that nobody supports.

PHILAMINTE. How suddenly you start to have these second
   thoughts!
   They came to you the moment that we lost our pile.

TRISSOTIN. I can't stand constant opposition—not my style.
   I'd rather not get tangled up in all this mess.
   I'm not prepared to marry, under such duress.

PHILAMINTE. This isn't to your credit. Now at last I know
   What I would not believe when they said it was so.   1720

TRISSOTIN. I don't care what you think of me. Go on, feel free
   To take it as you like! It's all the same to me.
   I'm not the sort of man to suffer the disgrace
   Of the rejections that you're throwing in my face;
   I'm worth much more than that, and I deserve my due.
   You don't want me. Goodbye—I kiss my hand to you.

                                        [Exit

PHILAMINTE. He wanted all our cash. How truly cynical!
   And walking out like that's not philosophical.

CLITANDRE. Take me. I'm not a scholar, but I'll stand by you.
   I'll help you out. Whatever happens, I'll be true.   1730
   I'm not well off, but what I have, you can command.
   I offer it to you, together with my hand.

PHILAMINTE. Monsieur, I'm really charmed. What generosity!
   Now, here is the reward for your fidelity.
   Yes, Henriette is yours. Come, take her, and you'll find...

HENRIETTE. No, mother, it's no use. You see, I've changed my
   mind.
   Don't make me marry him—my reasons are most grave.

CLITANDRE. What? won't you let me have the only thing I
   crave,
   When everyone says yes—at that moment, I'm scorned?

HENRIETTE. I know how little money you've got left,   1740
   Clitandre,
   I said I'd have you, but, at that point, I believed
   That, when we married, your distress would be relieved.

Our marriage was the object of my whole desire;
But now our luck has changed, I don't want to aspire
To make you bear the brunt of all these sudden blows—
I love you far too much to load you with our woes.

CLITANDRE. But poverty with you would be agreeable,
And living without you would be unbearable.

HENRIETTE. A man will say that, when his passion makes him
    blind.
But when his ardour cools, he'll often change his mind;   1750
For nothing's so disastrous to a married life
As poverty. It comes between husband and wife.
Each partner's quite convinced the other one's to blame
For what goes wrong when they no longer feel the same.

ARISTE. Is that it, then? Is this the only reason for
Your giving up Clitandre, or is there something more?

HENRIETTE. I tell you, but for that, I'd never let him go.
I've got to give him up, because I love him so.

ARISTE. In that case, go ahead, Clitandre, and claim your prize.
The bad news that I brought was just a pack of lies.   1760
I had to find some means of giving you support.
I planned this stratagem. It was a last resort.
I thought that we might get my sister on our side,
If she saw what her scholar did when he was tried.

CHRYSALE. Well, thank the Lord for this!

PHILAMINTE.   You've given us a thrill.
That hypocrite will swallow quite a bitter pill.
When he learns what a splendid wedding will take place,
He'll have his punishment. I'd love to see his face.

CHRYSALE. You see, I told you that I'd sort out all this mess.

ARMANDE. You plan to sacrifice me to their happiness?   1770

PHILAMINTE. No, not at all. Just look at it another way:
You've got philosophy, to be your prop and stay.
So chin up, and enjoy the wedding. You'll be fine.

BELISE. Clitandre, don't forget your heart is ever mine.
  If lovers marry when their hearts belong elsewhere,
  Then they'll live out their days in sorrow and despair.

CHRYSALE. Come on, Monsieur, I give the orders here. Obey,
  And write the contract out. I want it done my way.

THE END

EXPLANATORY NOTES

THE SCHOOL FOR WIVES

First performed on Boxing Day 1662, it was published in 1663, with a dedication to Henriette d'Angleterre, daughter of Charles I of England, and wife of Louis XIV's brother Philippe. For details of the controversy that followed the play's opening, see the Introduction.

2 *Arnolphe*: played by Molière himself, apparently in a farcical manner, with a wealth of grimaces, and a heavy black moustache. There is no record of what his costume was like. As for the name, St Arnulphius was traditionally regarded as the patron saint of cuckolded husbands. The story has it that he separated from his wife Scariberga by mutual consent, and that she too became a saint. The association between the saint and cuckoldry grew up in the Middle Ages.

Agnes: played by Catherine de Brie, aged 32 at the time. She was identified with the role, and continued playing it long after Molière's death. When eventually the troupe tried to replace her with a younger actress, the audience became so violent that she had to be fetched back immediately, and performed in her town clothes. She continued to play the part till she was 65.

Horace: played by La Grange, a faithful member of Molière's troupe, who kept a famous register detailing the day-to-day running of the troupe.

Alain: played by Brécourt, a playwright himself.

Georgette: probably played by Mlle La Grange.

Chrysalde: the so-called 'raisonneur', who presents a sensible view to offset against the eccentricities of the protagonist. He has his counterpart in the other plays—Cleante in *Tartuffe*, Philinte in *The Misanthrope*, and Ariste in *The Clever Women*. It is not known for certain who created this and the other minor roles.

a town square: this was an example of the 'décor multiple' still popular at the time. The set featured two houses, with an alleyway between them. The text alludes to particularities of the set. There is a house door, on which Arnolphe knocks, at the end of I.1. In I.4, Horace describes the house as having reddish walls. In V.2, Arnolphe says that the alleyway is dark. Props are mentioned in La Grange's register: a chair for III.2, and a purse with some counters to serve as coins for I.4; other props, not mentioned, are a letter for Horace to read in III.4 and the book of maxims for III.2.

3 *horns*: the traditional symbol for cuckolds.

5 *a fool*: the French word *sot* ('fool') also has the meaning of 'cuckold'.

game of 'box': in French the game is called 'corbillon', or 'basket'. Part of the joke is in the innuendo—'corbillon' itself is suggestive, and several of the words ending in -on, with which it rhymes, are obscene. I have slightly expanded the translation here, to explain the rules of the game.

6 *Yes, I'd prefer ... witty too*: this couplet is almost identical to one by Molière's contemporary François Scarron in his story 'The Fruitless Precaution' (1656), which is said to have inspired Molière.

Rabelais: François Rabelais (?1494–1553), a famous comic writer, much loved by Molière and his generation. The quoted remark was made by his eponymous giant Pantagruel in book III chapter 5.

7 *babies through the ear*: it was a seriously held religious belief that, during the Annunciation, Christ entered Mary's ear at the same time as she received the angel's message, as attested by the twelfth-century words: 'Gaude, Virgo, mater Christi, Quae per aurem concepisti.' Agnes, brought up in a convent, may have known of these theories.

8 *Monsieur de la Souche*: Arnolphe's new name, besides being crucial to the tangled plot, represents his attempt to rise in rank—since 'de' denoted noble birth. It is ridiculous, since 'la souche' means a stump or log. There is also an element of phallic innuendo, and a hint of contemporary satire (see note to *Monsieur de l'Isle*, below).

forty-two years old: Molière, playing the part, was nearly 41 when the play opened. Furthermore, he had recently married a woman of only 20, Armande. The similarity between the playwright and his character was striking, and many contemporaries commented on it maliciously.

Monsieur de l'Isle: a veiled allusion to the two famous playwrights Pierre Corneille (1606–1684) and his younger brother Thomas (1625–1709). Thomas, forgotten today but well known in his own day, had taken the name 'Monsieur de l'Isle': it was normal for a younger brother in a newly ennobled family to take a new name in this way. The brothers took this sly dig in bad part. The King had only recently (1661) proclaimed that people who unlawfully assumed noble titles would be punished. Corneille had difficulties being ennobled, while La Fontaine was forced to pay a fine for pretending to be noble.

I changed it for a reason: presumably, now that he is about to marry, Arnolphe is reluctant to bear a name associated with cuckoldry.

10 *won't get anything to eat*: Arnolphe's brutality towards his servants would have been perfectly normal at the time.

11 *But for the fleas ... the whole night through*: this line shocked Molière's contemporaries, and was attacked by Boursault in his satire *The Painter's Portrait* (1663): 'How skilfully [Molière] knows how to keep the audience awake! | For fear lest they should be overcome by sleep, | Did you ever see fleas appear at a more opportune moment?'

12 *nightcaps*: in the original, she has been making him 'coiffes', which were linings for nightcaps or hats.

you clever women: in the first of many soliloquies, Arnolphe attacks the *précieuses* (see Introduction). They clearly strike him as very threatening.

14 *a hundred pistoles*: a very considerable sum. G. Sablayrolles in his edition tells us that it represents considerably more than a night's takings for the play during its first run, although it was a sell-out.

I must. . . : Horace makes to give Arnolphe a receipt.

18 *please don't eat me up*: in the original production, Alain and Georgette fell on their knees six or seven times at this point. Molière's contemporary Donneau de Visé complained that the effect was too farcical.

20 *woman is a soup-bowl*: this comparison has a foundation in traditional peasant custom—a suitor would sit beside his girl and share her food from her bowl. Nevertheless, this was considered to be one of the most scandalous lines of the play—by most because it was too crude, but by some because it was too sophisticated, and not what Alain would have said.

21 *a certain Greek . . . on the rampage*: editors give two possible sources for this anecdote: Plutarch's *Apophthegms* and a play by Bernardino Pino.

25 *he... took...*: this innuendo was considered the most shocking element in the play. All Molière's enemies attacked it in their satires. Typically, Lidamont, in his *Panegyric on the School for Wives*, comments that the gentler sex 'is reduced to not knowing what is more seemly: to laugh or to blush'. Molière defends himself vigorously (and disingenuously) in *The School for Wives Criticized*, Scene 3.

26 *I'd have done anything, to help him in his need*: curiously, Molière's enemy Donneau de Visé, normally easily shocked, commented in his *Zelinde* that it was psychologically unconvincing for Horace to hold back when faced with such an easy conquest.

28 *a stone*: Molière's critics complained that the word he used, 'grès', meant a paving stone, which would be too heavy for a girl to lift.

I'm master here . . . obey: this is an absurdly inappropriate quotation of ll. 1867–8 of Corneille's tragedy *Sertorius* (1662), in which the speaker, Pompey, is sending an enemy off to his death. Corneille was not amused.

29 *breeches*: the fashion was for breeches ending at the knee, with a lace frill round the bottom, then stockings and shoes or boots.

30 *a problem with those two gold coins*: they were underweight. People used to shave bits off the edges of gold coins and try to pass them off as full-weight.

look at me right here: traditionally, Arnolphe points to his brow—the place where cuckolds grow their horns.

31 *her husband . . . and lord*: many of Molière's audience will actually have shared Arnolphe's views on the inferiority of women, who were, at the time, considered to be more or less the property of their husbands.

32   *a document*: Molière is believed to have been parodying St Gregory of Nazianzus' *Marriage Precepts* in the maxims that follow. They had been translated into French verse by Desmarets de Saint-Sorlin in 1640.

35   *Argus*: in Greek mythology, a monster with a hundred eyes.

37   *Love is the greatest teacher*: Corneille used the same expression in his play *The Sequel to The Liar*.

41   *I'm furious . . . slaps around the face*: Molière was famous for his comic portrayal of violent rage; contemporary accounts suggest that he milked lines like these for their farcical content.

43   *Scene 2*: at the time, this farcical scene was one of the most popular in the play. However, Molière's enemy Donneau de Visé commented: 'It's impossible for a man to talk for so long behind another man's back without being heard, and for the one who doesn't hear him to reply to what he says, up to eight times.'

      You fund her in proportion: in Molière's day, a wife's dowry normally passed into her husband's keeping. She could be provided for in a variety of ways should he predecease her, some of which the lawyer mentions later in the scene.

47   *The cobbler . . . at the corner*: apparently, cobblers, who worked in open booths right on the street, were notorious informers.

51   *don't go to extremes*: this is a message that Molière frequently reiterates, notably in *Tartuffe*, V. 1, ll. 1607–10.

52   *goes to law*: a litigious attitude was a regular target for mockery in Molière's day.

      cuckoldry . . . has its pleasures: critics are uncertain what to make of this speech. The audience can surely not have been expected to agree with such views. Was Chrysalde overstating his case to taunt Arnolphe? Or was Molière presenting the opposite extreme to Arnolphe's, to make the argument more balanced? Molière's contemporary Bossuet took the remarks at face value, and thundered that he 'exposes to the full light of day the advantages of a degrading tolerance on the part of husbands'.

60   *a . . . viper . . . bites its benefactor*: an allusion to a traditional fable. Molière's friend La Fontaine was to publish his version in 1668.

70   *Oh*: tradition has it that although he wrote 'Oh!', Molière, playing the part of Arnolphe, actually used the low register 'Ouf!', which suggests he had opted for a broadly comic interpretation of the scene. Apparently, the farcical interpretation was further enhanced by Alain and Georgette, who echoed Arnolphe's 'Ouf!', and rushed off after him. However, Molière's contemporary Robinet, focusing on Arnolphe's despair at the end, commented that 'one does not know whether to laugh or cry'.

71   *brother*: Molière frequently uses 'brother', 'sister' instead of 'brother-in-law' or 'sister-in-law'.

THE SCHOOL FOR WIVES CRITICIZED

74 *Uranie*: played by Mlle de Brie or Mlle Béjart. The name means 'marvellous' in Greek.

Elise: played by Molière's wife Armande. It was her first part. She was 21. The name means 'chosen one'.

Climene: played by Mlle du Parc. The name means 'renown'.

Galopin: a child actor took this part, probably the son of one of the actors.

Marquis: almost certainly played by Molière.

Dorante: played by Brécourt.

Lysidas: played by du Croisy. In Greek, the name means 'wolf's son'.

75 *Marquis*: The title was very different from the English marquess—the marquis were minor nobility, ridiculed for their pretension and stupidity, and a favourite butt of humour in Molière's day—the seventeenth-century Parisian equivalent of an 'upper-class twit'.

76 *the Louvre*: the King's palace in Paris.

the market place: Molière specifies the Paris market of Les Halles.

student quarters of Paris: Molière specifies La Place Maubert.

La Place Royale: the present Place des Vosges, then a fashionable meeting place in Paris.

Bonneuil: roughly pronounced Bonnoy, a village on the Marne, fairly close to Paris. The feeble pun is much the same in the original—people look on Uranie 'de bon œil', i.e. 'favourably'.

77 *précieuse*: see Introduction.

Damon: according to tradition, Molière's self-portrait follows. He was famous for his taciturnity.

79 *Palais Royal Theatre*: Molière's troupe had been performing at this theatre since 1661.

babies through the ear: see *The School for Wives*, I.1.

custard pie: see *The School for Wives*, I.1.

soup: see *The School for Wives*, II.3.

80 *he took her... You know*: see *The School for Wives*, II.5.

82 *obscenery*: in French, Climene says 'obscénité', which seems to have been an affected neologism at the time.

85 *frills and ribbons*: he specifies his *canons*, the lace frills round the knee, where the breeches ended. The ribbons were knotted above the lace frills.

86 *the pit*: the pit, or *parterre*, was standing room only. Tickets were cheap, and a mixed audience of servants, townspeople, and intellectuals frequented it.

the best seats: young gentlemen actually sat on seats round the side of the stage. The seats were expensive, and favoured by young, fashionable noblemen, who ogled the actresses, showed off their outfits, and continually interrupted the performance. Molière describes the situation and its problems in his play *The Bores*.

86 *a magnificent performance*: this is said to be modelled on the behaviour of a certain Plapisson.

Marquis de Mascarilles: Mascarille was a ridiculous valet pretending to be a marquis in Molière's play *The Ridiculous Précieuses* (1659).

89 *Lysidas*: the original of this character is said to be Donneau de Visé, who later became an admirer of Molière's, or, possibly, Boursault, who is attacked by name in *The Impromptu at Versailles*.

91 *Lots of actors*: in particular, Molière's rivals at the Hôtel de Bourgogne theatre, whom Molière mocks in *The Impromptu at Versailles*.

94 *a lace collar*: Molière specifies Venetian lace, which was very expensive and exclusive.

96 *Aristotle and Horace*: the Greek philosopher Aristotle (384–322 BC), in his *Poetics*, laid down the rules governing Greek tragedy. The Roman poet Horace (65 BC–AD 8) added further refinements in his *Art of Poetry*. These rules were adapted by seventeenth-century French theorists, and used as a blueprint for the French classical tragedies of the period.

the cookery book: Dorante specifies *Le Cuisinier français* (*The French Cook*), a seventeenth-century treatise on gastronomy.

THE IMPROMPTU AT VERSAILLES

The play was first performed at Versailles before Louis XIV in October 1663, then at the Palais Royal theatre in Paris in November.

104 *Molière*: clearly, the actors played themselves. The gloss for each name, taken from the first (posthumous) edition of 1682, indicates the parts they played in the 'play within a play'. The parts Molière has written for each of them in that section resemble their roles in *The School for Wives Criticized*.

La Thorillière: he did not have a part in *The School for Wives Criticized*.

Béjart: he did not have a part in *The School for Wives Criticized*.

Mademoiselle: in Molière's time, married women were frequently called 'Mademoiselle'. 'Madame' denoted a certain standing in society, to which actresses did not aspire.

108 *A year . . . ago, you wouldn't have said that*: they had been married for twenty months when this play was first performed.

109 *the same days as us*: Molière's troupe performed on Tuesdays, Fridays, and Sundays, as did the actors of the Hôtel de Bourgogne, the rival troupe targeted here.

since we've been in Paris: they arrived back from thirteen years touring the provinces in 1658.

That good-looking young man: according to tradition, the actor playing the King would have been La Thorillière, who was 37, but svelte and young-looking.

Corneille's Nicomède: the extracts mentioned in this scene are all from Corneille's verse tragedies. They are given, translated and in expanded form, in the notes—the French names for the characters have been kept.

Do you know . . . my power: in this speech, King Prusias is discussing the insubordination of Nicomède. The passage goes: 'Do you know what, Araspe? He's served me far too well. | By building on my power, he's taken it away. | He'll stay my subject only if he chooses to. | The man who helps me rule, rules over me instead.'

110 *Montfleury*: his enormous girth was a standing joke at the time—but he was annoyed at this attack. He was an immensely popular actor of tragedies.

Camille and Curiace: in Corneille's *Horace*. Camille is discussing the fact that her lover Curiace has been chosen to fight to the death in single combat. Molière slightly misquotes the first line. The whole passage, referred to here, and later in Molière's speech, goes as follows: Camille: 'Must you go, Curiace? This fatal honour—it | Delights you at the cost of all our happiness?' Curiace: 'Alas! I have no choice—I see now that my death | Must come, of sorrow, or inflicted by Horace. | I'm going off to fight: it feels like punishment. | I curse the way they've chosen me as champion. | The men of Alba love my courage, which I hate. | I'm in despair. My love is driving me to crime. | I blame the gods for this, I dare reproach them too. | I pity both of us. But still I have to go.' Camille: 'No. I know you too well. You want me on my knees. | Your country will excuse you, for you're in my power. | Already, you're well known because of what you've done. | You don't owe Alba anything, you've proved yourself. | You've been their champion through the whole of this harsh war. | You've killed more of the enemy than others have. | You've made your name, your reputation is assured, | So leave this task to someone else who wants to shine.'

111 *Pierced to the . . . heart*: from Corneille's *Le Cid*. The hero, Rodrigue, is soliloquizing about his predicament—he has learned that he has to fight a duel with the father of his beloved Chimène, who has insulted his own father. The first stanza goes as follows: 'Pierced to the depth of my heart | By an attack as unexpected as it is deadly, | Wretched avenger of an unjust quarrel, | Unhappy victim of a cruel rigour, | I stand here, motionless, and my downcast soul | Sinks under the deadly blow. | So near to seeing my love rewarded—| Oh, God! What a strange fate: | My father is the offended party, | And the offender is Chimène's father.'

The enmity . . . honour's due: Pompée is speaking: 'The enmity that reigns between our camps | Does not mean we forget our honour's due. | True merit has its own prerogatives | Which overcome the worst hatreds of all; | Even the fiercest enemies will feel | Respect and admiration, when deserved.'

Polybe is dead: the scene in which Oedipe discovers that he is not the son of Polybe, as he thought, and learns the secret of his parricide and incestuous marriage. The passage referred to, again misquoted by Molière, goes: Oedipe: 'So, Polybe, is he dead?' Iphicrate: 'My Lord, he is.' Oedipe: 'But why | Have you come here to help me mourn this tragedy? | You are chief counsellor, and at this time you should | Have stayed behind and ruled, until I came to you. | You took such care of me, you helped to bring me up. | You know I love you, and you know you've earned my trust. | I'm troubled and surprised. Tell me why you have come.'

when I cast you in The School for Wives Criticized: she played Climene.

112 *the same sort of part as you played in The School for Wives Criticized*: he played Dorante.

the same part as in The School for Wives Criticized: she played Elise.

115 *'Good day, Marquis'*: inverted commas indicate the play within a play.

116 *Custard pie*: see *The School for Wives Criticized*, Scenes 5 and 6.

a hundred pistoles: a considerable sum.

120 *lace frills*: Molière specifies 'canons'. See note to p. 85.

121 *improve on nature*: wearing make-up was frowned upon in Molière's day.

performed by the King's troupe: the play was Boursault's *The Painter's Portrait*. It was put on by the King's troupe at the Hôtel de Bourgogne theatre in September 1663.

Brossaut: Molière is said to have mispronounced the name here to make it sound as if he was spitting.

122 *devil-women, full of virtue*: see *The School for Wives*, IV. 8, l. 1296.

125 *in The School for Wives Criticized*: in Scene 6, Dorante accuses them of attacking other companies' productions.

The Ridiculous Précieuses: in Scene 9 of this play, which is an attack on pretentious society ladies with an interest in literature and refinement, the company is accused of forming a claque to drum up public enthusiasm for new plays.

126 *counter-criticisms*: the subtitle of Boursault's play was *A Counter-criticism of The School for Wives*.

attacking me . . . in their plays: two particularly damaging accusations were being spread about: first, that Molière was irreligious, witness his irreverent Maxims of Marriage in *The School for Wives*; secondly, that he had committed incest, and that Armande was the daughter, not the much younger sister, of his former mistress Madeleine Béjart.

TARTUFFE

The play was first performed in May 1664, at Versailles, before Louis XIV, in a shortened form; but it was not allowed to be performed on the public stage until February 1669. When the play was finally allowed, Molière was forced to change the title to *The Impostor*, which title was retained until 1734.

132 *Orgon*: played by Molière. He wore a black outfit of Venetian silk, trimmed with English lace, worth 60 livres.

Elmire: played by Molière's wife Armande.

Madame Pernelle: played by a man, Molière's brother-in-law Joseph Béjart, who had a pronounced limp, which he exaggerated in comic roles. Dressed too simply for her station, as befits a pious widow.

Mariane: played by Mlle de Brie, who also played Agnes in *The School for Wives*.

Tartuffe: Molière was made to change the character's name to Panulphe when the play was finally allowed. The role was taken by du Croisy. He was corpulent, with a ruddy complexion, as the text reveals. He may originally have been dressed as some kind of cleric; but later, he was dressed in simple black, as a layman. He is said by some to have been partly modelled on a contemporary of Molière's named Charpy; but the diarist Tallemant des Réaux mentions a hypocritical *abbé* named de Pons as 'the original of Tartuffe'. The name 'Tartuffe' traditionally meant a deceiver. The Italian for 'truffle', 'tartuffo', can be used as an insult.

Dorine: played by Molière's sister-in-law and former mistress, Madeleine Béjart. She was one of the most dynamic actresses in the company, but, by now in her forties, no longer played the young lead.

133 *Come on . . . Flipote*: this first, exposition, scene is one of Molière's most accomplished. By making this character angrily tell her relations home truths, Molière conveys the information necessary for the audience in a highly entertaining form.

a den of thieves: in the original, she claims the house is like the court of King Pétaud, the head of the beggars' guild.

134 *their late mother*: we learn that Elmire is Orgon's second wife.

135 *flat-footed*: in Molière's day, gentlemen wore shoes with heels, while the lower classes wore flat shoes.

138 *Babylon . . . babble on*: it is typical of Mme Pernelle to confuse the Tower of Babel (where people spoke in many different languages) with the Whore of Babylon. However, the mistake was a common one in Molière's day. Her suggestion for the etymological origins of 'Babylon' is ingenious.

you slut: despite her piety, Mme Pernelle uses coarse language.

civil war: the Fronde, a revolt of the nobility against the monarchy during Louis XIV's minority, from 1648 to 1653. We will remember this allusion later in relation to the secret documents in Orgon's possession dating from this time of civil unrest.

139 *This is a servant speaking*: Molière himself inserted this footnote. Although Dorine is well educated and uses a high register of speech, she is still only a lady's maid. No upper-class character would have been permitted to refer to the bodily functions in this crude way.

a hanky . . . in a holy book: small items of clothing were sometimes pressed between the covers of books instead of being ironed. See *The Clever Women*, II. 7, l. 562.

140 *With rosy cheeks . . . stout*: clearly this was a physical description of du Croisy, who created the role.

Poor fellow: this famous phrase is said to have been inspired by Louis XIV, commenting ironically on the eating habits of a greedy prelate.

141 *he bled her*: bleeding was probably the most common medical treatment practised in Molière's day. It could be done with a lancet, or by applying leeches. Healthy people were frequently bled at regular intervals to keep them well, and sick ones were bled copiously, even if they were clearly anaemic.

brother: Cleante is, of course, Orgon's brother-in-law. See note to l. 1775 on p. 71.

142 *The world would seem . . . manure*: Orgon warps a sentiment expressed, amongst others, by St. Paul (Philippians, 3: 8), that worldly advantages were contemptible.

couldn't care less: see Luke 14: 26.

143 *God*: in Molière's day, it was considered disrespectful to use the name of God. He uses 'le ciel' (Heaven) here.

144 *a Cato*: Cato the elder (232–147 BC). His writings were known for their austerity and wisdom.

145 *Oronte . . . Clitandre*: these elegant Grecian-sounding names were typical of the literary convention of the time. Molière's contemporary La Bruyère writes about the characteristics of his contemporaries in similar vein, using names like these. Oronte and Clitandre are characters' names in other Molière plays.

150 *a beard*: the common word for beard could also mean 'moustache'. Molière, playing Orgon, wore a heavy black stage moustache.

153 *Shut up . . . an outrage*: Orgon loses his temper here. In the original, he starts addressing Dorine as 'tu' instead of 'vous', showing that he has lost his sense of etiquette.

155 *A father can control . . . I confess*: fathers did indeed have absolute power over their daughters in Molière's day. See *The Clever Women*, I. 2, ll. 162–8.

156 *wipe his nose upon his sleeve*: Molière uses a vivid metaphor here, literally: 'He is not a man to blow his nose on his foot.'

scarlet ears: he exhibits all the signs of a sanguine temperament. The implication is that he is grossly sensual.

157 *a public coach*: in other words, a public conveyance, not a private carriage.

a stool: a person's rank was indicated by the type of chair they were offered. A stool was for the lowest of the low.

carnival: the beginning of Lent was carnival time, marked by wild festivities and practical jokes. In Molière's *The Hypochondriac*, for example, merrymakers dress up as doctors and trick the hero into believing that they have enrolled him into their learned company.

a performing ape: Molière names the ape as Fagotin, the most famous of his age. He belonged to a puppeteer called Brioché. The name was adopted by other owners of performing apes.

166 *My hairshirt . . . day by day*: the nineteenth-century critic Sainte-Beuve commented: 'The whole play up till now has been about [Tartuffe], but we have not yet seen him in person. The third act begins; he is announced, he enters, we hear him . . . This is the most admirable dramatic and comic entrance that could be invented.'

169 *a gift from Heaven*: Tartuffe is using the idea expressed in Cardinal Bellarmin's *The Spiritual Staircase* (1615), that nature's beauties reflect God's perfection, to aid his attempted seduction.

170 *Although I am . . . a man*: Molière parodies a line from Corneille's *Sertorius*: 'Although I am a Roman, I am still a man.'

173 *a guilty . . . man, I fear*: the way Tartuffe turns the tables on Damis by exaggerating his own guilt is reminiscent of an earlier play by Scarron, *Les Hypocrites*. Note that he acknowledges vague general guilt, avoiding any specific admission.

176 *where's my stick*: a stick was listed among the original stage properties for Molière's production.

178 *with . . . goods I'll you endow*: in French law, Orgon would not have been allowed to disinherit his son without good cause. He proposes to get round this by donating his property to Tartuffe during his lifetime.

181 *I must attend . . . I perceive*: it is time for vespers. Normally, people were expected to attend them on Sundays only.

182 *give mine . . . willingly*: presumably Mariane had inherited money from her late mother.

185 *I may seem rather odd . . . you're master in this place*: the earliest critics stressed the importance of this speech, which reminds the audience of Elmire's difficult position, and prepares them for the equivocal scene between her and Tartuffe.

186 *a very different tone*: Molière piles on the suspense—Tartuffe's reply is ambiguous; he still seems innocent to Orgon.

188 *a scoundrel speaking*: Molière himself inserted this note.

189 *he acted for the best*: a parody of the doctrine of 'laxism'. Pascal too had

mocked at theologians who claim that the intention is all that matters in his *Lettres provinciales*.

193   *his life and goods . . . at stake*: a traitor to the King, he was punishable by death. Orgon would have earned the same penalty for the crime of complicity and failing to denounce a criminal.

    without having to lie: Pascal, in his *Lettres provinciales*, parodies such casuistry: 'One can swear . . . one has not done something, although one has, while secretly meaning that one did not do it on a certain day, or before one was born, or some other similar circumstance.'

197   *his group*: we learn that Tartuffe forms part of a society. It has been suggested that Molière is here implying that his character is one of his enemies in the 'cabale des dévots', the religious secret society responsible for banning the play.

199   *a bailiff*: Loyal is a 'huissier à verge', literally a 'bailiff with a cane'. Writs were served by the bailiff touching his quarry with his cane.

202   *Has just gone . . . in the wrong*: Louis XIV prided himself on allowing his subjects free access to him.

203   THE OFFICER: he is called an 'exempt' soldier, originally a common soldier who was excused ordinary duties because he sometimes acted as an officer; but this character is clearly an officer and a gentleman, presumably in the King's bodyguard.

205   *By royal prerogative*: this was perfectly legitimate, as the King was the supreme judge.

THE MISANTHROPE

208   *Alceste*: the name means 'strong or bold'. Molière took the role himself. He played without the heavy black stage moustaches that had been his trademark for some time, but it seems that much of his performance was played for laughs. His costume was found among his effects after his death: 'breeches and a doublet of striped gold brocade and grey silk, lined with watered silk, trimmed with green ribbon; coat of gold brocade, silk stockings and garters.' It seems that both Molière and his wife liked the colour green, since numerous costumes were mainly green. Also, green was known as the colour of fools.

    Philinte: the name means 'friendly'. The role was probably created by La Thorillière.

    Oronte: probably played by du Croisy.

    Celimene: played by Molière's wife Armande: this was to be her most famous role.

    Eliante: probably played by Catherine de Brie, who created the role of Agnes in *The School for Wives*.

    Acaste: probably played by La Grange.

Clitandre: probably played by Hubert.

Arsinoë: probably played by Marquise du Parc, who later became the mistress of Racine.

Dubois: played by Louis Béjart.

The setting . . . Paris: Molière's register notes that 'six chairs, three letters and some boots' were required as props.

209 *hugged him without end*: the custom was to embrace instead of shaking hands.

212 *The School for Husbands*: in this play, first performed in 1661, Molière took the role of Sganarelle, a grumpy, misanthropic bachelor, determined to force his minx of a ward to marry him. His brother Ariste was reasonable, and believed in allowing young women more freedom. It is easy to see which brother Philinte thinks should be which.

with loathing . . . As they deserve: Molière is said to have been echoing Erasmus here: 'When Timon of Athens, known as the Misanthrope, was asked why he pursued all men with hatred, he said: "I hate the villains deservedly; and I hate the others for not hating the villains"' (*Apophthegms* 6).

213 *flat foot*: like Tartuffe, this villain is described as flat-footed because he is not a gentleman—only gentlemen wore shoes with heels.

can't conceal his sins: the portrait is reminiscent of Tartuffe, though the religious element in his hypocrisy is omitted.

214 *My phlegm . . . your spleen*: an allusion to the four humours, a medical model for viewing the body, popular in the Middle Ages, and still used in Molière's day. Philinte claims he is phlegmatic, with a calm temperament, while Alceste is acutely splenetic, suffering from black bile or melancholy, combined with yellow bile or choler.

Look, I agree . . . an aggressive ape: Philinte here accepts the truth of Alceste's observations on human nature, though he puts a different gloss on them. This is one of the differences between Alceste and the protagonists of other Molière plays: even his reasonable friend acknowledges that there is truth in what he says.

call upon the judge: it was customary to call on the judge both before and after the trial in Molière's day.

216 *his mistress*: in Molière's day, the word 'maîtresse' meant 'beloved' in a purely platonic sense, and was freely used in both comedy and tragedy.

220 *Hope, it is true . . . turns into despair*: this sonnet, probably composed by Molière himself, is far from being as ridiculous as the efforts of Trissotin in *The Clever Women*. However, it is precious, lacks originality, and, in particular, the paradox in the last two lines was a cliché at the time.

ALCESTE . . . to PHILINTE: Alceste moves from 'vous' to 'tu' in addressing Philinte here. He has clearly lost his temper.

221 *Expose yourself . . . with your debut*: Molière himself had very ambivalent

feelings about publication. In the preface to his play *The Ridiculous Précieuses*, he complains at being forced to publish by circumstances. He consistently mocks at pretentious writers (Trissotin in *The Clever Women* is a good example).

221 *throw the thing away*: Molière writes, throw it in the 'cabinet', which, then as now, could mean either a cupboard or a lavatory—a malicious play on words may be intended here.

222 *too far . . . from what real people say*: Molière was much in favour of the 'natural' in writing and theatre—see his comments on acting techniques in *The Impromptu at Versailles*.

If the King . . . my own dear with me: this verse is highly reminiscent of many genuine folk songs, but no precise source has been found.

226 *one long fingernail*: the practice of growing the little fingernail of the left hand had been in fashion with foppish noblemen since early in the century.

frilled with lace: Molière specifies that Clitandre wears 'canons'. See note to p. 85.

229 *the two marquis*: as in *The School for Wives Criticized*, and *The Impromptu at Versailles*, these marquis are minor noblemen, not the equivalent of the English title of marquess, and are portrayed as figures of fun, pretentious, silly fops.

230 *From head to toe . . . whispering 'hello'*: this portrait is said to have been modelled on a certain M. de Saint-Gilles, who importuned Molière.

234 *But if you listen . . . her most blatant flaws*: inspired by a passage from Lucretius, *De rerum natura*, 4, which Molière is said to have translated in his youth.

235 *an evening duty . . . at court*: Molière specifies that he is to attend the King's 'petit coucher', the ceremonial putting to bed attended only by select courtiers.

a smart coat: Molière specifies that it has full, pleated skirts.

236 *captain of the guard*: duels were banned by law. To enforce this, a tribunal of marshals of France had been set up, with a troop of soldiers to back up their authority. They summoned contentious noblemen to reconcile them, and prevent duels.

237 *Unless His Majesty insists . . . couldn't be worse*: tradition has it that the poet Boileau, Molière's friend, inspired this speech. He said much the same thing about his enemy Chapelain.

Oh, damn you . . . laughing stock: according to Boileau, Molière himself gave a bitter laugh as he spoke these last two lines.

238 *in the best seats*: see note to p. 86.

a jolly slim physique: Molière specifies that he has a tiny waist, which was very fashionable at the time.

247 *the Gazette*: *La Gazette de France*, the first French newspaper, founded in 1631.

254 *Scene 3*: many of Alceste's speeches in this scene have been adapted from Molière's earlier tragicomedy *Don Garcie of Navarre*. As a result, his lines seem serious and heartfelt, while Celimene's are flippant. Don Garcie was agonizingly jealous, but in his case it was without cause.

262 *he's telling everyone I wrote the thing*: this happened to Molière at the time of *Tartuffe*, according to his biographer Grimarest.

263 *man is nothing . . . to man*: a view made famous by the English philosopher Hobbes.

269 *spitting . . . to make ripples*: Henriette d'Angleterre, the wife of Louis XIV's brother Philippe, is said to have objected to this indelicate observation, but Molière refused to suppress it.

the green ribbons: see note to p. 208 for details of Alceste's costume.

the coat-tails: Molière writes 'the man in the coat'—presumably du Croisy, playing Oronte, had an unusual way of wearing his coat. One suggestion is that he wore his doublet over it. After Molière's death, the line was changed to 'the man who writes sonnets'.

THE CLEVER WOMEN

276 *Chrysale*: Molière himself took this role. We have a description of the clothes he wore, with doublet and breeches of black velvet and a coat of purple and gold. There were gold trimmings and touches of peachy yellow ('the colour of dawn'). The name Chrysale comes from the Greek word for gold.

Philaminte: from the Greek for 'love of science'. In Molière's production, the role was taken by a male actor, Hubert.

Armande: played by Mlle de Brie in the original production. She had created the role of Agnes in *The School for Wives*.

Henriette: played by Mlle Molière, in other words Molière's own wife. Curiously, she was called Armande.

Ariste: 'very good' in Greek. The role was taken by Baron, who was only 19 (Molière, his stage 'brother', was 50).

Belise: played by Mlle Villeaubrun. She was Molière's sister-in-law.

Clitandre: 'illustrious man', indicates nobility. The role was played by La Grange.

Trissotin: the name in French suggests stupidity (thrice *sot*, or 'fool'). This character was modelled on an enemy of Molière's, the Abbé Cotin. Charles Cotin (1604–81) was a prolific and successful society poet, known to be an arrogant pedant. Trissotin's two poems in Act III are genuine works by Cotin. Legend has it that for the première Molière's troupe managed to filch one of Cotin's coats, which the actor La

Thorillière wore. Cotin's reputation never recovered from Molière's ridicule. When he died, the following quatrain did the rounds: 'Do you know just how Cotin | Is different from Trissotin? | Cotin's days on earth are over, | Trissotin will live for ever.'

276 *Vadius*: it was believed at the time that he was modelled on the great grammarian Gilles Ménage (1613–92), a pedant known to plagiarize from the classics. Unsurprisingly, both he and Molière denied the charge.

Martine: it seems that she was played by Molière's actual servant-girl, also called Martine.

The scene . . . in Paris: an original document specifies that the scene is set in a room, and that the props required are 'two books, four chairs and some paper.'

277 *to discompose my mind*: the *précieuses*, a group of elegant women in Molière's day and earlier, established a cult of disdain for men. Some of them actually went to the lengths of Armande, refusing to marry and preferring celibacy. Apart from the novelist Mlle de Scudéry, the most famous example was Julie, the daughter of the Marquise de Rambouillet. Like Armande, she kept a suitor dangling for years. Armande is said to be modelled on her.

279 *coughs and spits*: the grossness of this line would have seemed quite shocking to a contemporary audience.

282 *A daughter's duty's to obey . . . that's criminal*: Armande is right. In Molière's day a father had complete control over his daughter's choice of husband. In *The School for Wives* Arnolphe, as Agnes's guardian, enjoys the same degree of power.

284 *And try not to seem clever . . . speaks*: the extent to which women were supposed to appear ignorant is demonstrated by one of the leading feminists of the time, the novelist Mlle de Scudéry. She wrote: 'I'm happy [for a woman] to know a great deal without showing off about it . . . but I don't want people to be able to say of her: she is a clever woman.'

wrap up . . . on market day: the market stall-holders at the Halles in Paris used to wrap up their wares in the discarded pages of books. Molière's satirical contemporary, the poet Boileau, also joked about this (*Satires*, 3 and 9).

You lovers have to do . . . the family dog: Plautus, whom Molière admired and imitated, has a character express similar views in his *Asinaria*: 'He wants to please his beloved, me, the lady's maid, the menservants and maidservants; and the new lover even caresses the little dog to make him pleased to see him.'

285 *He wouldn't change . . . an army general*: Cotin had a very high opinion of himself. In publishing his *Œuvres galantes*, he interspersed the poems with adulatory letters about them from admirers. Molière himself felt very differently. He is said to have told his friend Boileau: 'I have never in my whole life been completely satisfied with something I have written.'

a public place: Molière specifies that the place is the Gallery of the Palais de Justice in Paris—in other words outside the law-courts. It was a fashionable spot for meeting one's friends.

my suitor, like the rest: in her conviction that all men adore her Belise is partly modelled on Hesperie, a deluded character in Desmarets de Saint-Sorlin's comedy *The Visionaries* (1637), a play which the King was known to have enjoyed.

if you should attempt . . . banished from my sight: this adoring aphasia was a cliché among amorous *précieux*. Benserade, Molière's contemporary, wrote a poem beginning: 'Judge my martyrdom by my looks: Cloris, I am forbidden to explain myself more clearly.'

287 *The woman's mad . . . sensible*: this is the only soliloquy in this play. It will be noted that there are none at all in *The Misanthrope* and *Tartuffe*. Molière generally avoided them unless there was good reason for including them. In *The School for Wives*, *The Miser*, and *The Hypochondriac* the main character is living in a world of his own, so soliloquy is appropriate.

290 *Dorante . . . Lycidas*: these names, with their elegant, Grecian atmosphere, are typical of those of the romantic leads in Molière's plays. There are a Dorante and a Cleonte in *The Bourgeois Gentleman*, a Damis in *Tartuffe*, and a Lysidas (though not a heroic one) in *The School for Wives Criticized*.

293 *a clout . . . ear'ole*: in Molière's day, servants were regularly beaten by their masters.

295 *Vaugelas*: Claude Vaugelas (1585–1650), the celebrated grammarian and author of the much-admired *Remarques sur la langue française*. Vaugelas was much less dogmatic than Philaminte implies, and advocated relying on usage rather than on rigid rules.

296 *grandma*: this couplet gives us an insight into pronunciation in the seventeenth century. The French word 'grammaire' was pronounced 'granmaire', so rhymed with 'grand'mère' ('grandmother').

298 *Malherbe and Balzac*: the poet François Malherbe (1555–1628) was much admired for the elegance of his language. Louis Guez de Balzac (?1595–1654) was an elegant writer of prose.

Plutarch: Greek historian of the first century AD. His writings were very popular in Molière's day. It has been suggested that Molière's own father had a Plutarch for this purpose—a large volume was mentioned in the inventory of his books after his death. The habit of pressing linen in books may explain Tartuffe's discovery of a kerchief in a holy book (III. 2, l. 208).

299 *I ask for drink*: drinks were not available on the table during meals, but kept on the sideboard. The servants brought them on request.

300 *atoms, all too too bourgeois*: Belise is reflecting a contemporary revival of interest in atoms, inspired by the philosopher Gassendi.

306 *epigram and madrigal*: he uses 'madrigal' and 'epigram' to mean an elegant little love poem.

307 *a tasty piece*: Cotin composed a piece entitled 'A Poetic Feast', in which he talks of serving up to his lady-love a banquet of intellectual delights: a first course of solid reason, a ragout of epigrams, and so on.

SONNET . . . ON HER FEVER: The sonnet is taken word for word from Cotin's work, but Molière changes the title. Cotin had called it 'Sonnet. To Mlle de Longueville, now Duchesse de Nemours, on her tertiary fever'. Probably Molière thought it would be tactful not to associate the Duchess with such ridicule.

310 *ON A . . . CARRIAGE GIVEN TO A LADY-FRIEND*: again the poem is almost exactly the same as Cotin's original.

311 *Lais*: Lais was a famous Roman courtesan—so Cotin's use of the name is singularly inappropriate for a man of the cloth. Molière wickedly draws attention to it in l. 833.

too new: in Plato's *Republic*, book 5, he imagines an ideal community in which men and women are equal. Philaminte wants to take the idea further by creating an exclusively female Academy.

312 *time for language and . . . science to unite*: a transparent allusion to the two French Academies, the Académie Française (founded 1635) and the Académie des Sciences (founded 1666). In 1666 there had been talk of uniting the two in a single Academy, as Philaminte proposes to do with her feminine version.

peripateticism: Aristotle's world order, based on logic.

the vacuum: Epicurus' cosmogony was based on atoms and the vacuum. Descartes rejected them both. Belise accepts the one but not the other, so is partly Cartesian and partly Epicurean.

subtle matter: this and the next two lines refer to the world system of René Descartes (1596–1650). Roughly, he believed that the heavenly bodies move so fast that they throw off a kind of dust which fills the void between them.

Cartesian magnetism: Descartes claims that 'the whole earth is a magnet'.

vortices: Descartes wrote: 'The heavens are divided into a number of vortices, and the poles of some of these vortices touch the parts furthest away from the poles of the others.'

falling worlds: probably comets, though Descartes does not actually use this term to describe them.

313 *men upon the moon*: the science fiction of the period contains descriptions of journeys to the moon, though Descartes rejected the possibility of life in outer space.

the perfect . . . sage: the Greek philosopher Zeno described the ideal sage, who remained calm in the midst of misfortune.

sterilize our . . . verse: the Académie française was accused of trying to clean up the language in this way, strongly supported by the more prudish *précieuses*. They were particularly opposed to equivocal puns.

314 *an undertone*: apparently Ménage talked in a very quiet voice.

315 *speaks in Greek . . . in France*: Ménage was known as a very fine Hellenist.

in the salons or in town: Molière specifies the places in Paris where such writers are to be found: the Cour de la Reine and the Cours Saint-Antoine, restaurants or the *salons* or drawing-rooms of the *précieuses*.

Greek writer: it is actually a Roman writer, Horace, who is known to have expressed such sentiments, in his *Satires*, 1.73–4, his *Epistles* (2.90), and the last line of his *Art of Poetry*. No Greek writer seems to fit. Is Molière teasing his audience here?

316 *the three Graces*: the Graces or Charites were a trio of divinities, daughters of Zeus, who to the Greeks personified beauty: Aglaia, Thalia, and Euphrosyne.

ithos and pathos: terms of classical rhetoric. *Ithos* was the feeling which could touch the soul, *pathos* the passion which overwhelmed it.

eclogues: pastoral poems inspired by classical poets. Ménage had published a volume entitled *Eclogues and Idylls*.

Theocritus and Virgil: the Greek Theocritus (300–220 BC) and the Roman Virgil (70–19 BC) were masters of the eclogue.

odes: poems dedicated to a specific person. Ménage is known to have imitated odes by the Roman poet Horace (64–8 BC).

canzonets: in French, 'chansonnettes', or light-hearted verse.

roundels: in French, 'rondeaux', short poems with a refrain.

madrigals: see note to l. 750 on p. 306.

ballades: poems with three verses and a final couplet.

bouts-rimés: a fashionable parlour game at the time, *bouts-rimés* were verses composed to fit a rhyme which had been agreed beforehand, the more difficult the better.

317 *fails to admire . . . my pen*: Mme de Sévigné writes in a letter that Louis XIV composed a madrigal, and showed it anonymously to one of his courtiers, who expressed contempt. The King, however, thought this was a tremendous joke.

318 *Boileau*: Molière's close friend the great poet and court chronicler Nicolas Boileau-Despréaux (1636–1711) shared his dislike of Cotin and Ménage, and satirized both of them in his verse.

never leaves you any peace: Ménage is barely mentioned in Boileau's *Satires*, but Cotin, in *Satire* 9 alone, is attacked nine times.

Barbin's bookshop: Barbin was the publisher of Molière, and also of Boileau. His shop was near the Sainte Chapelle.

321 *Take off your glove*: ladies wore gloves for entertaining at home, but removed them to shake hands. Actresses, too, wore gloves on stage.

322 *form or matter*: the Peripatetics divided everything in this way—
     Philaminte is using philosophical language here.

324 *they don't deign . . . flesh and blood*: this idea of platonic love was a
     fashionable subject of debate at the time.

326 *another alien world*: a probable allusion to the comet that appeared in
     1664–5. Cotin had written a tedious dissertation about it.

328 *he . . . tries to laugh it off*: this was untrue of Cotin, who was known for his
     vicious attacks on his enemies. For instance, he called Boileau-Despréaux
     a 'vipereau', or 'little viper'.

329 *I think you should correct . . . their . . . savoir-vivre are immense*: compare
     Dorante's speech in *The School for Wives Criticized*, Scene 6.

     Rasius and Baldus: in inventing these pedants with Latinate names,
     Molière is poking fun: 'Rasius' is reminiscent of 'raseur' ('boring'), and
     'Baldus' of 'baudet' ('donkey'). However, there is also a topical allusion to
     the royal pensions scheme for writers, set up in 1663. Initially, foreign
     scholars (whose names often ended in -us) were included, but not after
     1671.

     their just reward at court: see previous note. Trissotin has presumably seen
     his pension removed, and is sniping at this system of patronage, which
     was almost the only way professional writers could make a living in the
     time of Louis XIV. Molière was, of course, in receipt of royal money, but
     then so was Cotin.

     three small-minded fools: Clitandre assumes Trissotin is talking about him-
     self as well as Rasius and Baldus.

330 *Horace, Virgil, Terence, and Catullus*: for Horace and Virgil, see note to
     p. 316. Terence was a Roman comic playwright (?185–160 BC); Catullus
     was a Roman lyric poet (?87–?54 BC).

333 *I'll go on a retreat . . . to marry anyone*: the convent was the only alterna-
     tive to marriage for many young women—witness Arnolphe's threat to
     Agnes at the end of *The School for Wives*.

335 *Philis, Iris, Amarante*: typical of the elegant names, inspired by the
     Greek, favoured by the *précieux*. Cotin was particularly fond of Iris and
     Amarante. In addition, 'Amarante' is reminiscent of the lavender-
     coloured carriage in Trissotin's epigram in Act III, in French 'un carosse
     de couleur amarante'.

     expressing love . . . is purely etiquette: Cotin confessed as much. He wrote
     to a friend: 'don't apply the names Iris and Amarante to the ladies of our
     acquaintance when you read what I have written about them: they are
     fictitious names.'

339 *écus, livres, and francs*: contemporary French currency. An écu was worth
     three livres or francs.

     in ides and in calends: Belise, thoroughly muddled, asks the Lawyer to use
     ancient Greek currency, but to date the contract according to the Roman

calendar. The calends were the first day of the month, the ides the thirteenth or fifteenth day.

342   *your brother*: see note to p. 71.

The Oxford World's Classics Website

www.worldsclassics.co.uk

- Browse the full range of Oxford World's Classics online

- Sign up for our monthly e-alert to receive information on new titles

- Read extracts from the Introductions

- Listen to our editors and translators talk about the world's greatest literature with our Oxford World's Classics audio guides

- Join the conversation, follow us on Twitter at OWC_Oxford

- Teachers and lecturers can order inspection copies quickly and simply via our website

www.worldsclassics.co.uk

American Literature

British and Irish Literature

Children's Literature

Classics and Ancient Literature

Colonial Literature

Eastern Literature

European Literature

Gothic Literature

History

Medieval Literature

Oxford English Drama

Poetry

Philosophy

Politics

Religion

The Oxford Shakespeare

A complete list of Oxford World's Classics, including Authors in Context, Oxford English Drama, and the Oxford Shakespeare, is available in the UK from the Marketing Services Department, Oxford University Press, Great Clarendon Street, Oxford OX2 6DP, or visit the website at www.oup.com/uk/worldsclassics.

In the USA, visit www.oup.com/us/owc for a complete title list.

Oxford World's Classics are available from all good bookshops. In case of difficulty, customers in the UK should contact Oxford University Press Bookshop, 116 High Street, Oxford OX1 4BR.